First World War
and Army of Occupation
War Diary
France, Belgium and Germany

24 DIVISION
Divisional Troops
Divisional Signal Company
1 March 1915 - 31 December 1916

WO95/2200A

The Naval & Military Press Ltd
www.nmarchive.com
Published in association with The National Archives

Published by

The Naval & Military Press Ltd

Unit 10 Ridgewood Industrial Park,
Uckfield, East Sussex,
TN22 5QE England
Tel: +44 (0) 1825 749494

www.naval-military-press.com

www.nmarchive.com

This diary has been reprinted in facsimile from the original. Any imperfections are inevitably reproduced and the quality may fall short of modern type and cartographic standards.

© **Crown Copyright**
Images reproduced by permission of The National Archives, London, England, 2015.

Contents

Document type	Place/Title	Date From	Date To
Heading	24th Division Divl Engineers 24th Signal Coy. R.E. Aug 1915-May 1919		
Heading	24th Div. 24th Signal Coy Vol 2 Aug & Sept 15 121/7198		
Heading	24th Division 24th Signal Coy R.E. Vol 1 August 15 To May 19		
War Diary	Cowshott	21/08/1915	29/08/1915
War Diary	Havre	30/08/1915	31/08/1915
War Diary	Aldershot District	21/08/1915	29/08/1915
War Diary	Southampton	29/08/1915	29/08/1915
War Diary	Havre	30/08/1915	31/08/1915
War Diary	Royon	01/09/1915	21/09/1915
War Diary	Bomy	22/09/1915	22/09/1915
War Diary	Bousnes	23/09/1915	24/09/1915
War Diary	Bethune	25/09/1915	25/09/1915
War Diary	Vermelles	26/09/1915	27/09/1915
War Diary	Sailly-Labourse	28/09/1915	28/09/1915
War Diary	Annequin	29/09/1915	29/09/1915
War Diary	St Hilaire-Cottes	30/09/1915	30/09/1915
War Diary	Blackdown	28/08/1915	28/08/1915
War Diary	Southampton	29/08/1915	29/08/1915
War Diary	Havre	30/08/1915	30/08/1915
War Diary	Montehort	31/08/1915	21/09/1915
War Diary	Molinghem	22/09/1915	22/09/1915
War Diary	Le Cornet Bordois	23/09/1915	23/09/1915
War Diary	Bethune	24/09/1915	24/09/1915
War Diary	Vermelles	25/09/1915	25/09/1915
War Diary	In The Field	25/09/1915	30/09/1915
War Diary	Black Down	30/08/1915	30/08/1915
War Diary	Havre	31/08/1915	31/08/1915
War Diary	Montreuil	01/09/1915	01/09/1915
War Diary	Huequecliers	02/09/1915	21/09/1915
War Diary	Reclinghem	22/09/1915	22/09/1915
War Diary	Berquette.	23/09/1915	23/09/1915
War Diary	Berquette.	24/09/1916	24/09/1916
War Diary	Bethune	25/09/1915	25/09/1915
War Diary	German 1st Line Trench	26/09/1915	27/09/1915
War Diary	Noeux-les-Mines	28/09/1915	28/09/1915
War Diary	Burquette	29/09/1915	30/09/1915
War Diary	Noeux. Les. Mines.	28/09/1915	28/09/1915
War Diary	Fontes	29/09/1915	29/09/1915
War Diary	Mazinghem	29/09/1915	30/09/1915
Miscellaneous	War Diary. No 4 Section. 24th Signal Coy. R.E. For The Month of September.		
War Diary	Havre	01/09/1915	01/09/1915
War Diary	Hesdin	02/09/1915	02/09/1915
War Diary	Torcy	02/09/1915	02/09/1915
War Diary	Torcy	03/09/1915	21/09/1915
War Diary	Laires	22/09/1915	22/09/1915
War Diary	Busnes	23/09/1915	24/09/1915

Type	Description	Start	End
War Diary	Beuvry.	25/09/1915	25/09/1915
War Diary	Hohenzollern Redoubt.	26/09/1915	27/09/1915
War Diary	Sailly La Bourse.	28/09/1915	28/09/1915
Heading	24th Division 24th Signal Coy RE. Vol 3 Oct 15 121/7517		
Miscellaneous	D.A.G. 3rd Echelon. Base.	11/11/1915	11/11/1915
War Diary	St Hilaire Cottes	01/10/1915	01/10/1915
War Diary	Steenvoorde	02/10/1915	06/10/1915
War Diary	Reninghelst	07/10/1915	31/10/1915
Diagram etc	Circuit Diagram 24th. Div. Sig. Co. R.E.		
War Diary	Ham-en-Artois	01/10/1915	02/10/1915
War Diary	Proven	02/10/1915	05/10/1915
War Diary	Oudermand	06/10/1915	12/10/1915
War Diary	Renninghelst	13/10/1915	16/10/1915
War Diary	Woodcote House	17/10/1915	31/10/1915
Diagram etc			
War Diary	Berguette	01/10/1915	02/10/1915
War Diary	Houtkerque	03/10/1915	06/10/1915
War Diary	Reninghelst	07/10/1915	15/10/1915
War Diary	Woodcote House	16/10/1915	18/10/1915
War Diary	Reninghelst	19/10/1915	31/10/1915
Diagram etc			
War Diary	Mazinghem	01/10/1915	02/10/1915
War Diary	Herzeele	03/10/1915	06/10/1915
War Diary	Proven	06/10/1915	11/10/1915
War Diary	H. 23. C. 52. Sheet 28	12/10/1915	31/10/1915
Diagram etc	Appendix I.		
Heading	24th Division 24th Signal Coy. Vol. 4 121/7724 Nov 15		
War Diary	Reninghelst	01/11/1915	22/11/1915
War Diary	Oxelaere	23/11/1915	23/11/1915
War Diary	Tilques	24/11/1915	30/11/1915
Diagram etc			
War Diary			
War Diary		01/11/1915	30/11/1915
Diagram etc			
Miscellaneous	Communication In 72nd Try Bde Area 29/11/15		
War Diary	Reninghelst	01/11/1915	04/11/1915
War Diary	H. 29.a.8.8	05/11/1915	22/11/1915
War Diary	Reninghelst	23/11/1915	23/11/1915
War Diary	Steenvoorde	24/11/1915	25/11/1915
War Diary	Noordpeene	26/11/1915	26/11/1915
War Diary	Ganspette	27/11/1915	27/11/1915
War Diary	Nordausques	28/11/1915	30/11/1915
Diagram etc			
War Diary	Dickebusche	01/11/1915	04/11/1915
War Diary	Reninghelst	04/11/1915	20/11/1915
War Diary	Eecke	20/11/1915	28/11/1915
War Diary	Eperlecques	29/11/1915	30/11/1915
Diagram etc	Communication 72 I.B.		
Diagram etc			
Diagram etc	Com 72-1 B		
Diagram etc			
Diagram etc	Communication 72 1B		
Diagram etc	Com 72 I.B.		
Diagram etc	Circuit Diagram		
Heading	24th Divl. Signal Coy Vol. 5 121/7931		

War Diary	Tilques	01/12/1915	03/12/1915
War Diary	Tilques	04/12/1915	07/12/1915
War Diary	Tilques	08/12/1915	11/12/1915
War Diary	Tilques	08/12/1915	16/12/1915
War Diary	Tilques	12/12/1915	16/12/1915
War Diary	Tilques	17/12/1915	21/12/1915
War Diary	Tilques	22/12/1915	28/12/1915
War Diary	Tilques	29/12/1915	31/12/1915
Diagram etc	Circuit Diagram		
Heading	WD		
Diagram etc	Communication Of 73 I.B At Eperlecques		
War Diary	Rest Camp	01/12/1915	31/12/1915
War Diary	Eperlecques	01/12/1915	31/12/1915
Miscellaneous	Commn 72.I.B. 1/12/15-31/12/15		
War Diary	Nordausques	01/12/1915	31/12/1915
Heading	24th. Signal Coy R.E. Vol. VI.		
Miscellaneous	D.A.G. 3rd Echelon Base.	04/02/1916	04/02/1916
Miscellaneous	Memorandum. OC. 24th Signal Co RE.		
Miscellaneous	O.C. 24th Divl. Signals.		
Heading	Signals 73 Inf Bde 24th Div		
Diagram etc			
War Diary	Tilques	01/01/1916	07/01/1916
War Diary	Renninghelst	08/01/1916	31/01/1916
War Diary	Rest Camp Bayenghem Lez-Eperlecques	01/01/1916	05/01/1916
War Diary	Rest Camp Ypres	07/01/1916	23/01/1916
War Diary	Rest Camp	24/01/1916	31/01/1916
War Diary	Nordausques	01/01/1916	06/01/1916
War Diary	Poperinghe	07/01/1916	07/01/1916
War Diary	Zillebeke Lake	08/01/1916	15/01/1916
War Diary	H 14 A.2.4	16/01/1916	21/01/1916
War Diary	Ypres	22/01/1916	31/01/1916
Map	Commn 72.I.B. 7/1/16		
Diagram etc	Diagram of Lines in Rest Area		
Diagram etc	Communication 72nd Inf Bde		
War Diary	Eperlecques.	01/01/1916	08/01/1916
War Diary	H.14.a. (Sheet 28)	09/01/1916	14/01/1916
War Diary	Zillebeke Lake	15/01/1916	31/01/1916
Diagram etc	Communications of 73. I.B. Eperlecques Appendix I. a		
Diagram etc	Communications of 73. I.B. in Rest Area. H.14.a. Sheet 28		
Diagram etc	Communications of 73. I.B. at Zillebeke Lake Appendix III a		
Diagram etc	Communications of 73. I.B. at Zillebeke Lake Appendix IV a		
Miscellaneous	24th Signals Vol. 7		
War Diary	Reninghelst	01/02/1916	14/02/1916
War Diary	Ad Reninghelst	14/02/1916	29/02/1916
War Diary	Zillebeke Lake	01/02/1916	16/02/1916
War Diary	Rest Camp H 14 A	17/02/1916	29/02/1916
War Diary	Ypres	01/02/1916	08/02/1916
War Diary	H. 14.A.24	09/02/1916	15/02/1916
War Diary	I 21.A.2.7	16/02/1916	23/02/1916
War Diary	I 14. b. 2.4	24/02/1916	25/02/1916
War Diary	Ypres	26/02/1916	01/03/1916
War Diary	H.14.a. Sheet 28	01/02/1916	08/02/1916
War Diary	Ramparts	09/02/1916	09/02/1916

War Diary	Ypres	10/02/1916	25/02/1916
War Diary	Poperinghe	26/02/1916	29/02/1916
Diagram etc	Sub Appendix I.		
Diagram etc	Sub Appendix II.		
Heading	24 Div Signals Vol 8		
War Diary	Reninghelst	01/03/1916	22/03/1916
War Diary	Fletre	23/03/1916	30/03/1916
War Diary	St Jans Cappel	31/03/1916	31/03/1916
War Diary	Rest Camp H 14 A.	01/03/1916	08/03/1916
War Diary	Zillebeke Lake	09/03/1916	23/03/1916
War Diary	Thieushouk	24/03/1916	28/03/1916
War Diary	T 21 DS. 2 Sheet 28	30/03/1916	30/03/1916
Diagram etc			
War Diary	Ypres	01/03/1916	04/03/1916
War Diary	Poperinghe	03/03/1916	09/03/1916
War Diary	H.14.a Ouderdom	10/03/1916	16/03/1916
War Diary	Ypres	17/03/1916	20/03/1916
War Diary	H.14.a Ouderdom	21/03/1916	21/03/1916
War Diary	R. 19. D. 1.5	22/03/1916	22/03/1916
War Diary	Mt Der Cats Map 27	23/03/1916	27/03/1916
War Diary	Buss FM.	28/03/1916	31/03/1916
Diagram etc	Commns 72.I.B.		
War Diary	Poperinghe	01/03/1915	03/03/1915
War Diary	Ypres	04/03/1915	16/03/1915
War Diary	H.14.a Sheet 28 (B)	17/03/1915	18/03/1915
War Diary	Meteren	09/03/1915	24/03/1915
War Diary	Petite Munque. Fm.	25/03/1915	25/03/1915
War Diary	Sheet 28. T.23.D. 6.9.	26/03/1915	31/03/1915
Diagram etc	Communication Of 73. Bde. in Ypres		
Diagram etc	Communications of 73rd Inf Bde. at. X.17.C 33. (Sheet 28)		
Diagram etc			
War Diary	St. Jans Cappel	01/04/1916	17/04/1916
War Diary	Bailleul	18/04/1916	30/04/1916
War Diary	Sheet 28 T 21 D 52	01/04/1916	06/04/1916
War Diary	Petite Munque Farm	06/04/1916	28/04/1916
War Diary	Bus Farm	01/04/1916	07/04/1916
War Diary	Dranoutre	08/04/1916	30/04/1916
Diagram etc	Office Diagram of 72nd Inf Bde. Commns. 18.4.16		
War Diary	Petite Munque Fm. T.23.d.6.9 Sheet (28)	01/04/1916	06/04/1916
War Diary	T.21.d.5.2 (28)	06/04/1916	30/04/1916
Diagram etc	Communication Of 73. Inf. Bde.		
Miscellaneous	Account Of Communication During Recent Gas Attack On 24th Division Appendix No. 4	30/04/1916	30/04/1916
Miscellaneous	Communication Within 24th Division Area Appendix No. 5		
Diagram etc	Westhof Farm. (24th Divnl. Advd HQ)		
Diagram etc	Plug Exchange		
Miscellaneous	D.A.G. 3rd Echelon.	03/06/1916	03/06/1916
War Diary	Bailleul	01/05/1916	31/05/1916
War Diary	Petite Munque Farm	01/05/1916	31/05/1916
War Diary	Dranoutre	01/05/1916	31/05/1916
Diagram etc	Lines 7.8.11.13 are comic Air. Lines		
War Diary	Sheet 28. T 21.d.52	01/05/1916	31/05/1916
Diagram etc	Communications Of 73 Inf Bde at (28) T.21.d.5.2		
Miscellaneous	The Officer i/c A.G.'s Office at the Base.	02/07/1916	02/07/1916

War Diary	Bailleul	01/06/1916	30/06/1916
War Diary	Petite Munque Farm. T. 23. D. 8.9. Sheet 28	01/06/1916	23/06/1916
War Diary	X 17 C4.3	23/06/1916	27/06/1916
War Diary	Locre	27/06/1916	30/06/1916
War Diary	Dranoutre	01/06/1916	30/06/1916
Diagram etc	Communication-Diagram		
Diagram etc			
Miscellaneous	Communications. No. 3 Sect 24th Divl. Sig. Co.		
War Diary	28 T.21.d.5.2	01/06/1916	17/06/1916
War Diary	St. Jans. Cappel	18/06/1916	20/06/1916
War Diary	Kemmel Hill (28) N 20.d. 2.4	21/06/1917	23/06/1917
War Diary	Kemmel Hill	24/06/1917	30/06/1917
Diagram etc	Communications of 73 Inf Bde at (28) T. 21.d.5.2		
Diagram etc	Communications of B. Inf Bde. At Kemmel Hill Sheet (28) No. 20.d.33		
War Diary	Bailleul	01/07/1916	04/07/1916
War Diary	Locre	05/07/1916	20/07/1916
War Diary	St Jans Cappel	21/07/1916	25/07/1916
War Diary	Cavillon	26/07/1916	30/07/1916
War Diary	Corbie	31/07/1916	31/07/1916
War Diary	Dranoutre	01/07/1916	25/07/1916
War Diary	Riencourt	26/07/1916	31/07/1916
War Diary	Dranoutre	01/07/1916	01/07/1916
War Diary	Locre	02/07/1916	08/07/1916
War Diary	Euglent Fm	09/07/1916	20/07/1916
War Diary	Mont des Cats	21/07/1916	25/07/1916
War Diary	Oissy	26/07/1916	31/07/1916
Diagram etc	Communication Diagram		
War Diary	Kemmel Hill Sheet 28. N.20.d.3.3	01/07/1916	11/07/1916
War Diary	T.21.d.2.10	12/07/1916	20/07/1916
War Diary	Thieushouck	21/07/1916	24/07/1916
War Diary	Molliens-Vidame	25/07/1916	31/07/1916
Diagram etc	Communications Of 73. Inf Bde. Sheet 28 N.20.d.3.3		
Diagram etc	Communications Of 73 Inf Bde. at (28) T.21.d.2.10		
Heading	24th Divisional Engineers 24th Divisional Signal Company R.E. August 1916		
Miscellaneous	Headquarters 24th Division.		
War Diary	Corbie	01/08/1916	02/08/1916
War Diary	Citadel. (F 21 B 4-3 Bray-Fricourt Road)	03/08/1916	03/08/1916
War Diary	Forked Tree	04/08/1916	08/08/1916
War Diary	Citadel.	09/08/1916	23/08/1916
War Diary	Forked Tree	24/08/1916	25/08/1916
War Diary	Buire	26/08/1916	31/08/1916
Diagram etc	Lines between Infantry Bdes & Minden Post 24th Signals.		
War Diary	Sand Pit E 18 D. 5.3 (Sheet b 2d) France	01/08/1916	16/08/1916
War Diary	Craters A 8b 2.9. (62c)	10/08/1916	17/08/1916
War Diary	Dummy Trench	17/08/1916	31/08/1916
War Diary	Morlancourt	01/08/1916	01/08/1916
War Diary	E. 18.d.4.0	02/08/1916	10/08/1916
War Diary	Chalk Pit	11/08/1916	16/08/1916
War Diary	Briqueterie	17/08/1916	18/08/1916
War Diary	Craters	19/08/1916	28/08/1916
War Diary	Briqueterie	21/08/1916	23/08/1916
War Diary	Citadel	24/08/1916	25/08/1916
War Diary	Dernancourt	26/06/1916	27/06/1916

Type	Description	From	To
War Diary	Ribemont	28/08/1916	30/08/1916
War Diary	Pommieres Redoubt.	31/08/1916	31/08/1916
War Diary	Vaux-Sur Somme	01/08/1916	02/08/1916
War Diary	Happy Valley Sheet 62.D. F. 27.C. 28	03/08/1916	08/08/1916
War Diary	62d. F22a	08/08/1916	17/08/1916
War Diary	Briqueterie	18/08/1916	20/08/1916
War Diary	62.c. A.8.b.2A	21/08/1916	22/08/1916
War Diary	62.d. E.24a.8.8.	23/08/1916	25/08/1916
War Diary	62.D. E 18.b.	26/08/1916	30/08/1916
War Diary	Pommiers Redoubt. 62.c. A.1.c.63	31/08/1916	31/08/1916
Diagram etc	Communications Handed Over by Sigs 98 Bde. to Sigs 73 Bde. 30/8/16		
Heading	Royal Engineers 24th Division 24th Divisional Signal Company September 1916		
War Diary	E 11 Central Bray-Albert Road.	01/09/1916	04/09/1916
War Diary	E II Central	05/09/1916	06/09/1916
War Diary	Longpre	07/09/1916	07/09/1916
War Diary	Ailly Le Haut Clocher (Somme)	08/09/1916	19/09/1916
War Diary	Longpre Stn	19/09/1916	20/09/1916
War Diary	Bruay	20/08/1916	20/08/1916
War Diary	Bruay (Pas de Calais)	21/08/1916	26/08/1916
War Diary	Camblain L'Abbe	26/08/1916	30/09/1916
War Diary	Rest Camp F 8 C 78 (France 62d)	01/09/1916	18/09/1916
War Diary	Gorenflos	19/09/1916	19/09/1916
War Diary	Pernes	21/09/1916	30/09/1916
War Diary	Pommieres Redoubt.	01/09/1916	05/09/1916
War Diary	F.8.d (Fricourt)	06/09/1916	06/09/1916
War Diary	Dernancourt	07/09/1916	07/09/1916
War Diary	Bois D.7. Abbey	08/09/1916	19/09/1916
War Diary	Valdhoun	20/09/1916	24/09/1916
War Diary	Ruitz	25/09/1916	26/09/1916
War Diary	Chateau De la Haie.	27/09/1916	30/09/1916
Heading	War Diary Of 4 Sec. 24 Signal Coy. R.E. For The Month Of September. 1916 Appendix No. 3		
War Diary	Pommiers Redoubt 62.C A.I.6.3	01/09/1916	02/09/1916
War Diary	F.8.C. (62.d)	03/09/1916	04/09/1916
War Diary	Dernancourt	05/09/1916	06/09/1916
War Diary	Vauchelles-Les-Domart.	07/09/1916	19/09/1916
War Diary	Marles-Les-Mines	20/09/1916	23/09/1916
War Diary	Villers-Au-Bois	24/09/1916	30/09/1916
Diagram etc	Appendix IV Communications of 73 1 Bde. at Pommiers Redoubt.		
Diagram etc	Appendix II		
War Diary	Camblain L'Abbe	01/10/1916	28/10/1916
War Diary	Bruay	29/10/1916	30/10/1916
War Diary	Noeux-Les-Mines	31/10/1916	31/10/1916
Miscellaneous	Appendix I Exchange Connections 24th Division		
Miscellaneous	Appendix II		
Miscellaneous	Appendix III		
Miscellaneous	Appendix IV 40th Division Exchange		
Miscellaneous	Appendix V		
Diagram etc	Diagram of Communications Camblain L'Abbe Appendix VI		
Miscellaneous	Appendix VII Reeled Up Cable		
Miscellaneous	Appendix VII		
Diagram etc	Appendix VIII		

War Diary	Chau D'Acq W 30 b 35 (France 36B)	01/10/1916	02/10/1916
War Diary	Chau de la Haie W12C89	03/10/1916	08/10/1916
War Diary	Villers Au Bois X19a 63	09/10/1916	24/10/1916
War Diary	Villers Au Bois	10/10/1916	27/10/1916
War Diary	W12C8.9 L23C21 L29a89	25/10/1916	27/10/1916
War Diary	Mazingarbe Chateau	28/10/1916	31/10/1916
War Diary	Chateau de La Haie	01/10/1916	02/10/1916
War Diary	Villa. d. Acq.	03/10/1916	18/10/1916
War Diary	Chateau De La Haie	19/10/1916	24/10/1916
War Diary	Mazingarbe	25/10/1916	25/10/1916
War Diary	Philosophe	26/10/1916	31/10/1916
Diagram etc	Appendix I		
Miscellaneous	War Diary Of 4 Sec 24 Signal Coy. RE For Month Of October 1916 Appendix XI		
War Diary	Villers-Au Bois	01/10/1916	01/10/1916
War Diary	Chau. De La Haie	11/10/1916	18/10/1916
War Diary	Chau D'Acq	19/10/1916	27/10/1916
War Diary	Chau De La Haie	28/10/1916	28/10/1916
War Diary	Les Brebis	29/10/1916	31/10/1916
Diagram etc	Diagram of Lines Sub-Appendix II		
Diagram etc	Loos Sector Appendix III		
Heading	War Diary 24th Divisional Signal Company R.E. November 1916 Vol 16		
War Diary	Braquemont (Noeux Les Mines)	01/11/1916	03/11/1916
War Diary	Braquemont	01/11/1916	05/11/1916
War Diary	Noeux Les Mines	06/11/1916	30/11/1916
Miscellaneous	Appendix I		
Miscellaneous	Appendix II		
Miscellaneous	Appendix III		
Diagram etc	Corps W/T Stations Appendix IV		
War Diary	Mazingarbe Chateau (L23C70 Sheet 36b France) "14 Bis Sector"	01/11/1916	14/11/1916
War Diary	Mazingarbe Chateau. 14 Bis Sector	08/11/1916	30/11/1916
War Diary	Philosophe	01/11/1916	30/11/1916
War Diary	Les Brebis (Sheet 36.b)	01/11/1916	11/11/1916
War Diary	Les Brebis	12/11/1916	30/11/1916
Diagram etc	Loos Sector. Appendix I		
Diagram etc	Loos Sector. Appendix II		
Heading	Cover for Documents. Nature of Enclosures. War Diary 24th Divisional Signal Company R.E. Vol 17		
War Diary	Braquemont Noeux-Les-Mines	01/12/1916	31/12/1916
War Diary	Mazingarbe Chau (Bde Hq) L23C80. (France 366) "XIV Bis" Sector	01/12/1916	09/12/1916
War Diary	XIV B15 Sector	11/12/1916	30/12/1916
War Diary	Philosophe	01/12/1916	31/12/1916
Heading	War Diary Of No 4. Section 24th Signal Coy. R.E. for the month of December 1916 Appendix No 3		
War Diary	Les Brebis	01/12/1916	31/12/1916
Diagram etc	Appendix 4 Communications Of 73rd Bde		

24TH DIVISION
DIVL ENGINEERS

24TH SIGNAL COY. R.E.
AUG 1915 - MAY 1919

24th Divn.

24th Divisional Coy
Vol 2

Aug & Sept 15

121/7/98

121/6489

24th Division

24th Div Signal Coy RE.
Vol I
August 15
to
May '19

Army Form C. 2118.

Headquarters
No 1 Section

WAR DIARY
or
INTELLIGENCE SUMMARY.
(Erase heading not required.)

August

Instructions regarding War Diaries and Intelligence Summaries are contained in F.S. Regs., Part II. and the Staff Manual respectively. Title pages will be prepared in manuscript.

Place	Date	Hour	Summary of Events and Information	Remarks and references to Appendices
Crowhurst	21st August		Received orders to prepare for embarkation. Culver (Captain) & 44 Ors. Detained cyclists attached to the coy.	FM Coy 2
"	22nd August		Sunday. Rested.	FM Coy 2
"	23rd August		Taking part in trench scheme at CHOBHAM COMMON. 1 Or Divorce at TURF HILL	FM Coy 2
"	24th August		Trench scheme CHOBHAM COMMON continued till 6 p.m. when company returned to camp	FM App 2
"	25th "		Picking up all cable lines laid for trench scheme. Received orders that 21st August was to be considered as 1st day of mobilisation.	FM App 2
"	26th "		Overhauling stores and repairing waggons	FM App 2
"	29th "		BROOKWOOD. Marched out at 9 a.m. to entrain at Brookwood station. 2nd Lt BROMWOOD & at 11.20 a.m. detrained SOUTHAMPTON. Embarked on H.M.T. ARCHIMEDES & "EMPRESS QUEEN" transferred	F.H. App 2
HAVRE	30th "		HAVRE at 8 a.m. 30°. Arrived No 1 Rest camp at 11 p.m.	
"	31st "		Left REST CAMP 4 a.m. entrained and left HAVRE 10.30 a.m. All day in train.	F.H. App 2

Army Form C. 2118

WAR DIARY
or
INTELLIGENCE SUMMARY.

(Erase heading not required.)

Instructions regarding War Diaries and Intelligence Summaries are contained in F. S. Regs., Part II. and the Staff Manual respectively. Title pages ___ 4th Signal Co. will be prepared in manuscript.

August 1915

Place	Date	Hour	Summary of Events and Information	Remarks and references to Appendices
Aldershot North Ca.	21	6pm	Received orders for mobilization to await instructions	
"	22		Ditto	
"	23		Taking part in Brick Scheme at Cobham Common	
"	24		Finished scheme continued	
"	24	5pm	" " finished Company return to above on camp	
"	25		Picked up all cable laid for Brick Scheme	
"	26		Overhauling stores and packing wagons	
"	27		Returning stores to Ordnance	
"	27	11am	Passed down to embark on 29 "	
"	28	8pm	Received orders to entrain at Farnborough	
"	29	11.20am	Entrained for SOUTHAMPTON	
"		1.15pm	Arrived SOUTHAMPTON embarked on H.M.T. "Inventor" leaving Queen's Quay	
Southampton		5pm	Left SOUTHAMPTON	
"	30	3am	Arrived at HAVRE	
HAVRE		9am	Disembarked and proceeded to No 1 Rest Camp	
"	31	10.27am	Entrained and left HAVRE arr. R. 2.7am	

2353 W: W3544/1454 700,000 5/15 D. D. & L. A.D.S.S./Forms/C. 2118.

Army Form C. 2118

WAR DIARY
or
INTELLIGENCE SUMMARY
(Erase heading not required.)

September 1915

Place	Date	Hour	Summary of Events and Information	Remarks and references to Appendices
ROYON	1	~~Sept~~	~~Entrained~~ Returned at HESDIN. No cyclone.	
		7am	Marched off for 24 Div HQ at ROYON	
		2am	Halted for breakfast	
		4am		
		9am	Resumed march	
		10am	Arrived ROYON. Took up billets. Room building, short form accommodation	F/A
		2pm	Opened Office. D.R communication with all units of Div. An line to I.S.C. D.R. & S	F/A
ROYON	2	2.15pm	Headquarters 24 Div asked for cable communication with all Brigades & Gp.R.N	F/A
ROYON	3	4am	All lines thro'. 4½ miles cable laid, and 10 total heavy rain and dark night.	F/A
ROYON	4	—	Maintaining communications	F/A
ROYON	5	—	Maintaining communication. On call was to C.R.E	F/A
ROYON	6	—	" Piche–Leh- was to 73 Div S to provide wire to [illeg] returns	F/A
"	7	—	" Took part in armoured scheme	F/A
"	8	—	" Relieved 2nd W 73 Div S and [illeg] around [illeg]	F/A
	9(a)	—	" for S.S.O. + R.T.O BEAURAINVILLE. Opened Office for same.	F/A
"	9(b)		Maintaining communication	
	10			

2353 Wt W2514/1454 700,000 5/15 D.D.& L. A.D.S.S./Forms/C.2118.

WAR DIARY
or
INTELLIGENCE SUMMARY.

Army Form C. 2118.

(Erase heading not required.)

Place	Date	Hour	Summary of Events and Information	Remarks and references to Appendices
ROYON	21/9/15	8.0 A.M.	Commenced packing up cable laid on coming to ROYON from Signal Hqrs to Brigades, 1/2 at MONTECHORT, 1/2 at HUCQUELIERS, 1/3rd at TORCY.	Both
		12.0 C.M.	Signal office closed, communication maintained by D.R.s.	
		4.0 P.M.	Signal Office opened at BOMY.	
		6.0 P.M.	Coy proceeded to march route to BOMY.	
BOMY.	22/9/15		Communication maintained by D.R.s to Brigades. 1/26 at MATRINGHEM. 1/2nd at REELINGHAM. 1/3rd at LAIRES.	
		8.0 A.M.	Cable section proceeded to BOUSNES to lay cable to Brigades	D.R.
			Hqrs 1/1st MOLLINGHEM. VIA 1/2nd at BERQUETTE.	
		4.0 P.M.	Signal office opened at BOUSNES	
		6.0 P.M.	Remainder of Coy proceeded to march route to BOUSNES	
BOUSNES	23/9/15		Reeled up 4 miles of buried cable to employ establishment. Laid behind by previous occupants. Communication maintained by	

Army Form C. 2118.

WAR DIARY
or
INTELLIGENCE SUMMARY.
(Erase heading not required.)

Instructions regarding War Diaries and Intelligence Summaries are contained in F. S. Regs., Part II. and the Staff Manual respectively. Title pages will be prepared in manuscript.

Place	Date	Hour	Summary of Events and Information	Remarks and references to Appendices
			Col. with 1/2 Brigade and 2/3 Brigade and by D.R.° to 1/3 rd Brigade at BOUSNES	
		4 P.M.	1/2 º Brigade move to LE-CORNET-BORDOIS line bent to LE-CORNET-BORDOIS.	
BOUSNES 24/9/15		10 A.M.	2 new telest Code received. Order section proceeded to BETHUNE to erect aerial from Divisional H.qrs to 1/2 and 1/3 rd Brigades in BETHUNE.	Both
		6.0 P.M.	Signal office established communication maintained by D.R. to 1/2 nd 1/3 rd in BETHUNE and 1/3rd at BEUVRY.	
BETHUNE 25/9/15		10 P.M.	Company proceeded to march route to VERMELLES via BEUVRY and NOYELLES	Both
		1.0 P.M.	Signal office opened at VERMELLES communication by D.R. to Brigades. During evening Divisional H.qrs heavily shelled by the enemy.	

Army Form C. 2118.

WAR DIARY
or
INTELLIGENCE SUMMARY.
(Erase heading not required.)

Instructions regarding War Diaries and Intelligence Summaries are contained in F.S. Regs., Part II. and the Staff Manual respectively. Title pages will be prepared in manuscript.

Place	Date	Hour	Summary of Events and Information	Remarks and references to Appendices
		6.30 PM	line laid from Sunrise Hyps to corner of Brewery. Picking up line already laid to that point, and from end of that line down to sunken road at W. Advanced Relay Point or Cuinchy.	P.H.
			NORTH of LE-RUTOIRE. Orders given to lay one pair as a. Advanced Relay Point on Cuinchy. This line of German trench.	
VERMELLES	26/9/15		Sunrise Hyps. still remaining at VERMELLES in spite of heavy shell fire from enemy. Communication maintained by Vel. and D.R's to Brigades via Advanced Relay Point mentioned before.	D.H.
VERMELLES	27/9/15	9.0 AM	Coy. formed between VERMELLES and NOYELLES. Signal office closed at VERMELLES and reopened at SAILLY-LABOURSE. Coy. parked at SAILLY-LABOURSE. Communication maintained by D.R's to Brigades.	

Army Form C. 2118.

WAR DIARY
or
INTELLIGENCE SUMMARY.
(Erase heading not required.)

Instructions regarding War Diaries and Intelligence Summaries are contained in F. S. Regs., Part II. and the Staff Manual respectively. Title pages will be prepared in manuscript.

Place	Date	Hour	Summary of Events and Information	Remarks and references to Appendices
SAILLY-LABOURSE	28/9/15	4 P.M.	Coy proceeded by route to ANNEQUIN. S.W. of BETHUNE	Oror
		8 P.M.	Signal office opened and reopened at ST. HILAIRE-COTTES. Communication by D.R.	
ANNEQUIN	29/9/15	12.00 A.M.	Coy proceeded to march route to ST. HILAIRE-COTTES via LILLIERS. Communication by D.R. Coy arrived at ST. HILAIRE-COTTES	Oror
ST. HILAIRE-COTTES	30/9/15		Cable laid to 73rd Brigade at MAZINGHEM. and to y et to HAM-EN-ARTROIS and from there by erecting cable to 72 Brigade at BURGUETTE. Communication maintained by tel and DR?	Oror

2333 Wt W2544/1454 750,000 5/15 D.D.&L. A.D.S.S. Forms/C 2118

WAR DIARY
or
INTELLIGENCE SUMMARY.

(Erase heading not required.)

Army Form C. 2118

No 2 Section
24th Sig Co RE
From 28/8/15 — 3/9/15

Instructions regarding War Diaries and Intelligence Summaries are contained in F. S. Regs. Part II. and the Staff Manual respectively. Title pages will be prepared in manuscript.

Place	Date	Hour	Summary of Events and Information	Remarks and references to Appendices
Blackdown	28/8/15	5 PM	Marched from Camp to Farnboro' Station, left 7-30PM arrived Southampton 10-15AM	
Southampton	29/8/15	7-30PM	Boat left for Havre, arriving there at about 4-0 AM	
Havre	30/8/15	10PM	Train left for Montechort	
Montechort	31/8/15	12Noon	Time of arrival two mile march to Bde HQ, then on to Chateau de Montechort	
— " —	1/9/15	—	Lines laid to 3 Batt. Dr cable being used, its enough wire to lay out to the 4 Bn's the 9th Suffolks being at Alette, 9th Norfolks at Montcauril, 11th Essex at Estrelle & Estrée, 8th Bedfords at Néuville. Line laid from Bde HD then to N.O.I. was laid by them, with their wire. Lines were laid out by S.U.I, N.O.I, and E.S.S.K.	

Army Form C. 2118

WAR DIARY
or
INTELLIGENCE SUMMARY.
(Erase heading not required.)

Instructions regarding War Diaries and Intelligence Summaries are contained in F. S. Regs., Part II. and the Staff Manual respectively. Title pages will be prepared in manuscript.

Place	Date	Hour	Summary of Events and Information	Remarks and references to Appendices
Monterhant	2/9/15			3rd page Summary C. Beauchamp(?)

Sketch:

- TOUTENDAL B. Coy.
- CLONLEU D. Coy.
- 71st Bde H.Q.
- (S.M.I.) Batt. H.Q.
- D.Coy. Farm House 50yds off Rd.
- B.Coy. Café 600yds from BN. H.Q.
- ESTRÉE (MAIRIE)
- C. Coy. Farm 20yds off Rd.
- E.G.S.K. Batt. H.Q.
- B.Coy. Farm just N of R. in CARNE. Le Camp du Carne ½ M. N. of MONTGAUREL.
- (M.O.I.) Batt. H.Q.
- C. Coy. Farm just E of X Rds ½ M. N. of N in ELENTTE

Army Form C. 2118.

WAR DIARY
or
INTELLIGENCE SUMMARY.
(Erase heading not required.)

Instructions regarding War Diaries and Intelligence Summaries are contained in F.S. Regs, Part II. and the Staff Manual respectively. Title pages will be prepared in manuscript.

Place	Date	Hour	Summary of Events and Information	Remarks and references to Appendices
Montchevret	18/9/15 to 19/9/15		Lines kept in working order. Posts were about wringed to fit in with the D.W. Posts what men were off duty and in any spare time. Stores were looked after and kept up to date and in order.	
	20/9/15	2 PM	All lines were taken in & a message in the morning. All Bde. lines needed in the morning. All Bde. lines needed in by 4-30 PM. Communication opened by D.R.	
	21/9/15	6 PM	The Bde. HQ with the Sig. Sec. marched from Montchevret to "Montchegrew" arriving there at 3-30 AM. Sig. office opened by D.R. only	
Molinghem	22/9/15	6 PM	Marched again to MOLINGHEM arriving in the early hours. Signal office opened on arrival and communication opened by D.R.	
Le bonnet Bondois	23/9/15	7 PM	Marched again to Le bonnet Bondois, arriving there at about 10-30 PM. Office again opened by D.R.	
Bethune	24/9/15	7-15 PM	Marched to Bethune through Choques. Office opened by D.R.	
Vermelles	25/9/15	11 NOON	Got the order to move & marched to 1 mile S. of Vermelles, at 5 PM we came evening we moved forward to brown roads about 1½ V.P. (Vermelles mining)	
In the field	26/9/15	8 PM	To the British line of trenches. All cycles were left at X Roads, impossible to bring them further, with horses and L.S. Bde. HQ taken up in Port line of British trenches. All communications were by D.R.	

Army Form C. 2118

WAR DIARY
or
INTELLIGENCE SUMMARY.
(Erase heading not required.)

Instructions regarding War Diaries and Intelligence Summaries are contained in F. S. Regs., Part II. and the Staff Manual respectively. Title pages will be prepared in manuscript.

Place	Date	Hour	Summary of Events and Information	Remarks and references to Appendices
In the field	26/9/15	—	During the advance Bde. H.Q. moved from 2nd line of "B" trenches to 2nd line German trenches, and in the evening to 3rd line of "B" trenches, during which time all communications were carried on by D.R. Div. H.Q. laid line up to within ½ of "Lone Tree", to which all D.Rs. from the trenches were sent.	
	28/9/15	5 A.M.	Left the trenches being relieved by the Guards Div; the Bde marched back to Vermelles, thence to Sailly-Labourse at about 11-0 A.M.	
	29/9/15		We were moved to road ½ to 2 M from our last area, that afternoon we were again moved to a position ½ M from Noeux-les-Mines; the same evening we moved again to & entrained at Noeux-les-Mines, left in camp at 7-30 PM & entrained on the 9-20 PM to Berguette. During move no lines laid at all. D.R. being used. Line of arrival at Berguette at 11-30 PM. Marched to Ham-en-Artois 2 miles.	
	30/9/15		Stay at HAM-EN-ARTROIS, communications by D.R. Office opened on arrival.	

Army Form C. 2118.

WAR DIARY
or
INTELLIGENCE SUMMARY.
(Erase heading not required.)

N° 3 Section
½ (Brigade)

Place	Date	Hour	Summary of Events and Information	Remarks and references to Appendices
Blackdown	30.8.15	—	Left Farnboro' L.S.W. Rly to Southampton on route for Havre	1000
Havre	31-8-15		Entrained Havre for Montreuil	5 p.m.
Montreuil	31-9-15		Left Montreuil marched to billets at Hucqueliers	3 p.m.
Hucqueliers	2-9-15		Lines laid to Batts. 8/Queens, 8/Buffs Manningham	9 a.m.
"			9/E Surrey, Avesnes. 8/R.W.K. Hucqueliers	
"	3.9.15		Halt.	9 a.m.
"	4.9.15		E Surrey moved Humbert. Buffs and Queens made responsible for line from Manningham to Humbert.	2 p.m. 9 p.m. 5 p.m.
"	5.9.15		Halt.	
"	6.9.15		Halt	
"	7.9.15		Tactical exercise. Attack for Corps Commander.	7 a.m.
"	8-9-15		Halt.	9 a.m.
"	9-9-15		Halt.	9 a.m.
"	10-9-15		Halt.	9 a.m.
"	11-9-15		Halt	9 a.m.

Army Form C. 2118

WAR DIARY
or
INTELLIGENCE SUMMARY.
(Erase heading not required.)

N° 3 Section
24 Div / 73 Bg

Instructions regarding War Diaries and Intelligence Summaries are contained in F.S. Regs., Part II. and the Staff Manual respectively. Title pages will be prepared in manuscript.

Place	Date	Hour	Summary of Events and Information	Remarks and references to Appendices
Hucqueliers	12-9-15		Halt.	S/M
"	13-9-15		Halt.	S/M
"	14-9-15		Halt.	S/M
"	15-9-15		Halt.	S/M
"	16-9-15		Halt.	S/M
"	17-9-15		Halt.	S/M
"	18-9-15		Halt.	S/M
"	19-9-15		Halt.	S/M
"	20-9-15		Halt.	S/M
"	21-9-15		Marched off to new area. Arrived 11 pm Reclinghem	S/M
Reclinghem	22-9-15		Marched off to new area. Arrived 2 AM Burguette	S/M
Burguette	23-9-15		Halt	S/M
Burguette	24-9-16		Marched off to new area. Arrives 11 pm. Bethune.	S/M
Bethune	25-9-15		Marched from billets. Concentrates at Courne-ne-Bully 2-15 pm. Moves 5 pm to be Reserve. 9.20 pm advances after deploying reached Lone Tree 11.5 pm. Occupies German 1st line trench 11-30 pm.	S/M
German 1st Line trench	26/9/15		2.10 pm H⁹ moves to dug out. 11 am attack launches. Retirement effected 1.30 pm. H.Q. retires nightmare dug out 5 pm.	S/M

Army Form C. 2118

N° 3 Section
24 Div / 72 Coy

WAR DIARY
or
INTELLIGENCE SUMMARY.
(Erase heading not required.)

Place	Date	Hour	Summary of Events and Information	Remarks and references to Appendices
German Lez-Vermelles	27-9-15	4 am.	Relieved by Guards Moralie – 28- Moves billets; Arrived 10 pm Mazeux – R.F. Mines	S/W
Houd-les-Mines	28-9-15		Moves new area by train. Arrived 11.30 pm Busquette.	S/W
Busquette	29-9-15		Halt.	S/W
"	30-9-15		Halt.	S/W

J.M. Mumby 2/Lieut
O.C. April 72nd Fd / R.E.

Army Form C. 2118

3

WAR DIARY
or
INTELLIGENCE SUMMARY

(Erase heading not required.)

Place	Date	Hour	Summary of Events and Information	Remarks and references to Appendices
NOEUX.LES. MINES.	28.	9 A.M.	Mounted portion of section marched in two stages to FONTES arrived at 4 p.m. 29th.	2/Lt Fletcher & 2/RE.
FONTES	29.		arrived at BERGUETTE STA. at 1 a.m. arrived FONTES 5 a.m. left FONTES 3 p.m.	2/Lt Ritchie 2/RE.
MAZINGHEM	29.		arrived at CHATEAU 4:30 p.m.	2/Lt Fletcher 2/RE.
	30		laid wire to 12 MIDDLESEX and 7 NORTHANTS.	2/Lt Ritchie 2/RE.

Army Form C. 2118

24 Dvy Syn
No 4 Sec
73rd Brigade

WAR DIARY
or
INTELLIGENCE SUMMARY.
(Erase heading not required.)

Instructions regarding War Diaries and Intelligence Summaries are contained in F. S. Regs., Part II and the Staff Manual respectively. Title pages will be prepared in manuscript.

Place	Date	Hour	Summary of Events and Information	Remarks and references to Appendices

WAR . DIARY.

No. 4 SECTION. 24th SIGNAL COY. R.E.

for the month of September.

Army Form C. 2118

WAR DIARY
or
INTELLIGENCE SUMMARY
(Erase heading not required.)

Instructions regarding War Diaries and Intelligence Summaries are contained in F. S. Regs., Part II. and the Staff Manual respectively. Title pages will be prepared in manuscript.

Place	Date	Hour	Summary of Events and Information	Remarks and references to Appendices
HAVRE	1	6 am	arrived at HAVRE. proceeded to rest Camp. Left at 10.30 pm	a.f. Ritchie, 2/Lt
HESDIN	2	3 pm	detained.	a.f. Ritchie, 2/Lt
TORCY	2	10.30 pm	arrived at TORCY.	a.f. Ritchie, 2/Lt
TORCY	3		opened Brigade signal office. Communicated with units by dispatch rider.	a.f. Ritchie, 2/Lt
	4		Cable communication with 24th Div opened. wires laid to 9. R. SUSSEX and 12 R. FUSILIERS. One man sent to Hospital injured.	a.f. Ritchie, 2/Lt
	5		wire laid to 13 MIDDLESEX and 7. NORTHANTS.	a.f. Ritchie, 2/Lt
	6. 7. 8. 9. 10.		maintained communication in Brigade area	a.f. Ritchie, 2/Lt
	11		maintained communication on tactical exercise by wire and dispatch rider.	a.f. Ritchie, 2/Lt
	12.			a.f. Ritchie, 2/Lt
	13.		reeled up wire to 13 MIDDLESEX and 9 SUSSEX.	a.f. Ritchie, 2/Lt
	14. 7 am		marched out for tactical exercise. exercise postponed.	a.f. Ritchie, 2/Lt
	15.		relaid wires to battalions	a.f. Ritchie, 2/Lt

Army Form C. 2118

WAR DIARY

Instructions regarding War Diaries and Intelligence Summaries are contained in F. S. Regs., Part II. and the Staff Manual respectively. Title pages will be prepared in manuscript.

(Erase heading not required.)

Place	Date	Hour	Summary of Events and Information	Remarks and references to Appendices
TORCY.	16			a.g. Ritchie, 2/RE.
	17.		reeled up wires to Battns. marched out for night tactical exercise at 7pm	a.g. Ritchie, 2/RE
	18.		maintained communication on tactical exercise. returned to Billets at 11 am.	a.g. Ritchie, 2/RE.
	19.		relaid wires to Battns	a.g. Ritchie, 2/RE.
	20.			a.g. Ritchie, 2/RE. a.g. Ritchie, 2/RE.
	21		reeled up wires. marched from TORCY at 6.45pm.	
LAIRES	22	1.30 am	arrived. maintained communication by D.R. left LAIRES 7pm	a.g. Ritchie, 2/RE.
BUSNES	23	2 am	arrived communicated with units by Dispatch rider.	a.g. Ritchie, 2/RE. a.g. Ritchie, 2/RE.
	24	7 pm	marched off from BUSNES. arrived at BEUVRY at m.t.	a.g. Ritchie, 2/RE.
BEUVRY.	25.	11 am	marched off. arrived VERMELLES 2pm. proceeded to trenches	
	24.	5 pm	took over from 27 BDE. wires laid to 9th DIV and 26 BDE.	a.g. Ritchie, 2/RE.
		11 pm	laid line to 13th MIDDLESEX.	
HOHENZOLLERN REDOUBT.	26	8 pm	BDE.H.Q. moved up to HOHENZOLLERN REDOUBT. Cable communication to 9th DIV and 26 BDE.	a.g. Ritchie, 2/RE.
	27.	2 pm	telephone communication with 9 DIV and 26 BDE broke down. relieved at 8pm by 65 BDE.	a.g. Ritchie, 2/RE.
SAILLY LA BOURSE.	28	2 am	reached SAILLY LABOURSE. 11.20 pm dismounted portion of section entrained at NOEUX.LES.MINES	a.g. Ritchie, 2/RE. 2/RE.

121/7517

24th A/5 Devain

24 K Signal Coy R.E.
Vol 3

Oct 15

D. A. G.
   3rd; Echelon.
         Base.

   Herein War Diary for the month of October . 1915. also Circuit Diagram of communication. Please acknowledge receipt hereon.

   also war diary for No 2 - 3 & 4 sections

                                Bradley Captain.
            Commanding 24th. Signal Co. R.E.

November 11. 1915.

Army Form C. 2118.

WAR DIARY
or
INTELLIGENCE SUMMARY.
(Erase heading not required.)

Instructions regarding War Diaries and Intelligence Summaries are contained in F.S. Regs., Part II. and the Staff Manual respectively. Title pages will be prepared in manuscript.

Place	Date	Hour	Summary of Events and Information	Remarks and references to Appendices
ST. HILAIRE, COTTES	1-10-15	11.00 AM	Company proceeded by march route to STEENVOORDE. Communication maintained by cable and D.R. to ST HILAIRE COTTES	
		4.0 PM	Company at STEENVOORDE. Wagons and horses parked and company billeted.	
STEENVOORDE	2/10/15		Signal office open at STEENVOORDE. Cable laid to 71st Infantry Brigade at PROVEN.	
			– Do – – Do – at HOUTKERQUE	
			– Do – 73rd – Do – at HERZEELE.	
			Also various trunk telephone circuits. 6th Corps turned telephone communication to 70th and 72nd Inf. Bdes.	
STEENVOORDE	3/10/15		Improved lines to Brigade and Zone telephone circuits. Communication maintained. Signalling and Buzzer instruction commenced for Infantry.	

Army Form C. 2118

Instructions regarding War Diaries and Intelligence Summaries are contained in F. S. Regs., Part II. and the Staff Manual respectively. Title pages will be prepared in manuscript.

WAR DIARY
or
INTELLIGENCE SUMMARY.
(Erase heading not required.)

Place	Date	Hour	Summary of Events and Information	Remarks and references to Appendices
STEENVOORDE	4/10/15		Maintaining communication by telephone and D.R. Put in ringing telephone to C.R.E.	
STEENVOORDE	5/10/15		Company engaged in signalling instruction. Communication maintained.	
STEENVOORDE	6/10/15		Company proceeded by march route to RENINGHEAST. Signal office closed at STEENVOORDE and re-opened at RENINGHEAST. Put in telephone to Divisional H.Q. Tapping over existing wires from 17th Signal Co. R.E.	
RENINGHEAST	7/10/15		Vibrator line erected to 17th Brigade at OUDERDOM. Put in telephone to C.R.E. Returning 17th Divisional lines. Company drilled and signal office communication by telephone. Reconnaissance for infantry recommenced.	

2353 Wt. W2544/1454 700,000 5/15 L.D.D.&L. A.D.S.S./Forms C. 2118.

WAR DIARY
or
INTELLIGENCE SUMMARY.
(Erase heading not required.)

Army Form C. 2118.

Place	Date	Hour	Summary of Events and Information	Remarks and references to Appendices
RENINGHELST	8/10/15		Put in telephone circuit to Commander officer Commanding ammunition column	
RENINGHELST	9/10/15		Repaired line to supply column at BUSSCHERE Communication maintained	
RENINGHELST	10/10/15		Put in telephone line to C.R.A. Also original Alpha having been moved.	
RENINGHELST	11/10/15		Ruled up old 75th Brigade line enemy and taking forward R.A. lines and laying three "core" and line.	
RENINGHELST	12/10/15		Commenced moving three "core" air line to TUE TUILE for communication to WOODCOTE HOUSE. Also commenced moving artillery wire to NEW HQRS	
RENINGHELST	13/10/15		Put in telephone to Divisional Ammunition Column and continued laying air line to WOODCOTE HOUSE.	

Army Form C. 2118

WAR DIARY
or
INTELLIGENCE SUMMARY.
(Erase heading not required.)

Instructions regarding War Diaries and Intelligence Summaries are contained in F.S. Regs., Part II. and the Staff Manual respectively. Title pages will be prepared in manuscript.

Place	Date	Hour	Summary of Events and Information	Remarks and references to Appendices
RENINGHEST	14/10/15		Regarding wires about camp. Putting through Vibrator and magneto tel lines from advanced R.A. Hqrs to R.A. Hqrs at RENINGHEST two lines laid from ZEVECOTEN to R.A. Hqrs at RENINGHEST. Laid one mile of cable from DICKEBUSCH to WOODCOTE HOUSE.	RASV
RENINGHEST	15/10/15		Ceased to supply telephone communication to 73rd Bde Hqrs at H.23.C.52 Map 28. Existing line to 73rd Bde at H.26.C.52 Map 28. Maintaining line to 73rd Bgde line. Running up 71st Brigade line alongside line to card over 17th Brigade. Infantry operations close. These men have been released from infantry Regiments and are able to mend wires in the trenches.	

2333 Wt. W3344/1454 700,000 5/15 L.D.& L. A.D.S.S./Forms/C. 2118.

WAR DIARY
or
INTELLIGENCE SUMMARY

Army Form C. 2118

Place	Date	Hour	Summary of Events and Information	Remarks and references to Appendices
RENINGHELST	16/10/15		They are being covered to resist the expected German assault, when they will then be attacked. They will return to their units. Reference order to R.A. Hqrs by "Comm" and lunch. Telephone and lunch to Ja 3rd Bayde at Woodcote House. Exchanged "Comms" not due to R.A. and 33rd Bayde. Arranged improved lines to Ja 3rd Bn at Woodcote House. Informed him about engine office. Put up one mile of insulated cable. Reninghelst to Boeschepe road.	DAA
RENINGHELST	17/10/15		Replaced cable lines to C.R.A. and D.A.D.O.S. in replace of "Comm" awaiting arrival of 2 miles of enveloped D.5.	
RENINGHELST	18/10/15		Rolled up 4 miles of enveloped D.5. returned cable damaged by enemy shells.	

Army Form C. 2118

WAR DIARY
or
INTELLIGENCE SUMMARY.
(Erase heading not required.)

Instructions regarding War Diaries and Intelligence Summaries are contained in F. S. Regs., Part II. and the Staff Manual respectively. Title pages will be prepared in manuscript.

Place	Date	Hour	Summary of Events and Information	Remarks and references to Appendices
RENINGHELST	20/10/15		Refitting line. Putting town clothing for troops maintaining communication.	
RENINGHELST	21/10/15		Peggys and tunnel line. Maintaining communication. Infantry refitting Class was consists of 35 men troops.	
RENINGHELST	22/10/15		Commenced trench for cable from 73rd Brigade at H23. C52. Map 28. to 1/4 Brigade at WOODCOTE HOUSE & Laying existing line from 18th Heavy Battery to C.R.A. Hqrs.	
RENINGHELST	23/10/15		Erected awnings from R.A. advanced dugout to existing trench line from YIR to 16th Brigade. R.F.A. turned complete line to 1/4 & 2 Sergeant topher try shell fire. Trench for carrying cable to 1/4 Brigade continuous.	

2353 Wt. W2544/1454 750,000 5/15 D.D.&L. A.D.S.S. Form.C 2118.

Army Form C. 2118

WAR DIARY
or
INTELLIGENCE SUMMARY
(Erase heading not required.)

Instructions regarding War Diaries and Intelligence Summaries are contained in F. S. Regs., Part II. and the Staff Manual respectively. Title pages will be prepared in manuscript.

Place	Date	Hour	Summary of Events and Information	Remarks and references to Appendices
RENINGHELST	24/10/15		Continued relieving in trenches & to R.A. Dugouts in Belgian artillery Hqrs. Carried on with trench & dugout work. Communication maintained.	
RENINGHELST	25/10/15		Connected Hqrs 106th Bde R.F.A. and Belgian Hqrs to trench work. Repairing and working at leads and generally strengthened all lines to Belgian artillery Hqrs.	
RENINGHELST	26/10/15		Continued digging trench for buried cable. Laying up of communication between R.A. and carrying out Keeling Bde Hqrs. trenching done.	
RENINGHELST	27/10/15		Moved telephone exchange to new telephone hut, installed exchange between by swinism including 6 men from 24th Signal Co. R.E.	

WAR DIARY or INTELLIGENCE SUMMARY

Army Form C. 2118

Place	Date	Hour	Summary of Events and Information	Remarks and references to Appendices
RENINGHELST			Continued work on lines and maintaining communication	
RENINGHELST	29/10/15		Reconnoitering Belgian trenches from RE 'dugout' to Belgian Artillery Hqrs. Continued work on Belgian lines from line gauges to YPRES for possible communication maintenance.	
RENINGHELST	30/10/15		Overhauling clips. Infantry class for operators continue. Very wet weather. 33 men now being instructed. Hqrs of Lahore Div. Signal office changed into Farmers Report. Airline arranged, continued work on trench to Lowan cable.	
RENINGHELST	31/10/15		Telegraphic communication again established with Administrative Staff. Work continued to lines to advanced Hqrs. Continued making trench stands for wires.	

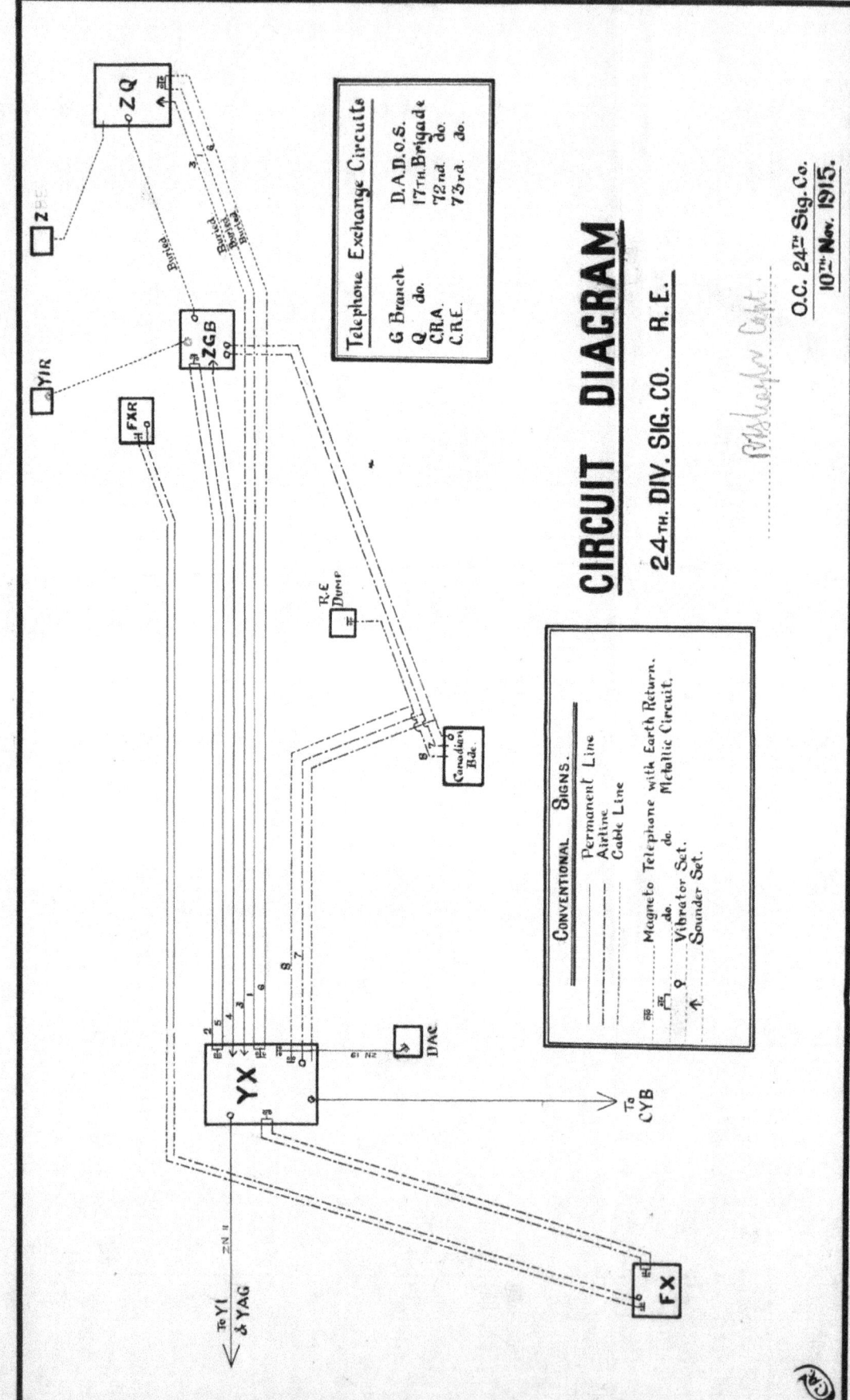

Army Form C. 2118

WAR DIARY

No 2 Section
24 Sig: Coy: R.E.

INTELLIGENCE SUMMARY.

From 1/10/15 — 31/10/15

(Erase heading not required.)

Instructions regarding War Diaries and Intelligence Summaries are contained in F. S. Regs., Part II. and the Staff Manual respectively. Title pages will be prepared in manuscript.

Place	Date	Hour	Summary of Events and Information	Remarks and references to Appendices
Hazen- brouck	1/10/15 – 2/10/15		Stood at Hazenbrouck by the 7/A Brigade H.Q. left at 9 A.M. train from Berguette for Gostewaerdt via Hazebrouck on arriving at Gostewaerdt at 12 o. we we marched to Proven 7 miles when all H.Q. was to be for the time being. 7BdeSig: Section was able to get hut. We were at once on arrival carried up with plans by Corps Signals. No huts land to Batt: because of men which was to be place at any time. Wats (Signal) arrived at by D.R. mounted at C. & M.C. DivSig: line was brought up and Office from Div H.Q.	Asternative
Proven	3/10/15 4/10/15 5/10/15		Work as usual, as well as seeing to and looking over all Sig: Sec: Stats.	
Proven			Marched at 10 men from Proven with 7Bde H.Q. to Guderman via Oppeninghe, H.Q. in farm houses. DivSig: brought in both Telephone & Sounder lines, but no lines again laid to Batt: because of men which was likely to come up shortly, and all SigSection was to join up with 7Bde 3rd Div: to huts and their lines.	
Oudezeem	6/10. 7/10		Went up to 7 Bde H.Q. to arrange for attaching my Section to them for a few days. Sent up 14 men to 7Bde H.Q. that night they were put into the trenches with 7Bde Sig: and to their last station. I went over 3rd Div. Sig: Office.	
	8/10. 9/10.		Went up to 7Bde Sig: Sec: and welcomed their lines. Brought in 15 men of my Sec: from 7Bde and Seek at some to better this place.	

Army Form C. 2118.

WAR DIARY
or
INTELLIGENCE SUMMARY.

(Erase heading not required.)

Instructions regarding War Diaries and Intelligence Summaries are contained in F. S. Regs., Part II. and the Staff Manual respectively. Title pages will be prepared in manuscript.

Place	Date	Hour	Summary of Events and Information	Remarks and references to Appendices
	9/10.		There is another move on. { *(signature)* O. Bernard	
	10/10.		Called all my Section in from 76sec on the night of the 10/10. Communication from 7/10 to 10/10 was carried on by D.R. with the help of Batt cyclists.	
	11/10.		71st Bde. H.Q. moved Mt to Poperinghe. day at 11:30 A.M. to march to Proven them Poperinghe. Later was trucked N.D.Y.Pres. 71st Bde was to join 6th Div. at Proven So Bde. Section did not join them with them. Got orders to join 17 Bde who would not be in Sn Sixte in three days, this place of 71st I.B. after 71.I.B. had moved Mb.R.S. was packed ready to move Mb to Div. H.Q. in the morning.	
	12/10.		Moved with 17 Bde. Section to 24th Sig. Coy: H.Q. at Reninghelst. to await 17 Bde. Bde section was moved with H.Q. to help in laying out line etc.	
Poperinghe Reninghelst	13/10.		Laying lines for H.Q.	
	14/10.			
	15/10.		Part of the 17 Bde arrived. So reported to H.Q. 17 Bde was in a 5th Batt ale. ; 71st was only to 4 Balta Bde. Put in few extra men and Stever at once. 17th Bde as soon made up of the following. 1st Roy Fus, 3rd R.B., 2nd London Regt. 12th Roy Fus. 28 Buffs.	
	16/10.		Move up and joined 17 Bde only 9 co+ from 24 Sig. H.Q. So no lines were laid out. except a telephone line no line to Batt. because we were again moving in two days. N.D. only did Air B the Change Camp in three days with all Batt. changed to the Div. the 8 Buffs came in again	

WAR DIARY
or
INTELLIGENCE SUMMARY.

(Erase heading not required.)

Army Form C. 2118.

Place	Date	Hour	Summary of Events and Information	Remarks and references to Appendices
Wardrecques Hinre.	16/10		72.1.B. the 17.1.B. running on Regular Balk. Put up Telephone in new Office and sent to all Stns.	
	17/10		Heard we were to letter and line now held by 72.1.B. went off early to see our new H.Q. and lines which were to be taken over. Phoned up from 72.1.B. H.Q. for linemen to come up as the enemy returned to our Old H.Q. in the evening. Re-laid up all Stns. Sent up rel. of OC & selrs with his linemen from each Batt to letter and all lines. New belongings to 72.1.B. Seelrs and Off. at 11.30 a.m. Waggon and Stores came up at night. with all transport. I went up and 2 P.M. to letter and lines. All linos letter & oral from 72.1.B. at 3.30 P.M. Sigs. Sec. and Seelrs & linemen were from head only been up here 3 days. the Batt helps there a b.g. 4 days and the rest of the troops there about 2 days. So Batl. ns we had been able to get all linos laid in hand things straighter all. If we are here long enough to get the ne in hand and finished. Went full Q lines from Batt to Bys.	
	18/10			
	19/10			
	20/10		Painter lines (all) from old H.Q. to Capt. Brand Signal Office, in a Sitting room of the house. Place made the in a day as lines, & a larger Room. Painting lines, and fitting up new Signal Office.	

WAR DIARY
or
INTELLIGENCE SUMMARY.
(Erase heading not required.)

Army Form C. 2118.

Place	Date	Hour	Summary of Events and Information	Remarks and references to Appendices
	22/10		Lines in hand. Cleaning up. Lines N.P. in use from Batt to Bde; in trenches and also N.P. of Div. Lines round Bde H.Q. Signal Office also well in hand. Safe to move in daylight.	
	23/10		Patrolling lines, replacing D³ by cable for BS¹⁰ on some of the lines.	
	24/10		Lines well advanced above Batt lines.	
	25/10		Patrolling lines. Refitting and wiring up Signal Office.	
	26/10		Chiefly rain. Managed to trace some of the tel. buried lines. Hope to move into new Signal Office tomorrow. Lines penetrated very bright – morning. Started on new line to our reserve Batt, but had to give it up, but Octr owing to aircraft. (German).	
	27/10		Nearly all lines rel. is in use as cleaned up Batt in support. Earl³ and Leury allied and buried track 300 yards from Grenade Rue. Hand in new Sig. Office at 4 p.m. all correct. 2ˣ Londons cannot come up to relieve our Regt. train to wait to-night. Heavy shelling of cross rds. ¾ mile N.W. of Rut and R.F.A. lines. Some trees have covered lines. Reserve Batt and Belgians	

WAR DIARY
or
INTELLIGENCE SUMMARY.
(Erase heading not required.)

Army Form C. 2118

Place	Date	Hour	Summary of Events and Information	Remarks and references to Appendices
	28/10.		Several lines cut, but all now in orders, buried lines in ground.	
	29/10.		Front line and Belgium line, and line back to Batt. at rest.	Approved
	30/10.		Lines patrols all round.	
	31/10.		Gott line have been strengthened cut- a L.P. at South have been brought ready to Batt H.Q. by means of trench cable. Gunner lines to batts a good shelter in places, but am am getting these strengthened up. Trenched sheltered lines (R&L) as handed over, but there are all wrong, as soon as all trees have been leaved map of Lindgren dug out, will be made and sent forward.	

WAR DIARY
or
INTELLIGENCE SUMMARY.
(Erase heading not required.)

Army Form C. 2118.

No 2 Section
24 Sig: Coy. R.E.

WAR DIARY
or
INTELLIGENCE SUMMARY.

No 3 Sect. 24 S.S. Coy. 1912

Army Form C.2118

(Erase heading not required.)

Place	Date	Hour	Summary of Events and Information	Remarks and references to Appendices
Busquett	1-10-15		Halted	9am
"	2-10-15		Train to Godewaersvelde - marched to new billeting area Houtkerque	9pm
		1-15 pm	arrived	
Houtkerque	3-10-15		Halted	9am
Houtkerque	4-10-15		Halted	9am
"	5-10-15		Halted	9pm
"	6-10-15		Moved new area - arrived Reninghelst 3 pm	9am
Reninghelst	7-10-15		Halted	9am
"	8-10-15		"	9am
"	9-10-15		"	9am
"	10-10-15		"	9am
"	11-10-15		"	9am
"	12-10-15		"	9am
"	13-10-15		"	9am
"	14-10-15		Moved to Woodcote House - took over from 27 IB - 72 IB holding Trenches 27.6-31 - relief completed 11-55 pm - Sp taken over 8 pm	9am
"	15-10-15			9am

Army Form C. 2118

WAR DIARY
or
INTELLIGENCE SUMMARY. No 3 Section 24th Sig Coy

(Erase heading not required.)

Instructions regarding War Diaries and Intelligence Summaries are contained in F. S. Regs., Part II. and the Staff Manual respectively. Title pages will be prepared in manuscript.

Place	Date	Hour	Summary of Events and Information	Remarks and references to Appendices
Woesten Hout	16-X-15		Line laid to batt. at Rest - at Dickebusch. Other lines walked.	Gpsd
"	17-X-15		Existing lines inspected and improved.	Gpsd
"	18-X-15		Lines inspected. Handed over to Sigs. N 1 B at 5 pm. Moved to rest - at RENINGHELST. arriving 6.30 pm	Gpsd
Reninghelst	19-X-15		Halted	Gpsd
"	20-X-15		"	Gpsd
"	21-X-15		"	Gpsd
"	22-X-15		"	Gpsd
"	23-X-15		"	Gpsd
"	24-X-15		"	Gpsd
"	25-X-15		"	Gpsd
"	26-X-15		"	Gpsd
"	27-X-15		"	Gpsd
"	28-X-15		"	Gpsd
"	29-X-15		"	Gpsd
"	30-X-15		"	Gpsd
"	31-X-15		"	Gpsd

1/11/15 [signature] Lt MR Pt
O/c No 3 Sec temp. 24 Div Sig Coy

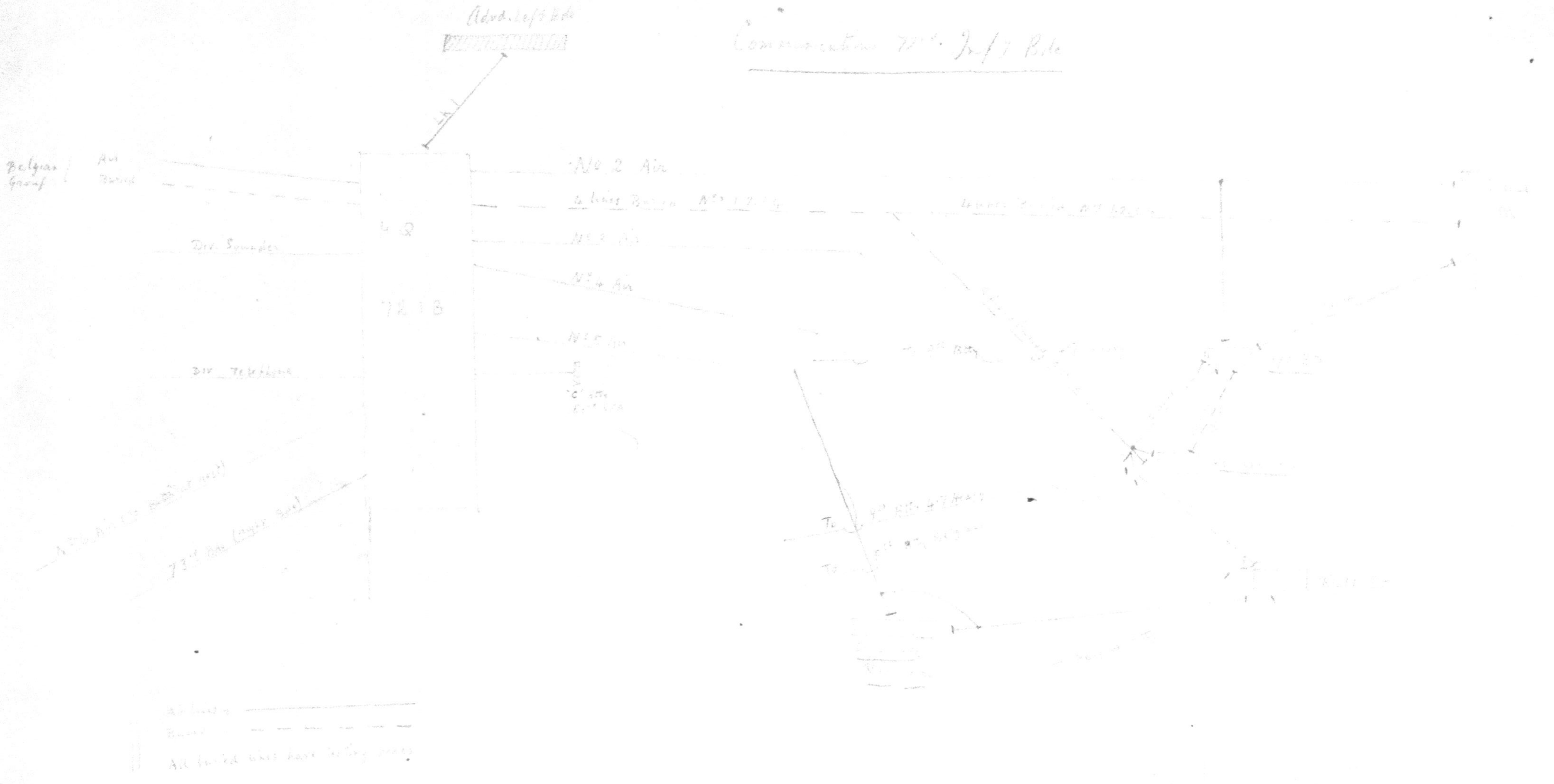

Communications 72nd Inf Bde
Advd. Left Bde
Belgian Group
Air
Buried
H.Q.
72 I B
No 2 Air
Div. Sounder
Div. Telephone
No 4 Air

Army Form C. 2118

WAR DIARY
or
~~INTELLIGENCE SUMMARY~~

(Erase heading not required.)

No 4. Sec. 2 4. Sig. Co.

Place	Date	Hour	Summary of Events and Information	Remarks and references to Appendices
MAZINGHEM.	1.		Picked up wires, mounted portion of section proceeded at noon to STEENVOORDE in two stages.	a.g. Ritchie
	2.	1.30 pm	Remainder of section entrained at BERGUETTE, arrived at GODEWAERESVELDE at 3.45 pm.	a.g. Ritchie
HERZEELE	3.		Marched to HERZEELE arrived at 9 pm.	a.g. Ritchie 2 R.E.
	4.		Laid wire to 7. NORTANTS.	a.g. Ritchie
	5.		One Sapper reported sick with Scabies, and went to hospital.	a.g. Ritchie 2 R.E.
	6.		Ruled up wire to 7. Northants. Marched from HERZEELE at 1 pm.	a.g. Ritchie 2 R.E.
PROVEN	6.	4 pm	arrived at PROVEN. Bell telephone installed to VI. Corps.	a.g. Ritchie 2 R.E.
	7.	9 A.M.	Laid enamelled wire to 7. Northants, 12. R.F. and 13 Middlesex. wire was broken in several places in the open country during the night.	a.g. Ritchie 2 R.E.
	8.	9 A.M.	Mended enamelled wire, and laid extra piece of D1 through the open country, leaving the enamelled wire through the village, where it can be safely laid along the tops of houses. Laid the D1 in a safe position along a tramway line.	a.g. Ritchie 2 R.E.
	9.	?	Maintained Communication	a.g. Ritchie 2 R.E.
	10.			a.g. Ritchie 2 R.E.
	11.	9.30 am	Left PROVEN - arrived RENINGHELST at 1 pm.	a.g. Ritchie 2 R.E.
H.23.C.52. sheet 28.	12.	Noon	Went to 43. 1. BDE at H.23.C.52. sheet 28 with 10 men to take over investigated lines	a.g. Ritchie 2 R.E.
	13.			a.g. Ritchie 2 R.E.
	14.	11 am	Took over communications from 43 I.B.	a.g. Ritchie

Army Form C. 2118

WAR DIARY

or ~~INTELLIGENCE SUMMARY~~

(Erase heading not required.)

Instructions regarding War Diaries and Intelligence Summaries are contained in F. S. Regs., Part II. and the Staff Manual respectively. Title pages will be prepared in manuscript.

2.

Place	Date	Hour	Summary of Events and Information	Remarks and references to Appendices
H.23.c.52. Sheet 28.	15.			
	16.			
	17.			
	18.			
	19.		maintained communication with lines as in appendix 1.	A.G. Ritchie
	20.			
	21.			
	22.			
	23.			
	24.			
	25.			
	26.			
	27.			
	28.		Lateral line to 17.1.13. broken by shell fire.	A.G. Ritchie
	29.			
	30.		buried line broken by shell fire.	A.G. Ritchie
	31.			

APPENDIX I.

WAR DIARY or INTELLIGENCE SUMMARY.

Army Form C. 2118

73 BDE COMMUNICATIONS at H 23 c 5.2.

Buried lines ---------
airlines ⎯⎯⎯⎯

Boxes shown: LBN, LCB, RCB, R Bn, TS, B HQ, ZGC, CZDR, RFA, YX

24th Div: Signal Coy:
Vol: 4

101/77D4

34th Division

Nov 15

Army Form C. 2118.

WAR DIARY
or
INTELLIGENCE SUMMARY.
(Erase heading not required.)

Instructions regarding War Diaries and Intelligence Summaries are contained in F. S. Regs. Part II. and the Staff Manual respectively. Title pages will be prepared in manuscript.

Place	Date	Hour	Summary of Events and Information	Remarks and references to Appendices
RENINGHELST	1-11-15		Used up new line exchange to Headquarters 106th Brigade R.F.A. Maintaining communication. Heavy rain.	
	2-11-15		Cannot commence truffle on the turned line. Put in new pyolin of earth to Signal office. Installing Cheveels for Groase line to R.A. Maintaining communication.	
	3-11-15		Extended existing wires to Headquarters 108th Brigade R.F.A. at DICKEBUSCH. Continued making Cheveels for Groase lines. Maintaining Communication.	
	4-11-15		Laid 3 truncl line from DICKEBUSCH ROAD to WOODCOTE HOUSE in our trench and covered them in. Maintaining communication.	
	5-11-15		New counted line to WOODCOTE HOUSE put through. New permanent route to SPIKE ISLAND road and got ready for work.	

WAR DIARY
INTELLIGENCE SUMMARY
(Erase heading not required.)

Army Form C. 2118.

Place	Date	Hour	Summary of Events and Information	Remarks and references to Appendices
RENINGHELST	6.11.15		All fronts in rear known route reviewed and remaining list been put in. Changed over Brigade lines to thousand yard continued felling in trench for buried cable. Maintaining communication.	
"	7.11.15		Extended existing twelve to Shaldraken 129 Field Co. R.E. also extended reserve to Kyoo Bestry Battalion 17th Infantry Brigade. Surrounds reported class @rhibow telegraphy. 25 Infantry men nominating hand oner through this class an from 12 6/4 noons for hours. Continued felling in trench and regulating reserve lines. Maintaining Communication.	
"	8.11.15		Put in telephone line from 104 Field Co R.E. to R.E. Divisn.	
"	9.11.15		Continued felling in trench for buried cable.	

Army Form C. 2118.

WAR DIARY
or
INTELLIGENCE SUMMARY.
(Erase heading not required.)

Instructions regarding War Diaries and Intelligence Summaries are contained in F.S. Regs., Part II. and the Staff Manual respectively. Title pages will be prepared in manuscript.

Place	Date	Hour	Summary of Events and Information	Remarks and references to Appendices
RENINGHELST	10-10-15		Work on filling in trenches continues. Working party strengthening existing Communication trenches maintained.	
-"-	11-11-15		Dug trench from ½ in Infantry Brigade Hqrs to point where trench from 1/2 Infantry Bde Hqrs Commences. Continued felling in trenches to 1/17th O.B. Maintaining communication.	
-"-	12-11-15		Completed digging trench from SPIKE ISLAND to last hut on 1/6 DICKEBUSCH ROAD laid in two D5 cables. Put in tool boxes and filled in trench.	
-"-	13-11-15		Laid army trunk army 6 gale and heavy iron Maintaining communication. Laid 1 the think phone line from SPIKE ISLAND to DICKEBUSCH ROAD Rfnewer the track mk by storm in "camp" airlines and permanent route.	

2333 Wt W.5244/1454 700,000 5/15 D.D.&L. A.D.S.S./Forms/C. 2118.

WAR DIARY
or
INTELLIGENCE SUMMARY.

(Erase heading not required.)

Army Form C. 2118.

Place	Date	Hour	Summary of Events and Information	Remarks and references to Appendices
RENINGHELST	14.11.15		Repaired "Emu" airlines damaged by gale. Burying line across DICKEBUSH-YPRES main road. Completed felling in trench from DICKEBUSCH RD to SPIKE ISLAND.	
"	15.11.15		Putting up lines into C.R.A. Hqrs from permanent lines in RENINGHEST. Commenced burying cable from grounds of SPIKE ISLAND to first but occupied by 147th S.B. turned route.	
"	16.11.15		Putting additional strip on "Emu" airline. Commenced putting in permanent poles from RENINGHERST to CRA Hqrs.	
"	17.11.15		Constructing new permanent pole to service route subway from work of permanent route to SPIKE ISLAND. Continued digging trench from SPIKE ISLAND to WOODCOTE HOUSE (french route).	

Army Form C. 2118.

WAR DIARY
or
INTELLIGENCE SUMMARY.
(Erase heading not required.)

Place	Date	Hour	Summary of Events and Information	Remarks and references to Appendices
RENINGHELST	18.11.15		Maintaining Communication. Infantry operators Class continues satisfactorily. It was found that the effect of the close was very difficult to remove entire. On the return of three men of such troop, ahead, and looking the which men to their Regiments they were working knowledge of telegraphy neither this was rectified by means of L.S. Orderly Regulating & reporting all lines into Signal Office. Shaking and overhauling our Stationary Communication.	
	19.11.15		Preparing to hand over the hut & hen-huts of Communication to 3rd Signal Co. R.E.	
	20.11.15		Maintaining Communication.	

Army Form C. 2118.

WAR DIARY
or
INTELLIGENCE SUMMARY.
(Erase heading not required.)

Instructions regarding War Diaries and Intelligence Summaries are contained in F. S. Regs., Part II. and the Staff Manual respectively. Title pages will be prepared in manuscript.

Place	Date	Hour	Summary of Events and Information	Remarks and references to Appendices
RENINGHELST	26.11.15		Cleaning up Camp and Project lines and relaying up all broken cable. Maintaining communication	
— " —	22.11.15	9.00 A.M.	Company proceeded by march route to OXELAERE via STEENVOORDE arrived at OXELAERE 5:30 PM. Company billeted at Chateau, wagons and horses parked in adjoining field. All lines made up and standing equipment handed over to 3rd Sigs Co. R.E. at RENINGHELST.	
OXELAERE	23.11.15	9.00 A.M.	Company proceeded by march route to TIRQUES via ST. OMER. arrived at TIRQUES 3.00 PM. Coy billeted in farm buildings, wagons and horses parked in adjoining field. Signal office established and taken over communication maintained by D.R.	

2353 Wt. W2544/1454 700,000 5/15 L. D. & L. A.D.S.S./Forms/C. 2118.

Army Form C. 2118.

WAR DIARY
or
INTELLIGENCE SUMMARY.
(Erase heading not required.)

Place	Date	Hour	Summary of Events and Information	Remarks and references to Appendices
TILQUES	24-11-15		Despatching equipment and establishing local events. G.H.Q. twelve Metallic circuit to 43rd Infantry Bde at EPERLECQUES. Metallic circuit and single line to 72nd Infantry Bde at NORDAUSQUES.	
"	25-11-15		Maintaining communication. Tie line to H.Q. Divison "Q" Branch.	
"	26-11-15		Ordinary cleaning ways. Maintaining communication. Held telephone line to 6 C.R.E. and "E" Branch. Ground H.Q. Maintaining communication. Extended line erected by No. 26 Airline team to 17th Infantry Bde at BAYINGHEM and 72 nd Infantry Bde at NORDAUSQUES.	
"	27-11-15		Continued extending equipment. Maintaining communication.	

Army Form C. 2118.

WAR DIARY
or
INTELLIGENCE SUMMARY.
(Erase heading not required.)

Place	Date	Hour	Summary of Events and Information	Remarks and references to Appendices
TILQUES	28-11-15		Extended single line erected by G.H.Q. to R.A. Farm Headquarters at [?] E.M. Cleaning and overhauling equipment. Maintaining Communication.	
" "	29-11-15		Continued cleaning and overhauling equipment. Company reconnoitred instructions in Visual signaling. Maintaining Communication.	
" "	30-11-15		Overhauling equipment and stores. 12 operators sent from 14th Corps to relieve Company operators. Instruction in Visual signalling continued. Maintaining Communication.	

Army Form C. 2118.

WAR DIARY
or
INTELLIGENCE SUMMARY.
(Erase heading not required.)

Instructions regarding War Diaries and Intelligence
Summaries are contained in F. S. Regs., Part II
and the Staff Manual respectively. Title pages
will be prepared in manuscript.

Place	Date	Hour	Summary of Events and Information	Remarks and references to Appendices

Army Form C. 2118.

WAR DIARY
or
INTELLIGENCE SUMMARY.
(Erase heading not required.)

Summary

Place	Date	Hour	Summary of Events and Information	Remarks and references to Appendices

1st Roy Fus .... BOYENGHEM.
12th Roy Fus .... EST MONT, WEST MONT, WESTROVE.
8. Buffs .... LA COMMUNE, LA PANNE, LE COMMUNAL.
3rd Rifle Bde .... NORTBEULINGHEM.
2 London Regt .... RICQUES.
103rd Field Coy R.E. ...... MONNESCOVE.
202 Coy Div. Train ...... "   "
74 Field Amb. .... CHAU. de la VIEGETTE. (WESTROVE).
17. I. B. H.Q. .... 1/4 M. North ? in WESTROVE. (Chau).

8 Batts.   12 R.F.
                        12 F.
                  Bde H.Q.

Ammi as now laid out by Batts.
Also emclose Sketch? lunis, that was drawn of left Horse & Hovers.

31.

No 2. Section. 2 4 Army Form C. 2118.
Signal Coy. 24 Div
WAR DIARY
or
INTELLIGENCE SUMMARY.   Nov: 15. 1/11/15 — 30/11/15
(Erase heading not required.)

Instructions regarding War Diaries and Intelligence
Summaries are contained in F.S. Regs., Part II.
and the Staff Manual respectively. Title pages
will be prepared in manuscript.

Hour, Date, Place	Summary of Events and Information	Remarks and references to Appendices

1/11
2/11 } Div patrols, laid cable from Sheet 51A, D: C13c
3/11 } relieved by D5 in same div. frontage.
4/11
5/11
6/11
7/11   Took over Sect. line from 26 Bde in trenches
       33–35 and handed over to 72 I.B. my nos
       of wire laid. Laid cable to new Batt H.Q.
       from new forward left Bde. Div air line in
       e.T. Also air line lair (air) laid at from
       Bde H.Q. to Batt H.Q.
8/11   Area woke on lewis mount Pole H.Q delayed
       by German air craft.
9/11 }
10/11 } all lines patroled.

WAR DIARY or INTELLIGENCE SUMMARY

Army Form C. 2118.

Place	Date	Hour	Summary of Events and Information	Remarks and references to Appendices
	11/11			
	12/11		Divn festival, no load cemetery owing to the wet.	
	13/11			
	14/11			Reharsing
	15/11		Divn holism returned flown by staff five.	
	16/11			
	17/11		Divn holism, cies in view.	
	18/11			
	19/11			
	20/11		Stand to how 1/38 Bde covt opened to bathe and divs, the funnel into the Bde war At Reberry Boesflers of the 17.Bde Luis men from 76 Bde came up to go over my lines Luis lectures one by 76 Bde at 4.30 P.M. Life without Home at 7.30 P.M.	
	21/11		mogt Spend at Renuinghelet	
	22/11		Marched to EECKE at 4.30 P.M. via BOESCHEPE and GODEWAERSVELDE amvrig there at 10 P.M. Office opened at 11 P.M. by D.R.	
	23/11		Day Spent at EECKE. Communication by D.R.	

Army Form C. 2118.

WAR DIARY
or
INTELLIGENCE SUMMARY.
(Erase heading not required.)

Instructions regarding War Diaries and Intelligence Summaries are contained in F.S. Regs., Part II. and the Staff Manual respectively. Title pages will be prepared in manuscript.

Place: S.M.

Date	Hour	Summary of Events and Information	Remarks and references to Appendices
24/11		Marched at 9.45 a.m. to ARNEKE via CARSEL arriving at 12.30 p.m. Officers synced 1 p.m. by D.R.	
25/11		Marched at 9.45 a.m. to (GASPETTE) ECERLECQUES via Ruhrouda. Officers synced at 2 p.m.	
26/11		BROXEELE, and Watten arriving at 2 p.m. Officers synced at 2.30 p.m. by D.R.	
27/11		Marched at 12.30 p.m. to leave 1/4 N.B. of WESTROVEN arriving there at 1.30 p.m. Officers synced at 2 p.m. by D.R. Communicated by S.R.	
28/11			
29/11		Lid laid out to three Batts within about 2½ miles, leaving the Horse Station on Battn. Hd. Line	
30/11		all correct.	

Right Sector

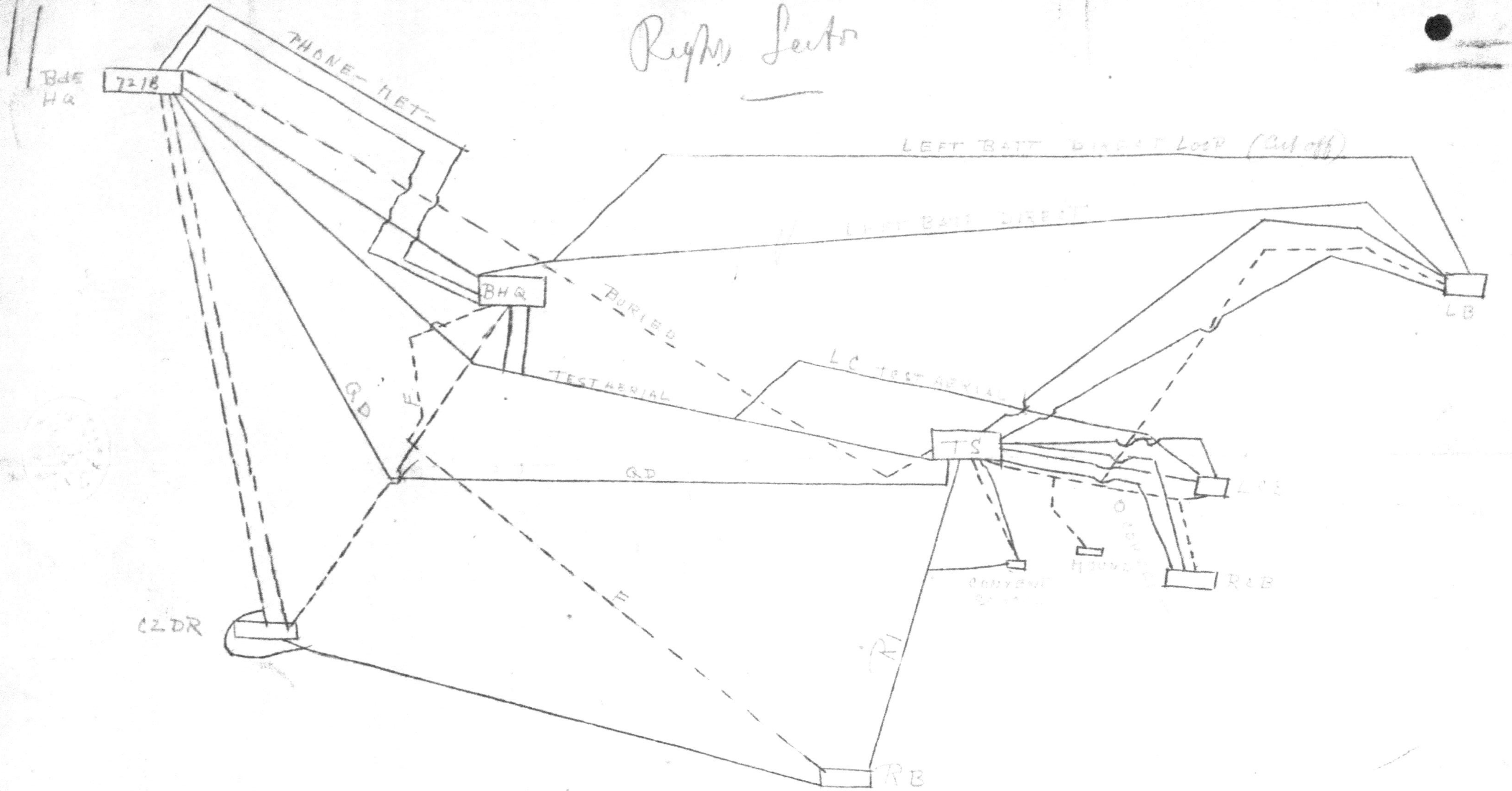

Lines as taken over from Sigs 73/B

5/11/15

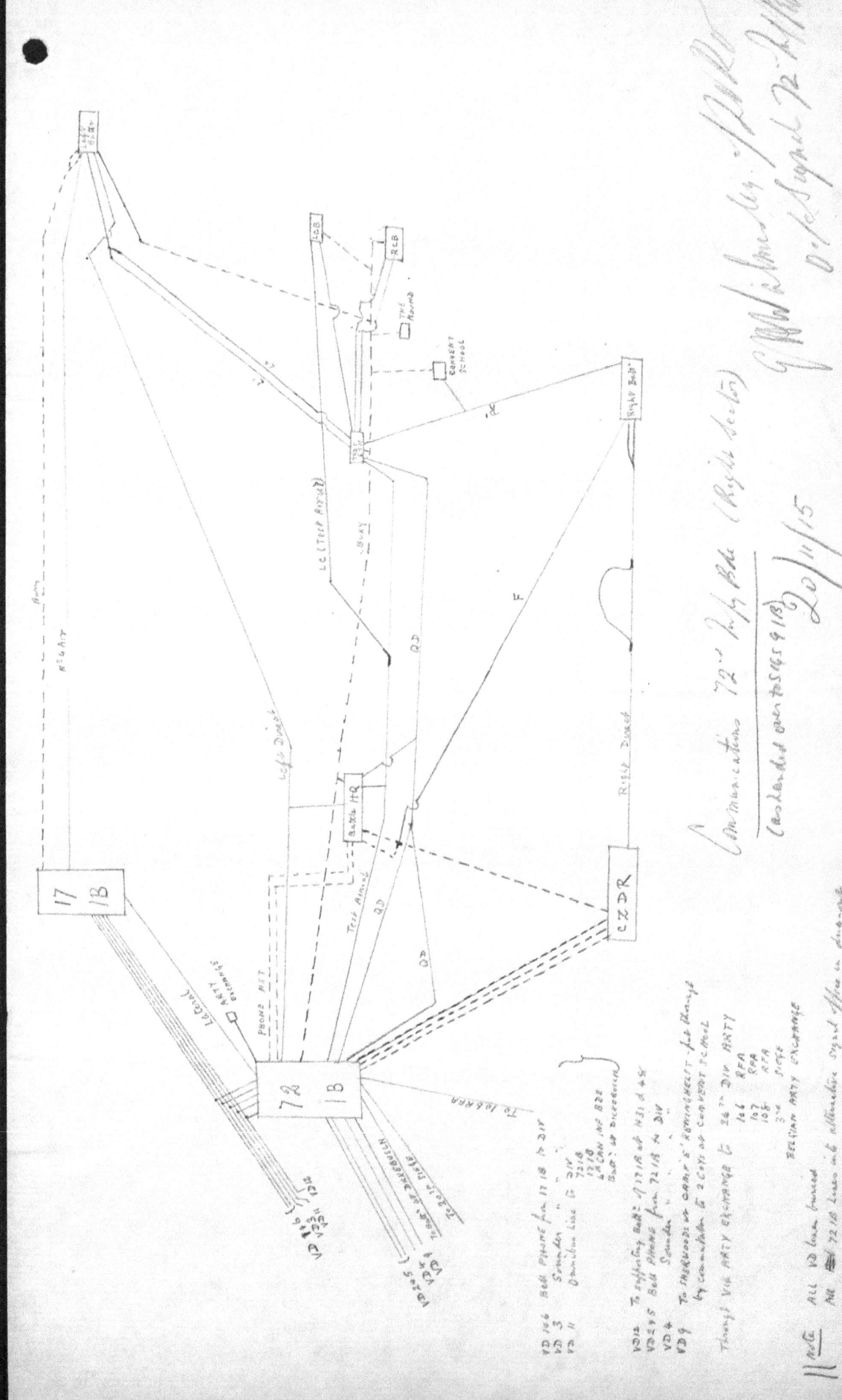

Communications in 72nd Inf Bde Area 29/4/15

———— = Airline
~~~~~~ = Arrangements for talking only

SQDRN = Despatch Riders
NS = 1st N. STAFFS
QUH = 8/QUEENS
ESI = 9/E. SURREYS
RWK = 8/R.W. KENT
JJD = 106TH FD Coy R.E.

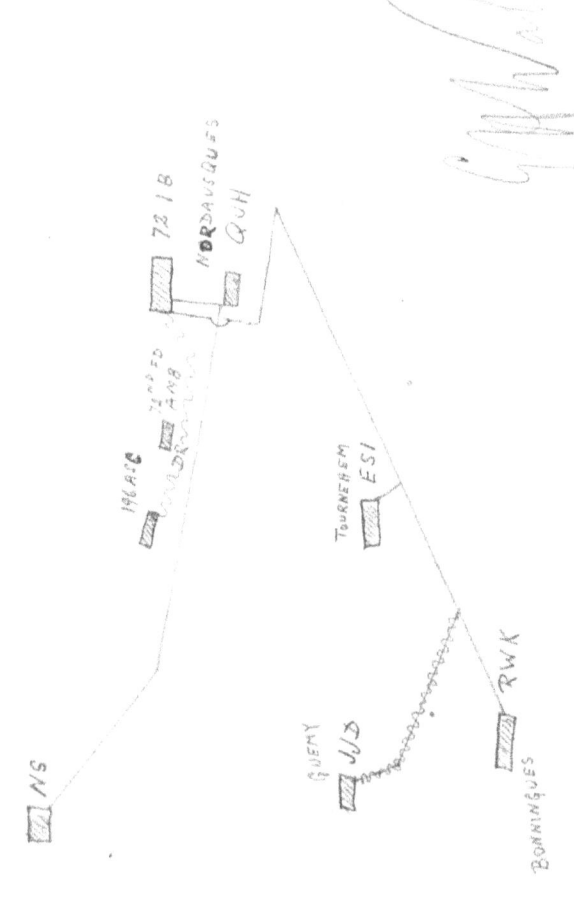

Army Form C. 2118.

WAR DIARY
or
INTELLIGENCE SUMMARY.

No 3 Section 24th Div. Signal Coy RE

(Erase heading not required.)

Instructions regarding War Diaries and Intelligence Summaries are contained in F. S. Regs., Part II. and the Staff Manual respectively. Title pages will be prepared in manuscript.

Place	Date	Hour	Summary of Events and Information	Remarks and references to Appendices
Reminghelst	Nov 1/915		Halted	
"	2 "		Halted	
"	3 "		Halted	
"	4 "		Marched to Chateau at H.29.a.9.8. Ref. map 28. Took over from Signals 73 I.B. Diagram of lines taken over attached.	
H.29.a.9.8.	5-14		Lines patrolled and necessary alterations and improvements made.	
"	6 "		"	
"	7 "		"	
"	8 "		"	
"	9 "		"	
"	10 "		"	
"	11 "		"	
"	12 "		"	
"	13 "		"	
"	14 "		"	
"	15 "		"	
"	16 "		"	
"	17 "		"	
"	18 "		"	
"	19. "		"	

Army Form C. 2118.

WAR DIARY
or
INTELLIGENCE SUMMARY. No 3 Section 24th Div
Signal Coy R E

(Erase heading not required.)

Instructions regarding War Diaries and Intelligence Summaries are contained in F. S. Regs., Part II. and the Staff Manual respectively. Title pages will be prepared in manuscript.

Place	Date	Hour	Summary of Events and Information	Remarks and references to Appendices
H.Q.D.88	20.Nov/15		Lines patrolled and necessary alterations made	9 A.W
" "	21 "		" "	9 A.W
" "	22 "		Handed over to Signals 9th I.B. (diagram of lines as handed over attached) Marched to camp at RENINGHELST arriving at 5pm.	9 B.W
RENINGHELST	23.11.15		Marched to new billeting area at STEENVOORDE arriving 10 pm.	9 A.W
STEENVOORDE	24.11.15		Halted	9 A.W
" "	25.11.15		Marched to new billeting area at NOORDPEENE arriving at 2 pm	9 A.W
NOORDPEENE	26.11.15		Marched to new billeting area at GANSPETTE arriving at 1 pm	9 A.W
GANSPETTE	27.11.15		Marched to new billeting area at NORDAUSQUES arriving at 12.30 pm	9 A.W
NORDAUSQUES	28.11.15		Lines laid to units in group as per diagram attached	9 A.W
" "	29.11.15		Training	9 A.W
" "	30.11.15		Training	9 A.W

3.

RCB — MIM

RSVI

NRG.

ZGC

YX

COMMUNICATIONS of 731.B. at EPERLECQUES.

27/11/15.

agritcha

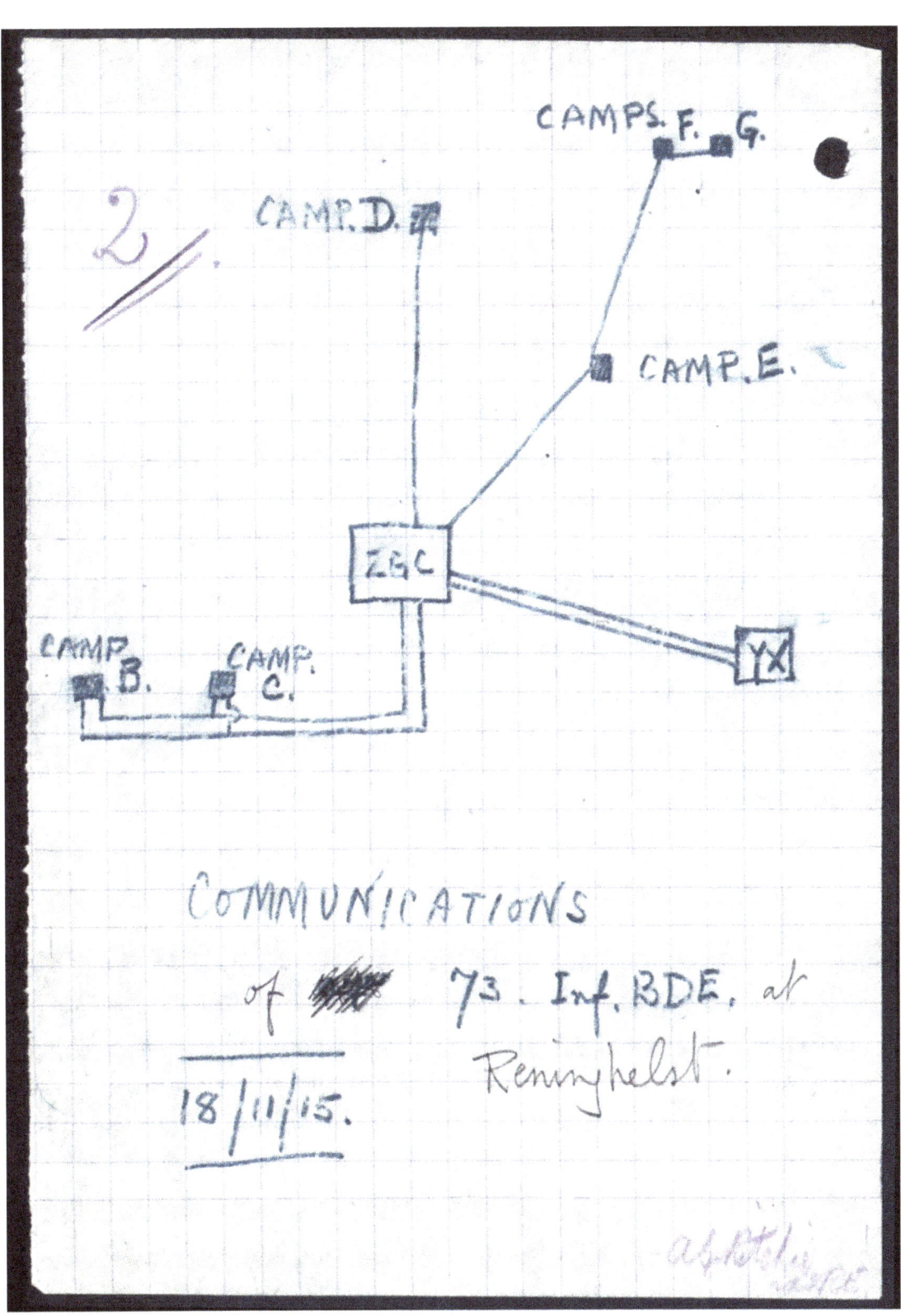

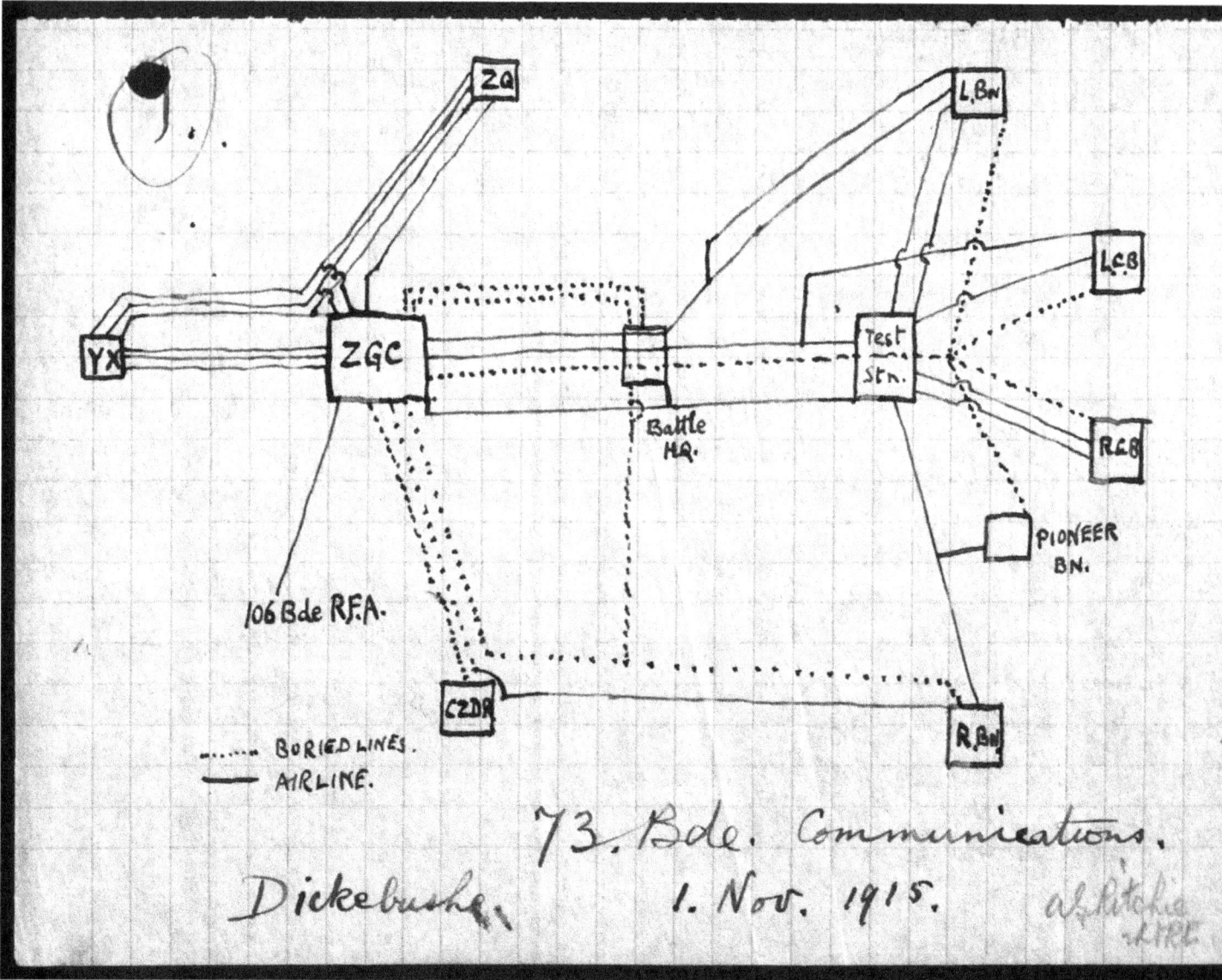

Army Form C. 2118.

WAR DIARY

NOVEMBER 1915.

No. 4. sec. 24 Signal Coy.

(Erase heading not required.)

Place	Date	Hour	Summary of Events and Information	Remarks and references to Appendices
DICKEBUSCHE.	1.		Maintained communication as in Appendix 1.	A.G. Ritchie 2/Lt R.E.
	2.			A.G. Ritchie 2/Lt R.E.
	3.		Lateral line to ZQ broken by shells. Test aerial broken.	A.G. Ritchie 2/Lt R.E.
	4.	3pm.	72nd Bde Signals took over at DICKEBUSCHE.	A.G. Ritchie 2/Lt R.E.
RENINGHELST.	4.	5.30 pm.	arrived Reninghelst	A.G. Ritchie 2/Lt R.E.
	5.		Kept up communication with 4 battalions at rest and the Transport of 73rd and 72nd Bdes, by orderly.	A.G. Ritchie 2/Lt R.E.
	6.		provided working party of 10 men for divl. Signal Coy to build buried line.	A.G. Ritchie
	7.			
	8.		again provided working party of 10 men.	A.G.R.
	9.			
	10.		Moved to huts in Reninghelst. Laid lines to Camps B and C	A.G.R. appendix 2.
	11.		Laid line to Camps F and G.	A.G.R. appendix 2.

Army Form C. 2118.

WAR DIARY
or
~~INTELLIGENCE~~ SUMMARY.
(Erase heading not required.)

November.

2.

Instructions regarding War Diaries and Intelligence Summaries are contained in F. S. Regs., Part II. and the Staff Manual respectively. Title pages will be prepared in manuscript.

Place	Date	Hour	Summary of Events and Information	Remarks and references to Appendices
RENINGHELST.	12.		laid line to Camp D.	a.g.R. Appendix 2.
	13.			
	14.			
	15.		maintained communication.	a.g.R.
	16.			
	17.			
	18.			
	19.			a.g.R.
	20.	4.45.	left RENINGHELST. Camps taken over by 76th Bde.	a.g.R.
EECKE.	20.	11 p.m	arrived EECKE.	
	21.			
	22.	9 A.m.	left EECKE. arrived OCHTEZEELE 2.35 p.m	a.g.R.
	23.	9 A.m.	left OCHTEZEELE. arrived EPERLECQUES 3.30 p.m. Maintained communication	a.g.R.
	24.		by orderly while on the move.	a.g.R.
	25.		laid line to 13 Middlesex at NELLEBROUCQ.	a.g.R. Appendix 3.
	26.			
	27.		laid wire to Leinsters at GANSPETTE. and 9 Sussex. at HOULLE	a.g.R. Appendix 4.
	28.			a.g.R

Army Form C. 2118.

November 3.

WAR DIARY
or
INTELLIGENCE SUMMARY.
(Erase heading not required.)

Instructions regarding War Diaries and Intelligence Summaries are contained in F. S. Regs., Part II. and the Staff Manual respectively. Title pages will be prepared in manuscript.

Place	Date	Hour	Summary of Events and Information	Remarks and references to Appendices
EPERLECQUES	29.–30.		Started training in Visual signalling for those men not employed in maintaining communication.	a.g.R

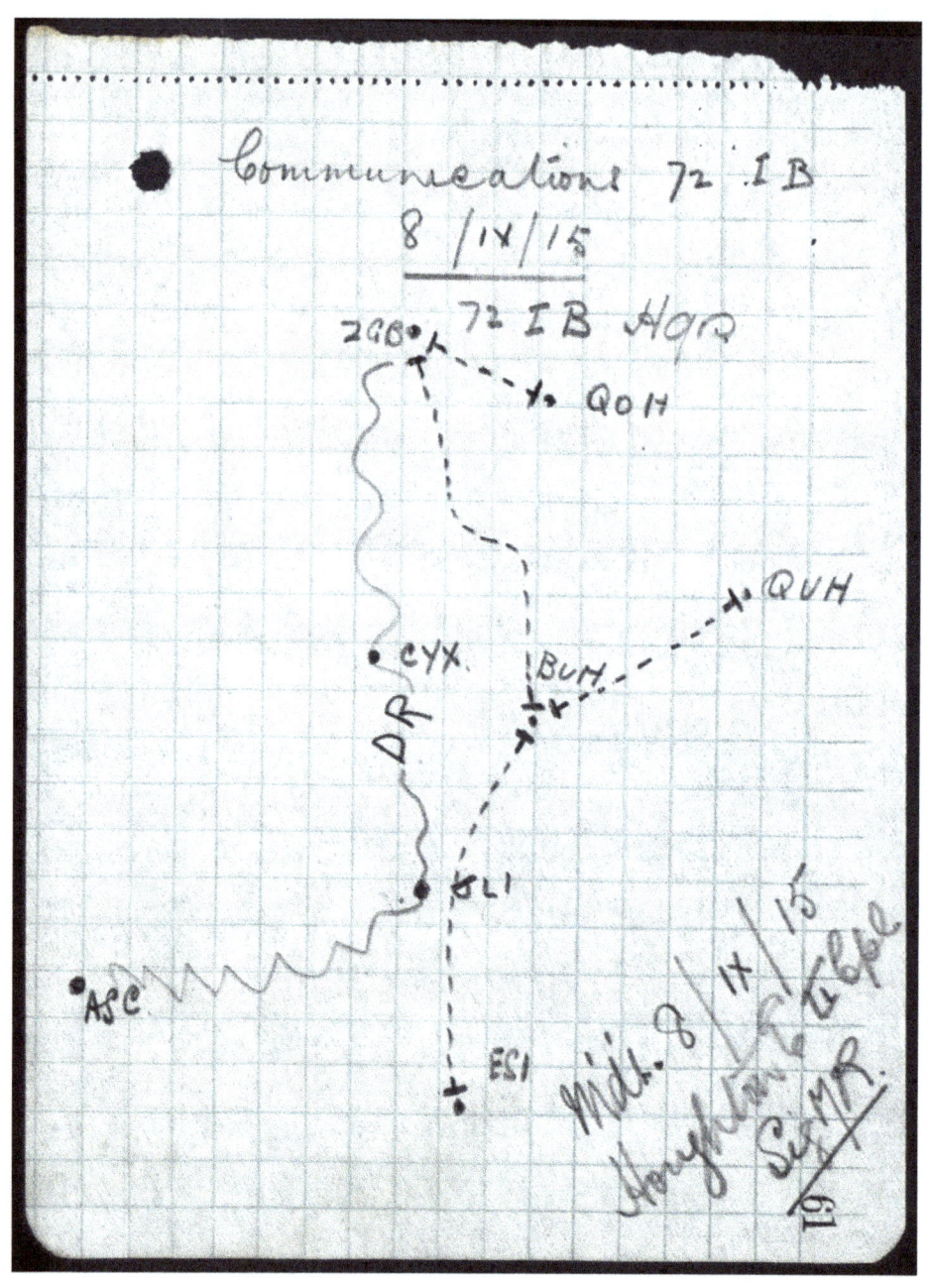

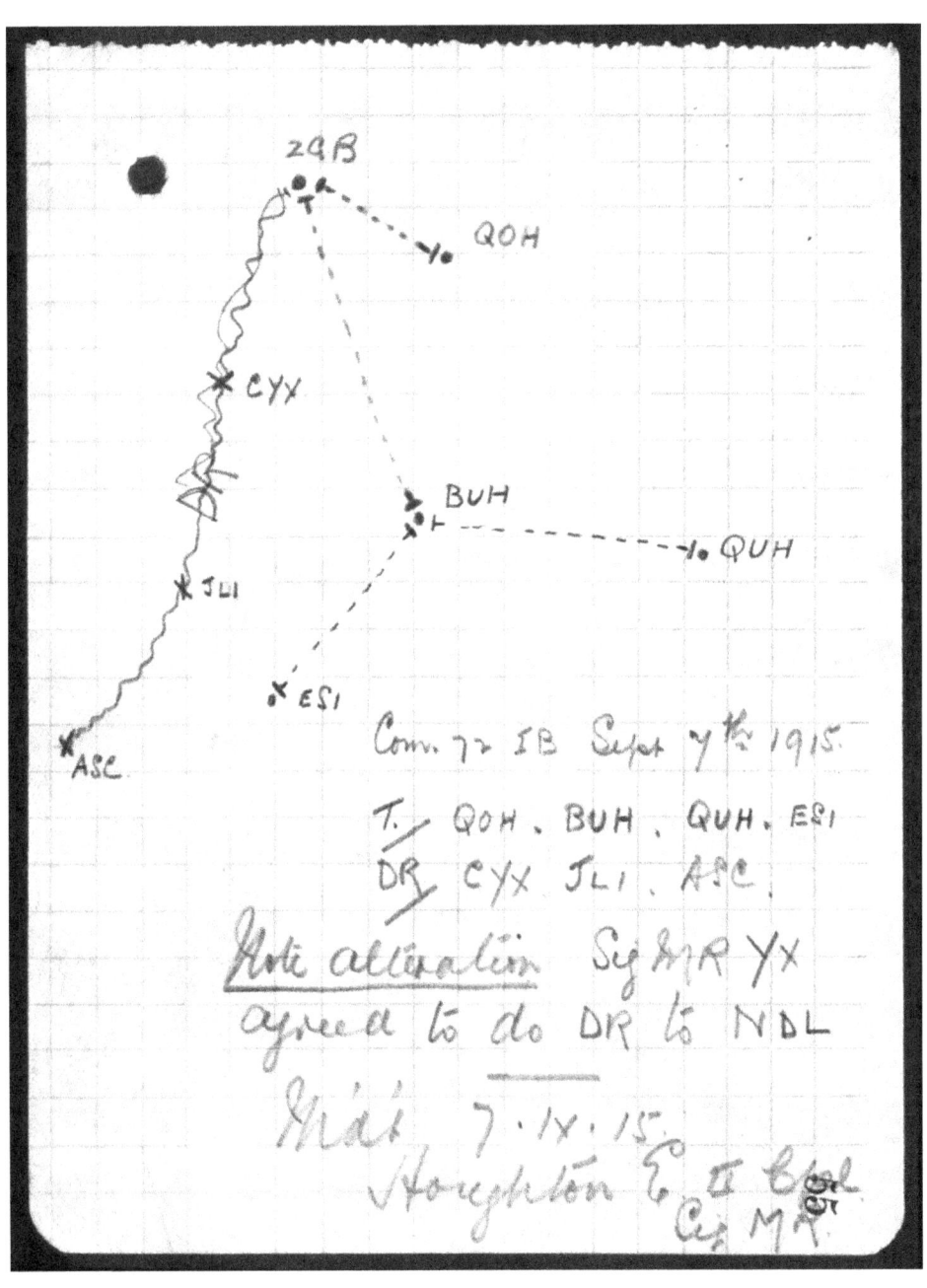

Conn. 72 IB Sept 7th 1915.

T/ QOH. BUH. QUH. ES1
DR/ CYX. JLI. ASC.

Note alteration Sig MR YX
agreed to do DR to NDL

Miåt 7.IX.15.
Houghton E. I Cpl
Cg MR

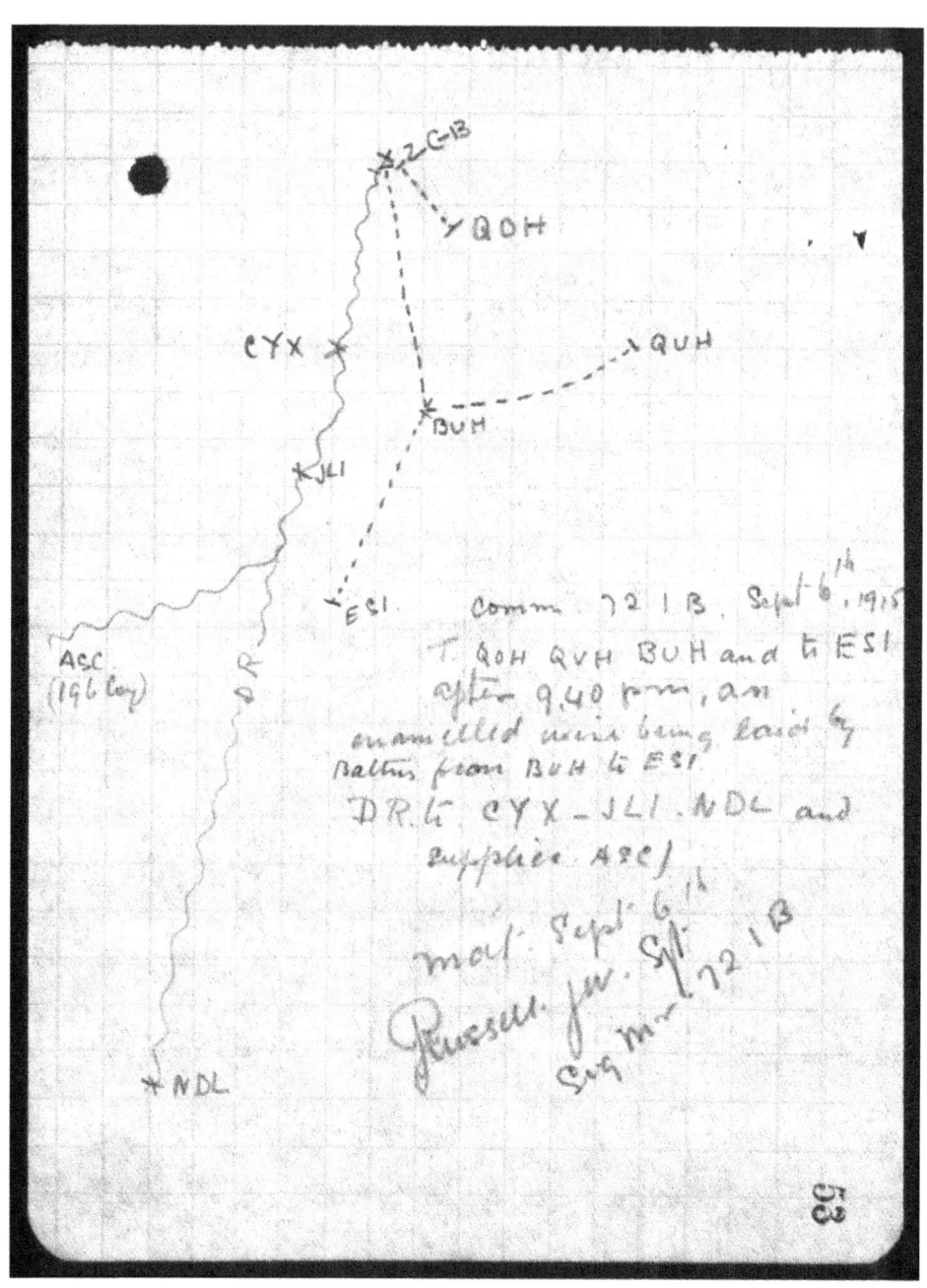

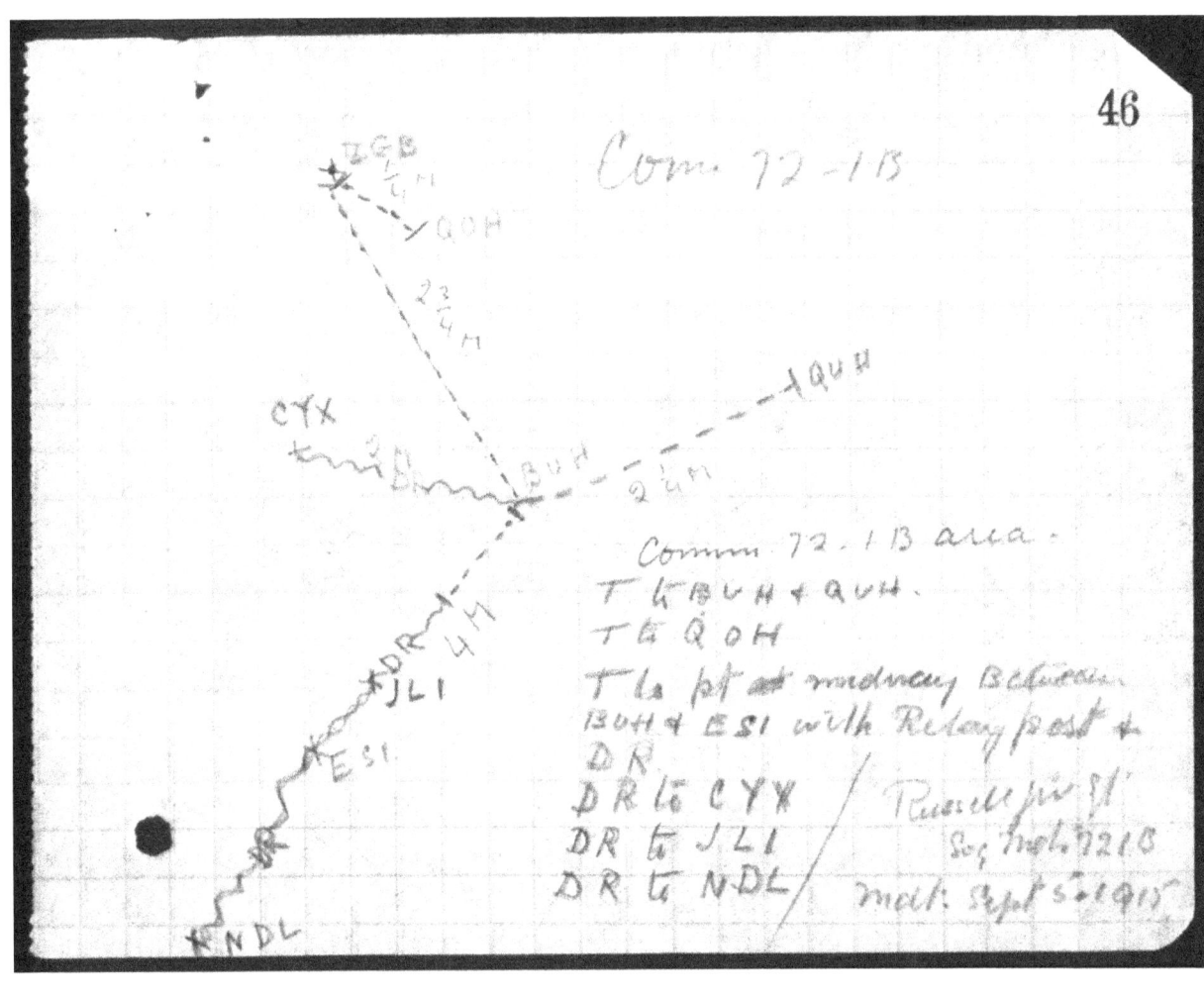

Comm 72-1B

Comm 72-1B area.
T to BUH & QUH.
T to QOH
T to pt at midway between
BUH & ESI with Relay post &
DR
DR to CYX / Russell jr 81
DR to JLI / Sgt. Ingl. 7218
DR to NDL / mah. Sept 5 1915

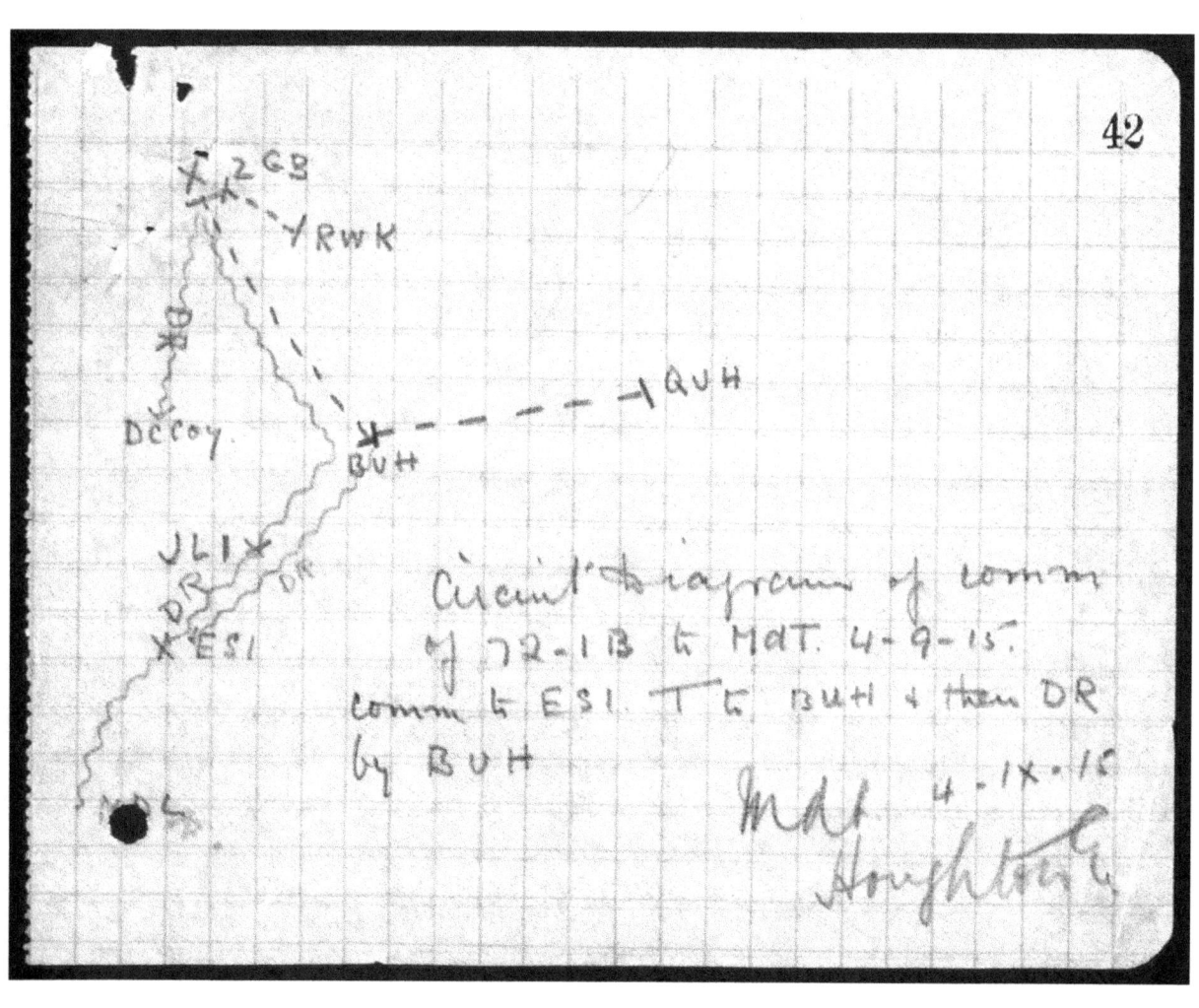

- Communications 72-1B
  9/14/15

  2 GB
       -1 QOH
            -1 QUH
  CYY
       BUH

  JLY

  196 ASC
       ⊥ ESI

  mdl 9-1X-15
  Russell f W. S/L
  Sig mx 72-1B

Communications 72 1B
10 - IX - 15

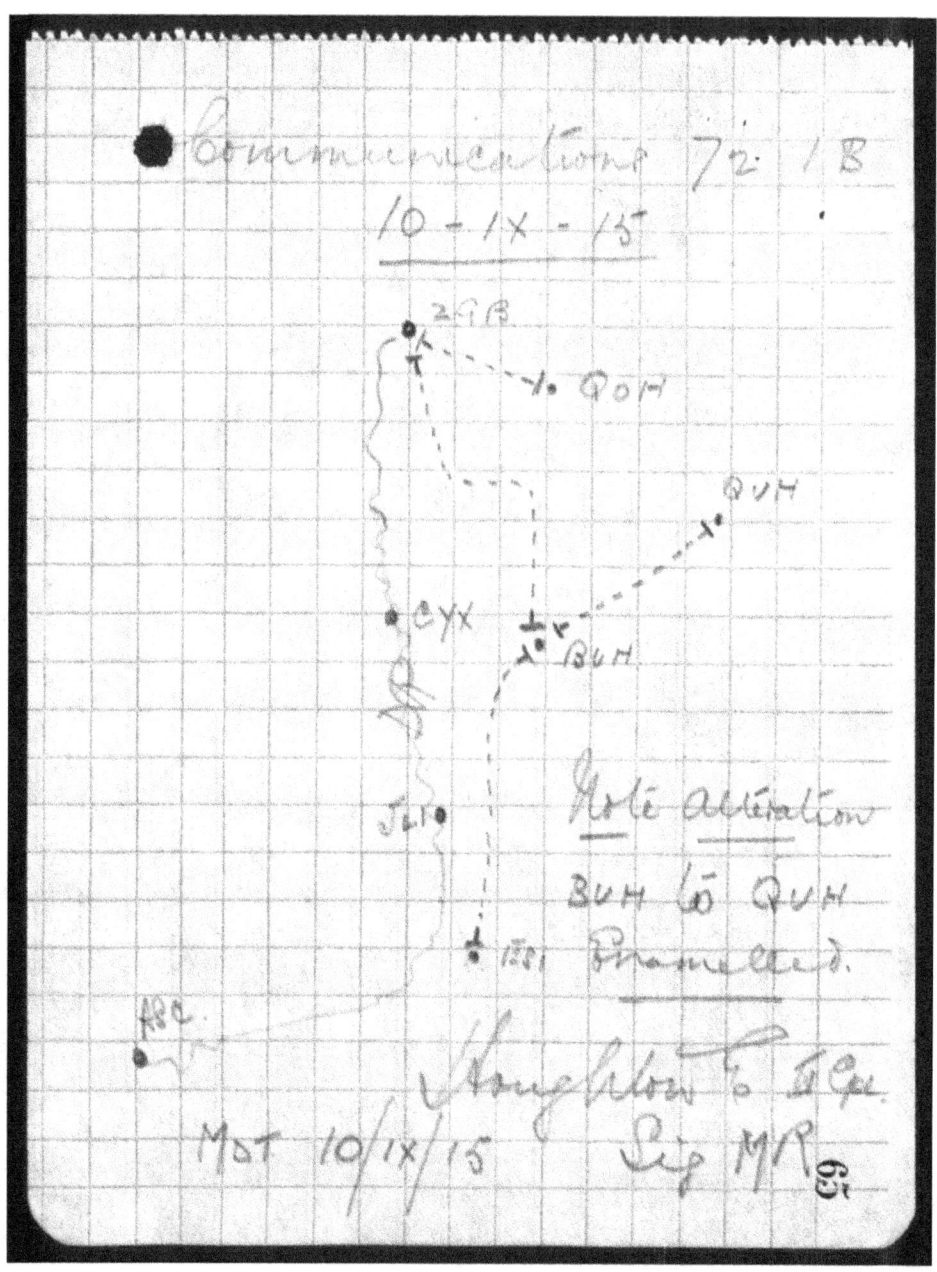

Note alteration
BUH to QVH
cancelled.

Stoughton to OC

MoT 10/IX/15   Sig MR

● Communications 72/13
    11/IX/15

        ✱ 29B
         ↘ QOH

     ⟨YK
       ✚ BUH ---------- ↑QOH

              Th QOH - BUH QOH EST
              DR LCYK - LLI - ACC
    ⟨ESI

ACC

    md1/11g/05
        Russell

Communications 72 IB
12/IX/15

2GB

QOH

CYX

QUH

BOH

Tb QOH BOH QUH FSI
DR E, CYX, JLI, ASC

JLI

FSI

mat. 12-9-15
Russell Jr S/
Sig Dr 72 IB

ASC

Communications of 721B
13/14/15

• 26B

QOH

BUH — — — QUH

JLI

T to QOH QUH BUH ESI
DR to JLI ASC

ESI Note alteration —
CYX moved to D group
mat 13/1X/15
Russell JW sgt 721B

ASC

Communications 72.1B
14/IX/15

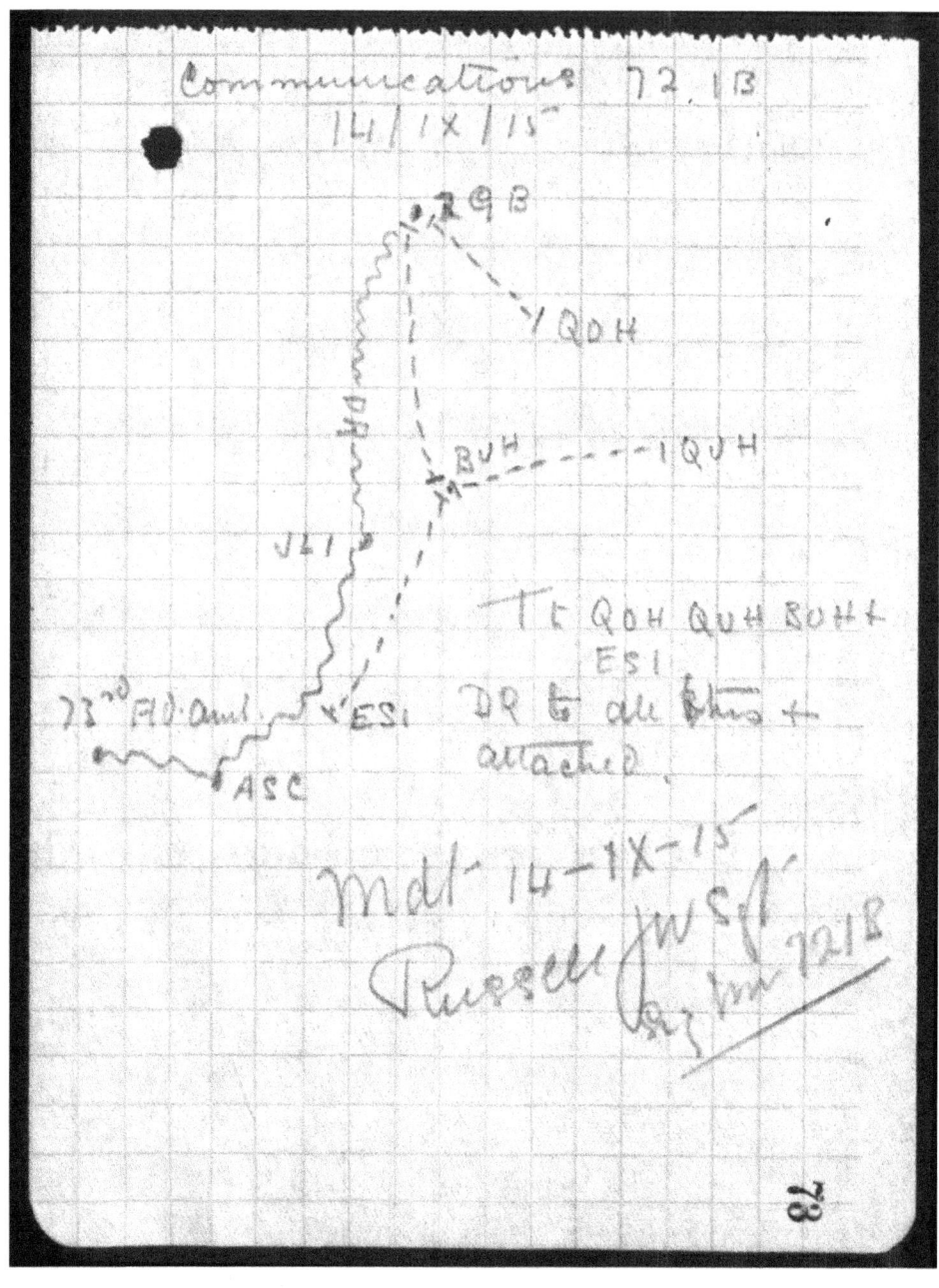

To QOH QUH BUHL
ESI
DR to all others +
attached.

mdt - 14-IX-15
Russell JWS
Sig ln 721B

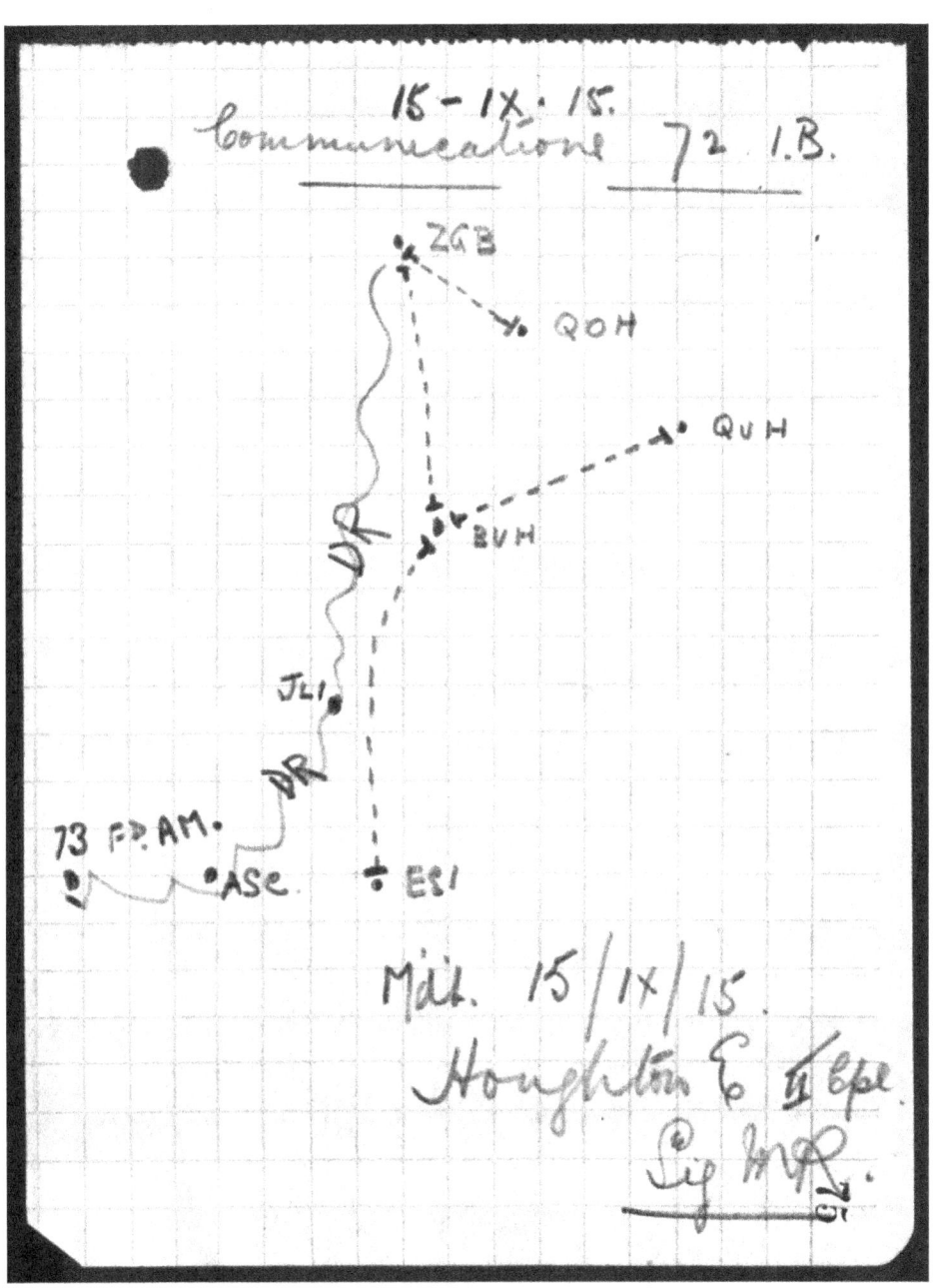

15 - IX - 15.
Communications 72 I.B.

Mât. 15/IX/15.
Houghton E. II Cpl.
Sig MR.

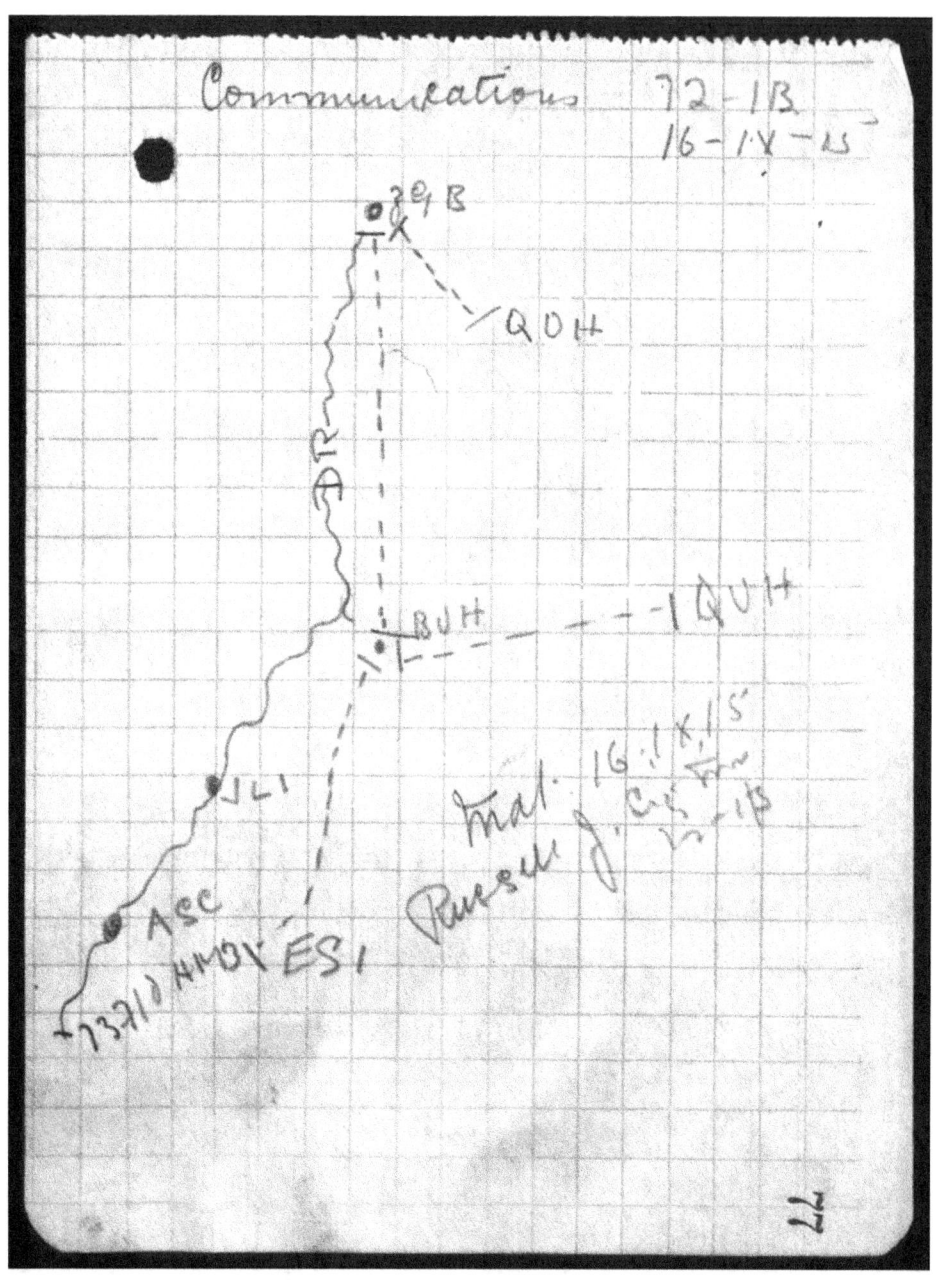

Communications 72 IB
20. IX. 15

Communication with all
units in the 72nd Bde
area is being carried out by
D.R.

* 2 CB
n.aut.   * QOH

BuH
            QOH
       JJC
JJD BGS
     ES1

196 asc

mat 20-IX-15
Russell pr S/ Sig mr
72 IB

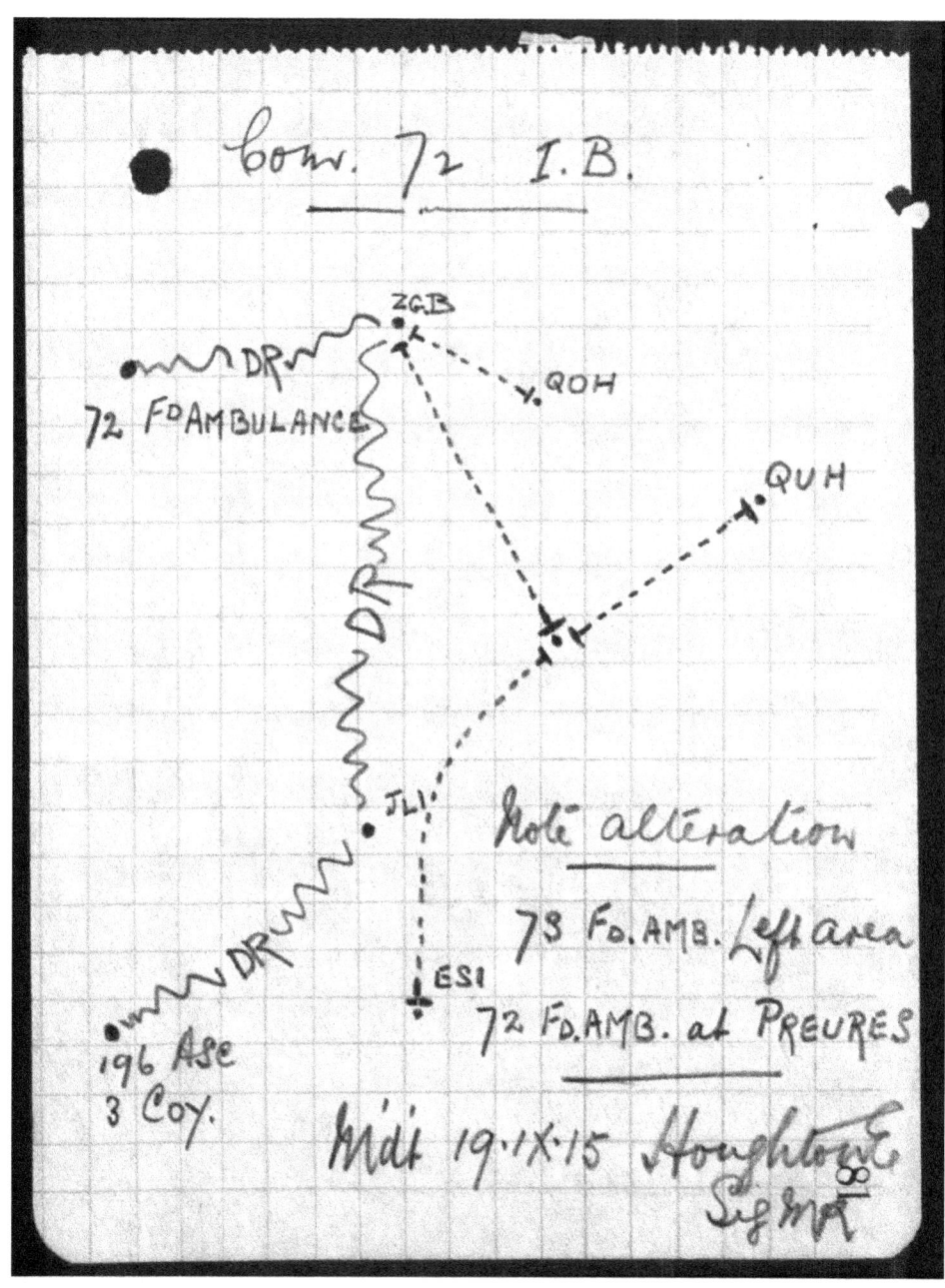

Circuit Diagram

- QOH
DP
- JLI — BUH — — QVH
- ASE
  E91
To Amb.

mat NHX/15
Russell Jor Sf
Sig nbr 12/15

24th Bat: Signal log
Vol: 5

121/7931

Army Form C. 2118.

WAR DIARY
or
INTELLIGENCE SUMMARY.
(Erase heading not required.)

Instructions regarding War Diaries and Intelligence Summaries are contained in F. S. Regs., Part II. and the Staff Manual respectively. Title pages will be prepared in manuscript.

Place	Date	Hour	Summary of Events and Information	Remarks and references to Appendices
TILQUES.	1.12.15		January in Town Regimental continued Instruction in construction of trench mortars and cable wagon lines. Maintenance communications.	Dhuth
	2.12.15		Cable laid from R.A. Sigs at CoULEM to 109th Brigade R.E. at D.A.C. also to and in Cange of 106th Brigade H.Q. LATENHEM exchange of Army Signals. Instruction in "Conference" and engineering continued. Commenced laying of telephone line from main Calais Road to right Bde H.Q. at BAYENGHEM. Evacuation in trenches and round continued. Maintenance communications.	
	3.12.15			

WAR DIARY
or
INTELLIGENCE SUMMARY.
(Erase heading not required.)

Army Form C. 2118

Place	Date	Hour	Summary of Events and Information	Remarks and references to Appendices
TILQUES.	1.12.15.		Journey in Vienne. Signalling continued instruction in construction of bonnet antenna and cable wgn circuit. Maintaining communication.	
	2.12.15.		Cable laid from R.A. Hqrs at COULEM to 109th Brigade R.F.A. at and on to 6 D.A.C. at. 8 men in engcd. 106th Brigade at TATENHEM trying on Army Signals exchange. Instruction "One"card" and Vienne signalling continued. Commenced between of telephone line from main Calais Road to 17th Bde Hqrs at BAYENGHEM. Instruction in Vienne and Vienne continued. Maintaining communication.	
	3.12.15.			

WAR DIARY
INTELLIGENCE SUMMARY

Place	Date	Hour	Summary of Events and Information	Remarks
TILQUES	4.12.15		Ref schm erected from R.A. H.Qrs to 10/ and 108th Bties and extension of main telephone line from CLERCQUES to HQ Calais Rd to 17/HQrs also to BAYENGHEM. Information continues to arrive from time to time concerning the enemy and also intelligence maps.	Dyball
	5.12.15		Reconnaissance of continuing from car. Infantry suggestions still continue. Ordinary bombing reports from the line. Advanced training by 7 Bde.	
	6.12.15			
	7.12.15		Visibility continuing today. Bty 75 shoots commenced by G.O.C.	

WAR DIARY or INTELLIGENCE SUMMARY

Army Form C. 2118.

Place	Date	Hour	Summary of Events and Information	Remarks and references to Appendices
TILQUES	4.12.15		Nil item reported from R.A. HQrs to 10th and 108th Bde at — and CLERCQUES by G.H.Q. Extension of main telephone line from Calais Rd to 17th D.13 HQrs at BAYENGHEM. Instruction contained in manual and rise one communication.	[initials]
	5.12.15		Entire wagon line Instruction in maintaining Lines of communication.	
	6.12.15		Training continued. Horses and cars. Wagon lines Infantry targets can still continue maintaining communication.	
	7.12.15		No one returned to 17 D.B. damaged by gun fire. Continued training in horse and line and air line communication. Bridget Class commences for D.A.C.	

WAR DIARY
or
INTELLIGENCE SUMMARY.

(Erase heading not required.)

Army Form C. 2118

Place	Date	Hour	Summary of Events and Information	Remarks and references to Appendices
TIDWORTH	Thurs 8.7.15		Usual regular work and line operation Care major training Somewhat foggy Class continues 35 men having passed out through the class to date 12 to return for more instruction Company Organisation Left up New 13 line change after Refereny got out 13th O.R. sent Drainetion in trench table waggon and Gunnery to train regiment and course also training Equitation Instruction continued in mounted and dismounted Commerce return	[illegible]
	9.7.15			
	10.7.15			
	11.7.15			

WAR DIARY
or
INTELLIGENCE SUMMARY.

Army Form C. 2118

Place	Date	Hour	Summary of Events and Information	Remarks and references to Appendices
Tilques	6.7.15		Viewed Regimental and Sur Line transport carts, wagons, limbers, Divisional supply Close continuing 35 men having been out through the class as from 12 to it months boy recruit	
			Returning communication	
	9.7.15		Lytted the No 13 Army exchange in Signal office. Returning to France took wagon and Cable wagon and travelling in recent engineering and came all time	
	10.7.15		Maintaining communication between Divisions continuing in recent and in wagon lines maintaining Communication	
	10.7.15			

Army Form C. 2118

WAR DIARY
or
INTELLIGENCE SUMMARY.
(Erase heading not required.)

Place	Date	Hour	Summary of Events and Information	Remarks and references to Appendices
TILQUES	12/12/15		Training continued. Issued orders for Brigade action. Lewis gun commenced maintaining communication.	
	13/12/15		Continued work and only major return which happened to fly by.	
	14/12/15		Successful in a understanding to the Corps covering a visit inspection in honour	
	15/12/15		Regimental and Cable Wagon work. Maintaining communication. Training continues.	
	16/12/15		Training continues. Company attended Divisional gas instruction. Party of one company attended gas instruction at Moringhem	

Army Form C. 2118

WAR DIARY
or
INTELLIGENCE SUMMARY.
(Erase heading not required.)

Place	Date	Hour	Summary of Events and Information	Remarks and references to Appendices
TILQUES	12/12/15		Training continued. Harness & Cooks Wagon Mill Class for Bngade. Both became Competent. Maintaining Communication.	[signature]
	13/12/15		Continued Harness and Only Wagon Scheme which proves to be very preventative, and instruction to the Company resorted to continued instruction in recent Regulating and Cable Wagon drill. Maintaining Communication.	
	14/12/15		Continued Regulating and Cable Wagon Drill. Maintaining Communication.	
	15/12/15			
	16/12/15		Training continued. Party of men from Company attended Gas demonstration at Wizerne.	

Army Form C. 2118.

WAR DIARY
or
INTELLIGENCE SUMMARY.
(Erase heading not required.)

Place	Date	Hour	Summary of Events and Information	Remarks and references to Appendices
TILQUES	17/12/15		Continued training of units. Repairing huts & flat roof. Painting windows & remembering store. Continued issue of ordnance, clothing materials etc.	
	18/12/15			
	19/12/15		Ordnance Office opened for Infantry of the Reserve & to 73rd Infantry Bde throwing in reserve and Othee regiments there	MWh
	20/12/15		Issuing of Ordnance stores and automobile construction. Refixing of Ebro government wagons. I.C.O. of general workshops repairing Issuing of ordnance on large	
	21/12/15		scale to units still maintaining	

Army Form C. 2118

Instructions regarding War Diaries and Intelligence Summaries are contained in F. S. Regs., Part II. and the Staff Manual respectively. Title pages will be prepared in manuscript.

WAR DIARY
or
INTELLIGENCE SUMMARY.
(Erase heading not required.)

Place	Date	Hour	Summary of Events and Information	Remarks and references to Appendices
TRAQVES	17.12.15		Continued training of N.C.O's & men. Parading wagons & unloading Stores	
	18.12.15		Continued move. Agnelling instruction	
	19.12.15		Ordnance officer sent on intermediate deposit letter to 73 Infantry Bde. Training in manner arc Exec.	
	20.12.15		10 gm turn training. Continued Hand and arms Loading. Rifling Class. Gunnery served J.C.O. & gunlayers for army Contribution to Reserve air Cadre begun will continuing commutation.	
	21.12.15			

Army Form C. 2118

WAR DIARY
or
INTELLIGENCE SUMMARY.
(Erase heading not required.)

Instructions regarding War Diaries and Intelligence Summaries are contained in F. S. Regs. Part II. and the Staff Manual respectively. Title pages will be prepared in manuscript.

Place	Date	Hour	Summary of Events and Information	Remarks and references to Appendices
THEVES 22.12.15			Continued training in Horse and Cart exercise in small Riding class. Continue maintain Horsemanship exercise	
"	23/12/15		Gunnery ordinary Value and Riding drill	
"	24/12/15		Maintaining Communication training as usual. Infantry intended for Bugger instruction returned to Units.	W.W.W.
"	25/12/15		Having no usual work done.	
"	26/12/15		Wagon drill. Riding School & usual continued.	
"	27/12/15		Nothing being collected until 5 p.m. Bugger class resumed. Technical class continued.	
"	28/12/15		Wagon drill. Visual signalling below having as usual. Carried out successfully Lamp, Signalling practice at Coys for Inf: and Arty: Class. Class doing Flag drill.	

Army Form C. 2118.

WAR DIARY
or
INTELLIGENCE SUMMARY.
(Erase heading not required.)

Instructions regarding War Diaries and Intelligence Summaries are contained in F.S. Regs., Part II. and the Staff Manual respectively. Title pages will be prepared in manuscript.

Place	Date	Hour	Summary of Events and Information	Remarks and references to Appendices
TIGUES	22.12.15		Continued Gunnery in Horse and Pack wagon drill. Riding Class continued. Maintaining communication.	
"	23/12/15		Gunning continued. Maintaining Telephone communication. Riding drill.	
"	24/12/15		Maintaining Communication. Having as usual. Infantry attached for Buyer Instruction returned to Units. Having no usual until noon.	
"	25.12.15			
	26.12.15		Wagon drill. Riding school & usual continued. Watching boats extended until 5 p.m. Buyer Class resumed. Technical class continued	
	27.12.15			
	28.12.15		Wagon drill. Visual signalling scheme hiring up Brigade carried out successfully. Lamp- Signalling practice at 6 p.m. for Inf. and Arty. Classes doing Flag Drill.	

Army Form C. 2118.

WAR DIARY
or
INTELLIGENCE SUMMARY.
(Erase heading not required.)

Instructions regarding War Diaries and Intelligence Summaries are contained in F. S. Regs., Part II. and the Staff Manual respectively. Title pages will be prepared in manuscript.

Place	Date	Hour	Summary of Events and Information	Remarks and references to Appendices
T. LAVES	29/12/15		Training as usual. Wagon drill. Infantry drill. (Bugges & Vicarat).	
"	30/12/15		Training as usual. Instruction to keep men on	
"	31/12/15		-do-	
			Locating & repairing faults in Overhead Cable, in preparation for next Divst Area.	

Army Form C. 2118.

WAR DIARY
or
INTELLIGENCE SUMMARY.
(Erase heading not required.)

Place	Date	Hour	Summary of Events and Information	Remarks and references to Appendices
FLEURES	29/12/15		Training as usual. Wagon drill. Infantry classes (Buglers & Visual).	
"	30/12/15		Training as usual.	
"	31/12/15		-do- Instruction to learners on locating & repairing faults in Quadruple Cable, in preparation for new Divl. Area.	

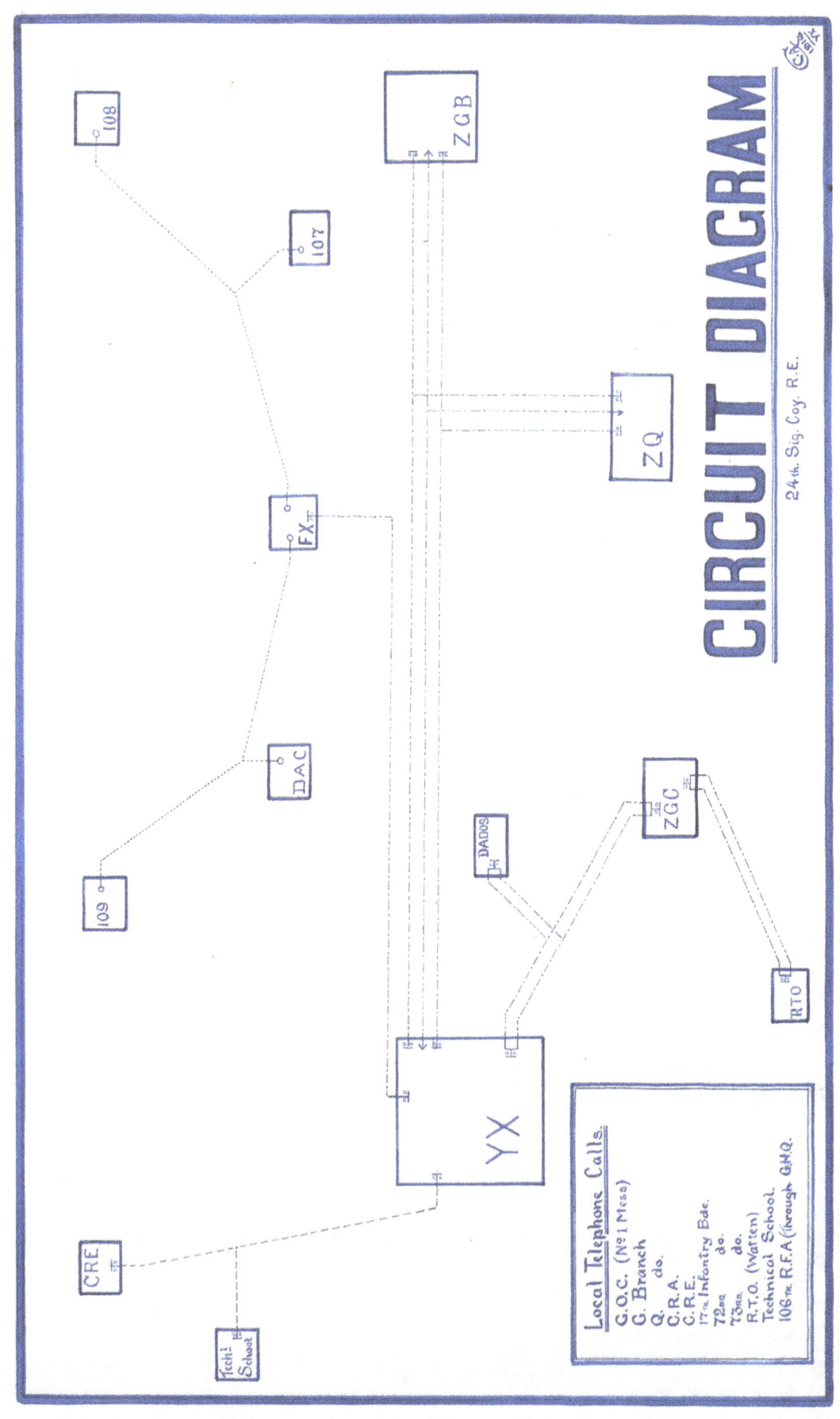

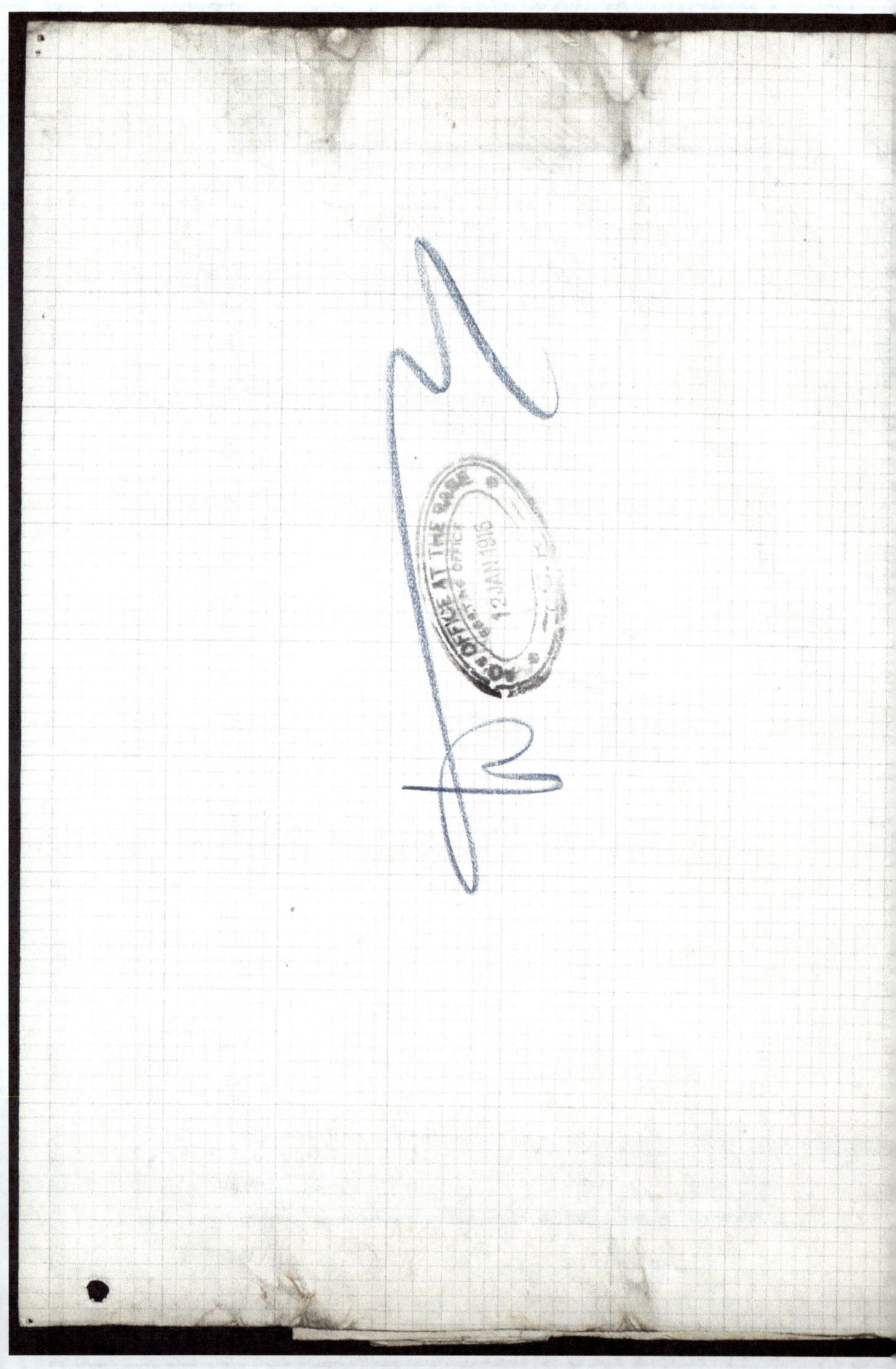

RCB MIM   R.T.O. WATTEN!

                    RSU
                    73. F.AMB.

          NRG.

          ZGC

          YX   COMMUNICATIONS
129   of 73 I.B. at
Field Coy   EPERLECQUES.

                    12/12/15.   a.g.ritchie

Army Form C. 2118.

WAR DIARY

No 2 Section

INTELLIGENCE SUMMARY.
(Erase heading not required.)

Place	Date	Hour	Summary of Events and Information	Remarks and references to Appendices
Rest Camp	1/12/15 to 24/12/15		Communication kept up by D.R. and cable, D.R. to 2 Kendals & 3 Rifle Bde., cable to 1st Roy. Fus., 12 Roy Fus. and 8 Buffs. In bath with Div. by Sounder and phone, all lines patrolled and all in order. Station overhauled and seen to. Rel. in batteries half an hour. Helio work delayed by rain day and night.	
do	25 – 31·12·15		Came as above, except 'phone suspended in order of F. Div. Sig. during last 3 days. Training carried on with addition of day + night schemes (transmitting) with flag (M +S), helio. Lamp; weather rather better for this work.	

2333 Wt. W2344/1454 700,000 5/15 D.D.&L. A.D.S.S./Forms/C. 2118.

WAR DIARY
or
INTELLIGENCE SUMMARY.
(Erase heading not required.)

Army Form C. 2118.

December 1915.
A Sec= 24. Sig. Co.

Place	Date	Hour	Summary of Events and Information	Remarks and references to Appendices
EPERLECQUES	1-31.		Maintained communication with units as in Appendix 1. The line to 13th Middlesex and 2nd Leinsters was once broken by a motor-bus coming along a road, on which one would not expect such things to travel. Otherwise lines to Battalions have always been through. D.R.L.S. posts were run from Brigade to Battn at 9.30 a.m. 3 p.m. and 6 p.m. Visual signalling was practised daily by those men not employed in maintaining communication	A sketch is to RE.

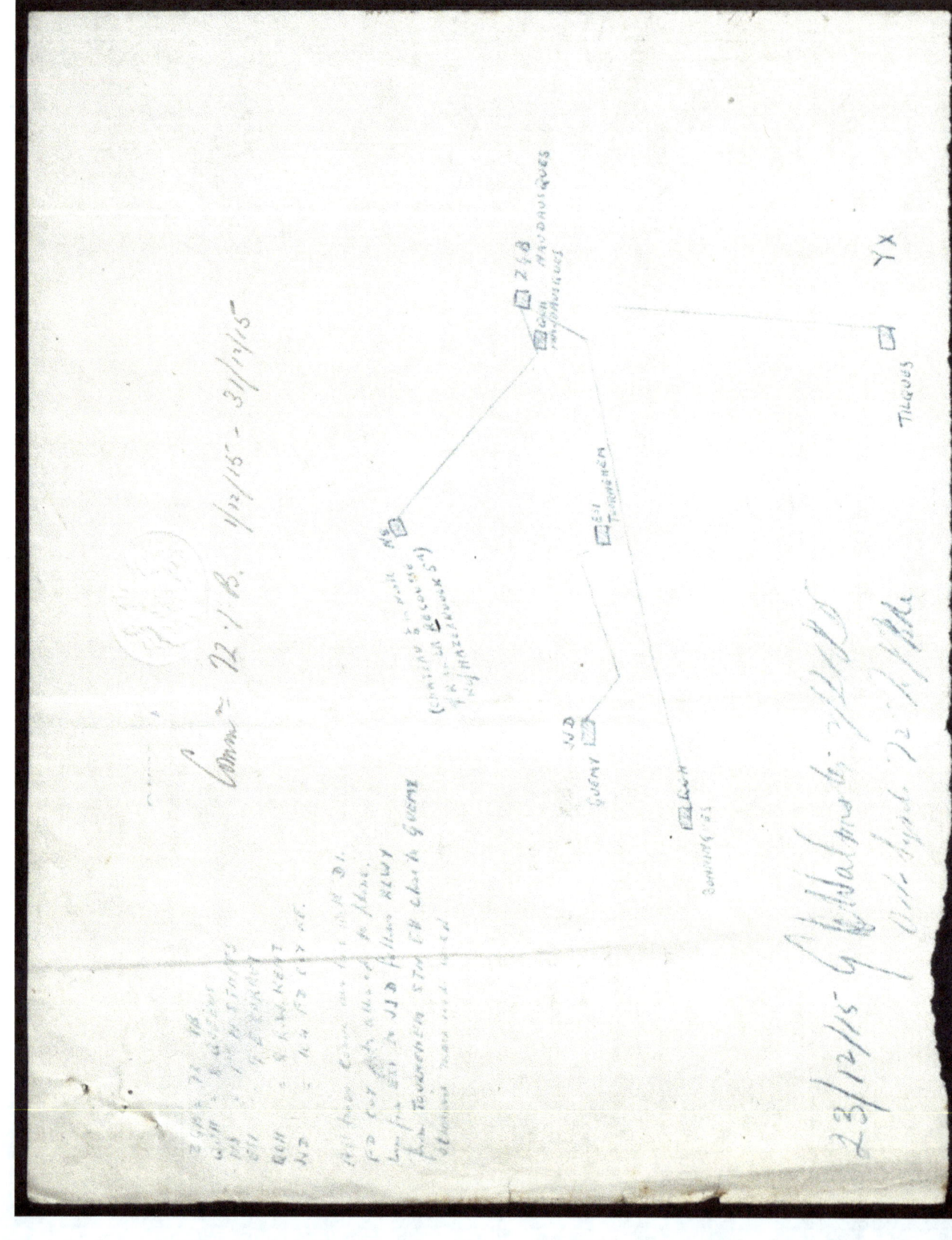

Army Form C. 2118.

WAR DIARY
or
INTELLIGENCE SUMMARY.

(Erase heading not required.)

No. 3 Section 26 Sig Coy R.E.

Instructions regarding War Diaries and Intelligence Summaries are contained in F. S. Regs. Part II. and the Staff Manual respectively. Title pages will be prepared in manuscript.

Place	Date	Hour	Summary of Events and Information	Remarks and references to Appendices
NORDAUSQUES	1/12/15		Training	7/12/15
"	2/12/15		"	8/12/15
"	3-12-15		"	6/12/15
"	4-12-15		"	6/12/15
"	5-12-15		"	6/12/15
"	6-12-15		"	6/12/15
"	7-12-15		"	6/12/15
"	8-12-15		"	6/12/15
"	9-12-15		"	6/12/15
"	10-12-15		"	6/12/15
"	11-12-15		"	6/12/15
"	12-12-15		"	6/12/15
"	13-12-15		"	6/12/15
"	14-12-15		"	6/12/15
"	15-12-15		"	6/12/15
"	16-12-15		"	6/12/15
"	17-12-15		"	6/12/15
"	18-12-15		"	6/12/15

Army Form C. 2118.

WAR DIARY
or
INTELLIGENCE SUMMARY. No. 3 Sect. 24 Sig Coy R.E.

(Erase heading not required.)

Place	Date	Hour	Summary of Events and Information	Remarks and references to Appendices
NORDAUSQUES	19-12-15		Training	
"	20-12-15		"	
"	21-12-15		"	
"	22-12-15		"	
"	23-12-15		"	
"	24-12-15		"	
"	25-12-15		"	
"	26-12-15		"	
"	27-12-15		"	
"	28-12-15		"	
"	29-12-15		"	
"	30-12-15		"	
"	31-12-15		"	

C. Wadmilton [?]
No 3 Section
B.E.F. No 24 Div Sig Coy

24th Signal Coy / R.E.

Vol. VI

Sigs24/154.

D. A. G.
3rd. Echelon,
Base.

    Herewith War Diaries for the month of January 1916, for Headquarters, No. 2. 3. and 4 Sections of the 24th Signal Company R.E.

    Kindly acknowledge.

4th February 1916.

[signature] Captain,
Commanding 24th Signal Co. R.E.

MEMORANDUM.

From OC.
  24th Signal Co
    RE

To O i/c
  A G's Office Base

From

To

ANSWER.

24th Febry. 1916.

Reference attached memo.
The instructions appear to have been complied with.
The Diaries of Headquarters, No 1, 2, 3 & 4 sections are attached, and may be regarded as Appendices.

Capt.
O/C. 24th Signal Co.

Sent

O.C. 24th Divl: Signals.

Please cause the
diaries of Sections
to be forwarded
with your war
diary — and if
necessary they can
be regarded as
Appendices to the
diary of the Divl:
Signal Coy.

14 FEB 1916

C.R. No. 140/881

?
Signals
73 Inf Bde

24 D

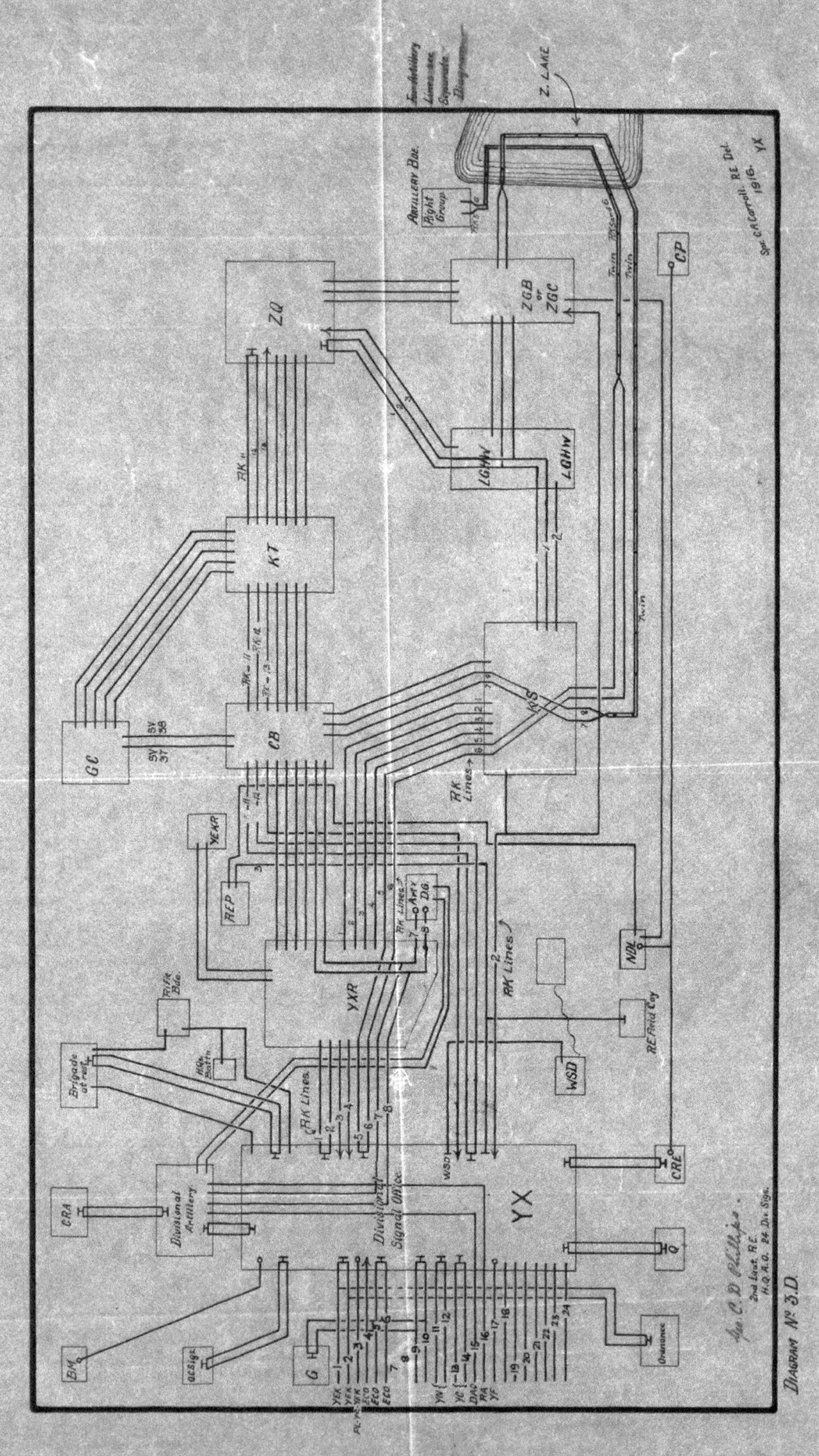

Army Form C. 2118.

WAR DIARY
or
INTELLIGENCE SUMMARY.
(Erase heading not required.)

Place	Date	Hour	Summary of Events and Information	Remarks and references to Appendices
TILQUES	1/1/16		Training as usual. Two Linesmen proceed to RENINGHELST (the new Billet Area) to take over lines.	
- do -	2/1/16		Training as usual. One NCO & 6 Linesmen proceed to new Area.	
- do -	3rd		Training as usual.	
- do -	4th		- do -	
- do -	5th		- do - Some Units moving to War Area.	
- do -	6th		- do - Cleaning Camp.	
- do -	7th		Fatigues. Leave TILQUES. Column rest at HARDIFORT for the night.	
RENINGHELST, 8th			Coy arrive at RENINGHELST 4.30 p.m. Main line to 72.I.8 cut in 4 places by shell fire. All latrel lines between 17.I.8 & 72.I.8 cut. These lines were all repaired with the exception of the Quad, which was not needed owing to darkness.	
- do -	9th		Quad repaired. DM's at RE Dump & 129th FOL Co replaced by Bell Telephone.	

Army Form C. 2118.

WAR DIARY
or
INTELLIGENCE SUMMARY.
(Erase heading not required.)

Place	Date	Hour	Summary of Events and Information	Remarks and references to Appendices
RENINGHELST	10/1/16		Clearing up Camp. Paths made & improving conditions.	
-do-	11/1/16		Preparing cable for new route to RT Bde. Telephone line to 17.1.B cut by shell fire. Advanced HQ shelled at 4 p.m. Signal office hit by a large fragment. Commence digging in new buried route to Right Side. Working party of 500 men. 2000 yds dug. 3 cables laid in. One GP (Storm) one 5 substitute, and one D5. and trench filled in again.	Ashleigh Capt.
-do-	12/1/16		Preparing cable for laying tonight. Wkg party of 150 men carry on with trench. 900 hundred yds buried and filled in.	
-do-	13/1/16		Preparing cable for laying tonight. Working party of 150 men bury and fill in 600 yds.	
-do-	14/1/16		Lt. Mitchell (17th Bde) at Ramparts YPRES wounded in thigh by H.E. shell. Advanced RE party killed with 8 inch	
-do-	15/1/16		Relaid part of line from GPO to Wipers. Montague Tuttle Line. About 120 eight inch shells fell in neighbourhood of Advanced HQ.	

Army Form C. 2118.

WAR DIARY
or
INTELLIGENCE SUMMARY.
(Erase heading not required.)

Instructions regarding War Diaries and Intelligence Summaries are contained in F.S. Regs. Part II. and the Staff Manual respectively. Title pages will be prepared in manuscript.

Place	Date	Hour	Summary of Events and Information	Remarks and references to Appendices
REMNGHAST	15/1/16			
-do-	16/1/16		New route to ZILLEBEKE POND Buried with from YXR to KS Cut. New route to ZILLEBEKE POND completed. Armoured & trans taped cable being put across pond. Reserve buried line from advanced Hqrs to corner of BEKE Cut by shell fire.	
-do-	17/1/16		Preparing cable and supplying camp.	
-do-	18/1/16		Diverted line to Resting Bde. so as to avoid Bombing Practice Ground. Putting new Test Boards at KS (Dugout). Commence tying permanent joints in new buried route.	
-do-	19/1/16		Soldering joints on new buried route	
-do-	20/1/16		Soldering joints & completing putting through on new buried route which gives very good speaking. Metallic Circuit erected from YXR to TRE Dump.	
-do-	21/1/16		Pegging out narrow buried route.	
-do-	22/1/16		Pegging out route. Added Airline from Signal Office to trestle route. Established manual between KS and Bde Hqrs on BEKE Pond.	

WAR DIARY
or
INTELLIGENCE SUMMARY.
(Erase heading not required.)

Army Form C. 2118.

Place	Date	Hour	Summary of Events and Information	Remarks and references to Appendices
RENINGHELST	23/1/16		Completing permanent joints on New Buried Route.	Ratley Capt
-do-	24/1/16		Permanent joints put in line from YxR to CB and KS.	
-do-	25/1/16		Remainder of new route proceded out from ZILLEBEKE POND to KS.	
-do-	26/1/16		Improving & maintaining lines. Dug-out at YxR fitted up.	
-do-	27/1/16		Improving joints & labelling lines. Work on Visual Scheme.	
-do-	28/1/16		Line from KT to Ramparts (YPRES) labelled. Metallic loop from point where new buried route entered pond, to RT Bde HQs. Continued relabelling lines.	
-do-	29/1/16		Commenced laying new line in BEKE from CB to KT. Commenced digging in new loop on LGHW line to avoid Bdge 14. Continued labelling lines & staking out buried line. New DS cable run from BEKE to KT and started ads of steam.	
-do-	30/1/16		RE Dump line put OK. 4 working parties & reinforced route Exchange opened at YxR. Two telephone operators	
-do-	31/1/16		Completed new loop on LGHW of ½ mile. Putting through new loop. 115 men digging.	

WAR DIARY

INTELLIGENCE SUMMARY.

Army Form C. 2118.

17th Inf. Bde
N° 2 Section
Appendix I

Place	Date	Hour	Summary of Events and Information	Remarks and references to Appendices
REST CAMP BRANDHOEK EZ-EPERLECQUES	1 – 3.1.16		Went up on 3rd to 51st Bde HqrS in ramparts of YPRES to look over their lines.	
	4		4 Linesmen went up to 51st Hqrs to take over lines	
	5		Section marched to RUBROUCQ & entrained to POPERINGHE, marched to rest camp at OUDERDOM – VLAMERTINGHE road at H.14.a (map pg)	
REST CAMP	7 – 12		Section took over from 51st Bde (17 Divn) in ramparts.	
YPRES	13		Lines patrolled & improved. Casualties 1 OR wounded by HE	
	14 – 23		RAILWAY WOOD communication through RAMPARTS satisfactory working in close weather otherwise not reliable. Buried wire on extreme left but into new from Ede Hqrs to Fyfr Bde. 72 I.B. Linesmen came up on 21st Bde relieved by 72 I.B. Signals relieved by 7 I.B. & proceeded to Rest camp H.14.A. Casualties nil. Visual line from Coy hqr on MENIN RD to Bn-Coy HQ	
REST CAMP	24 – 28		Came with wD linesmen of 17 I.B. & 18 I.B. also Bn sig. Staff of all 3 Bdes try wire on orderly. Section meeting & refitting. Linesmen went to take	
	31		over 73 I.B lines at ZILLEBEKE RAMPARTS (51) Section moved up & took over from 73 I.B 7 P.M.	

Appendix 1

WAR DIARY N°3 Section 24th Div Sig Co
or
INTELLIGENCE SUMMARY. (Sub Sector 72.I.B.)
(Erase heading not required.) Appendix II.

JANUARY 1916

Army Form C. 2118.

Place	Date	Hour	Summary of Events and Information	Remarks and references to Appendices
NORDAUSQUES	1/1/16		Training	
	2.1.16		Training	
	3.1.16		Training	
	4.1.16		Training	
	5.1.16		Training	
	6.1.16		Training - placed r.o.v. of 6 km ZUDCOOTE LAKE LANO	
℞ POPERINGHE	7.1.16		Move to new billetting area POPERINGHE. Bde N° 2 Bde Depots	
ZILLEBEKE LAKE	8.1.16		Took over signals at ZILLEBEKE LAKE from Sigs 50th Inf'y Bde 7/1/16. Lines as per plan N°1 attached. Bde H'qr's T.E. & B.C. (inclusive)	
	9.1.16		Patrolled our infored lines	
	10.1.16		Patrolled and repaired lines	
	11.1.16		Patrolled and repaired lines. Road for new bury to ZOUAVE WOOD via HALFWAY HOUSE shown	
	12.1.16		Patrolled and repaired lines. Working party on new bury	
	13.1.16		Patrolled and repaired lines. Worked on bury. Cable rec'd	
	14.1.16		Patrolled and repaired lines. Work on bury continued	
	15.1.16		Patrolled and repaired lines. Work on bury continued	
H 14. A. 2.6.	16.1.16		Bde HR H14A2.4. Signals 6. Sigs 72BX Z.B. 5/m. Bury dug from Bde Hd to Zouave wd and dugouts to ZILLEBEKE SWITCH. Moved to reserve area	
	17.1.16		Stoves overhauled	
	18.1.16			
	19.1.16			
	20.1.16			
	21.1.16		Lewis post of 6 lines laid in YPRES rain	
	22.1.16		Stoves overhauled	
YPRES	23.1.16		Took over Signals in YPRES section from Sigs 17.I.B. 5/30 pm. Lines as per office diagram attached (Plan n° 2)	
	24.1.16		Line patrolled. Road for new bury to F 13 C shown	
	25.1.16		Line patrolled. Working party on new bury	
	26.1.16		Line patrolled. Working party on new bury	
	27.1.16		Line patrolled. Working party on new bury	
	28.1.16		Line patrolled.	
	29.1.16		Line patrolled. Working party on new bury	
	30.1.16		Line patrolled and work on new bury continued. Working party on trestling	
	31.1.16		Line patrolled and work on new bury continued	

PLAN I

Common 72/B. 7/1/16.

YPRES
MENIN GATE
LILLE GATE
AIR & RAMPARTS
PHONE, 2 AIR
HAR
AIR E RESERVE BTN. at KRUISTRAAT
QUEEN D. 16
HALFWAY HOUSE BTN HQ
N? AIR ANNEXE RANGE
2 AIR
ETANG DE ZILLEBEKE
2 DL
INCOMPLETED RLWY.
2OU: BTN HQ

——— = AIR
----- = Bury

PLAN II. Diagram of Lines in Rest Area.

9ᵗʰ E. SURREYS. CAMP "A"

8ᵗʰ QUEENS CAMP "B"

1ˢᵗ N.STAFFS "C" (MET. C.I.R.)

17 INF. BDE. HQRS.

12ᵗʰ SHERWOOD. FOR. CAMP.

2ⁿᵈ LONDONS CAMP "F"

3ʳᵈ RIFLE BDE. CAMP "E"

R.W. KENTS. CAMP "D"

12ᵗʰ R. FUS. CAMP

Communication to all transports by DR
Also by DR to the following:-
5ᵗʰ LAB. BATTN.
2ⁿᵈ ENT. BATTN.
O.C. HUTTING.
R.E. DUMPS at H.13 & 9.2. and H.16 & 11

...... Airline

[signature]
10/1 Sep 1916

PLAN III

Communication 72nd Inf. Bde 23/1/16

MR = Visual & Telep'n (N°59 Medium Road)
HORN CELLARS = HQ of Battn in Reserve & enemy attack
Pc = Coy of Left Battn in Rkwy Wood.

—— = Buzz
- - - = Air
→ = Visual

NB. The line 'B' was handed over dis' Bde who intend to front of MR 30 1/2 and G.T. takes us to Horn Cellars. The line from Right Battn to Right Battn to MD HQ is just a field line. A new buried line from Bde to Left Battn HQ is being laid.

WAR DIARY

Army Form C. 2118.

JANUARY 1916.

No 4 Sec= 24 SIG. COY.

Place	Date	Hour	Summary of Events and Information	Remarks and references to Appendices
EPERLECQUES.	1 2 3 4 5 6		Maintained Communication with lines as in Appendix I.	A.S.R.
	7	6.45am	Pack and riding horses proceeded by road to POPERINGHE in two stages.	A.S.R.
		9 pm	handed over to SIGS 52ND BRIGADE	A.S.R.
	8	1.30am	entrained at AUDRICQ. 7.30am wagon detrained at GODEWAERSVELDE.	A.S.R.
		8.am	dismounted portion of Section detrained at QUINTEN	
H.14.a. sheet 28.		2.30pm	took over at H.14.a sheet 28. lines as in Appendix II.	
	9 10		patrolled lines	
	11 12		relaid pair of lines to Camps B.&C. movement extended them to Camp A and used them as a metallic circuit.	
	13.		relaid line to Camp D and teed off to Camp F.	A.S.R.

Army Form C. 2118.

WAR DIARY

Sheet II of
4 Sect. 24 SIG. COY.

(Erase heading not required.)

Place	Date	Hour	Summary of Events and Information	Remarks and references to Appendices
H.M.Q (Locre)	14		Laid line to 12. Notts & Derbys.	a.g.R.
ZILLEBEKE LAKE.	15	6:30pm	Took over from SIGS. 72. I.B. Lines as in Appendix III z signals on lines to right battalion very weak. Aerial line from Halfway house to Zouave Wood untraceable.	a.g.R.
	16		Patrolled lines. Dug in 200' of new buried line in continuation of the portion dug in by SIGS 72. IB on North side of LAKE.	a.g.R.
	16/17		Laid D.1. line from Halfway House to Zouave Wood.	
	17		Line to BELGIAN CHATEAU broken. Dug in 1/4" only buried line starting from HALFWAY HOUSE working towards ZOUAVE WOOD	a.g.R
	18		Line to BELGIAN CHATEAU broken and repaired.	
	18/19		Relaid and poled new D.1. line from ZOUAVE WOOD to HALFWAY HOUSE.	a.g.R.
	19		Old buried line to right and left battalions broken, and found to be not in a fit state to repair	a.g.R

WAR DIARY
INTELLIGENCE SUMMARY

Jan. 1916. Sheet III.

A Secn. 24 SIG. COY.

Army Form C. 2118.

Place	Date	Hour	Summary of Events and Information	Remarks and references to Appendices
ZILLEBEKE LAKE.	20.		Old No.1. aerial from HALFWAY HOUSE to ZOUAVE WOOD broken, and found untraceable. Continued burying line Halfway Ho. to ZOUAVE WD.	AGR
	21.		Line to BELGIAN CHATEAU broken and repaired. Continued burying cable.	AGR
	22.		Finished buried line from HALFWAY HOUSE to ZOUAVE WOOD and started to work on it.	AGR
	23.		Line to BELGIAN CHATEAU. Broken.	AGR
	24.	11am	No 2 aerial to Halfway House broken by shell in two places. No 1. aerial also broken. Relaid and poled No 2 Aerial.	AGR
	25.		Continued buried line from ZILLEBEKE LAKE to HALFWAY HOUSE. Laid armoured cable in trench from right Coy in HOOGE SECTION back towards support Coy for distance of 300x.	AGR
	26.		Continued laying armoured cable in HOOGE SECTION from left Coy towards Support Coy. LINE to BELGIAN CHATEAU broken.	AGR

Army Form C. 2118.

WAR DIARY
or
~~INTELLIGENCE SUMMARY~~

4 Sec 24 SIG. COY

Jan 1916.   Sheet IV.

(Erase heading not required.)

Instructions regarding War Diaries and Intelligence Summaries are contained in F. S. Regs., Part II. and the Staff Manual respectively. Title pages will be prepared in manuscript.

Place	Date	Hour	Summary of Events and Information	Remarks and references to Appendices
ZILLEBEKE LAKE.	27.		Continued laying armoured cable in HOOGE SECTION back to Support Coy and towards Battn Hqrs.	a.g.R.
	28.		Continued laying armoured cable in HOOGE SECTION towards battn Hqrs.	
	29.		Continued laying armoured cable in HOOGE section. Completed buried line from Bde Hqrs to left Battn at Halfway House.	a.g.R.
	30.		Labelled buried line from ZILLEBEKE LAKE to HALFWAY HOUSE and ZOUAVE WOOD.	a.g.R.
	31.	11am	sent N.C.O. and four men to take over from SIGS Z.Q. at H.14.a.	
		6:30pm	Handed over to Sigs S.Z.Q. lines as in Appendix IV.2	

A.J. Pitcher
i/c 2/Lt RE.
SIGS 73-1-15

COMMUNICATIONS of 73.I.B.
at.
EPERLECQUES.

Appendix I a.

RJP.
WATTEN.

RCB.

MIM

NRG

ZGC.

Yx

RWI

5/1/16.
A J Ritchie 2.Lt. R.E.

Appendix II 2

COMMUNICATIONS OF 73 I.B.
in REST AREA. H.14 a.
Sheet 28.

13/1/16

A.G. Ritchie
2 Lt. RE.

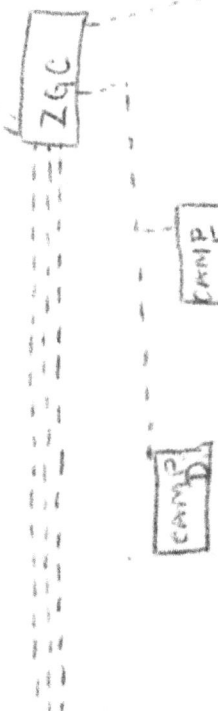

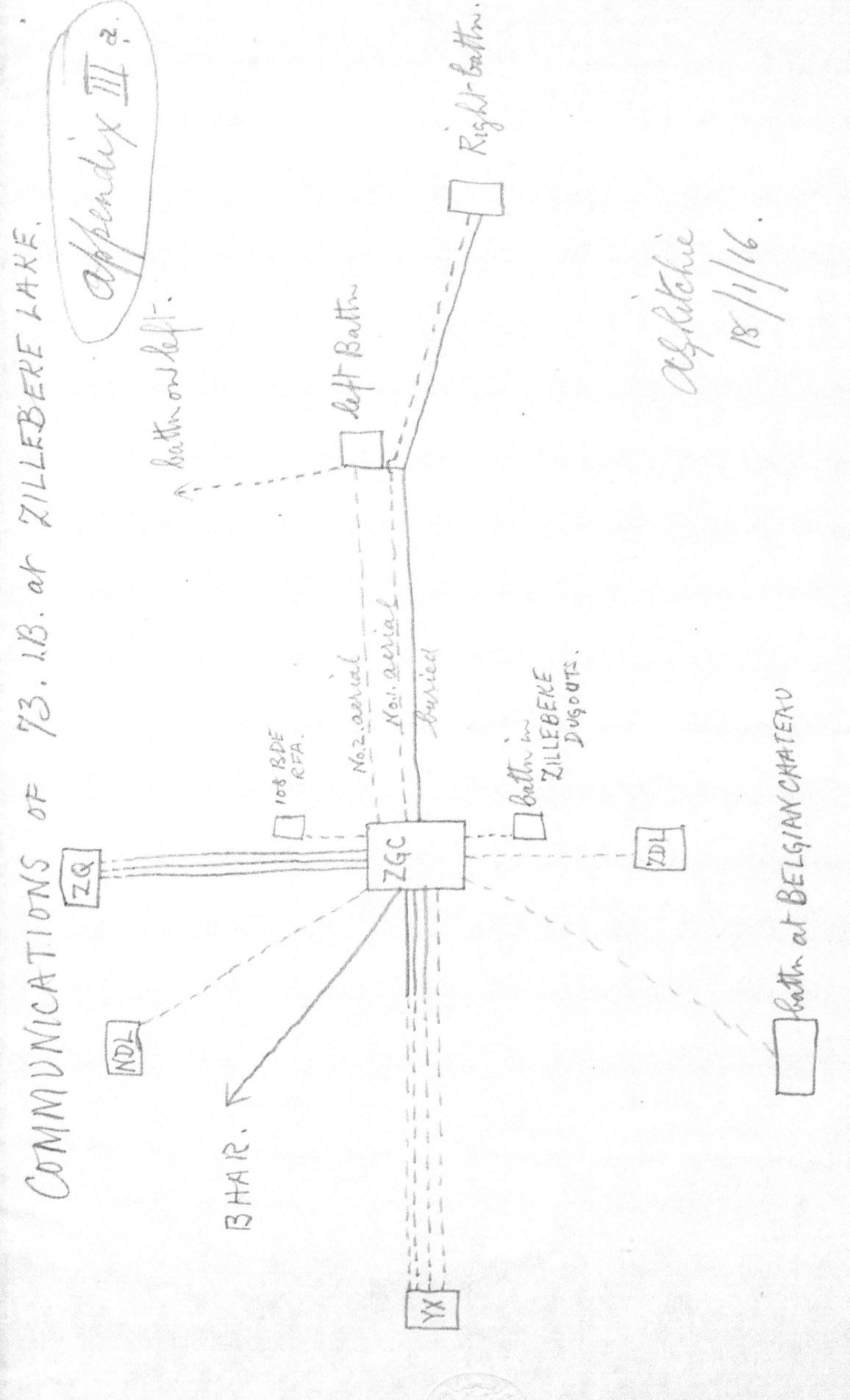

COMMUNICATIONS of 73.I.B. at ZILLEBEKE LAKE.

Appendix IV.

- Rt batt.
  - to batt. on right.
- Left batt.
  - to batt. on left.
- 108 RDF RFA
- ZGB
- NDL
- BHAR
- ZGC
- batt. in ZILLEBEKE LAKE DUGOUTS
- ZDL
- batt. at BELGIAN CHATEAU
- YX

28/1/16.

Sketch by
2/Lt R.E.

24th Signals
Vol: 7

Army Form C. 2118.

WAR DIARY
or
INTELLIGENCE SUMMARY.
(Erase heading not required)

2nd/1st Dur. Signal Coy RE

Place	Date	Hour	Summary of Events and Information	Remarks and references to Appendices
RENINGHELST	1/2/16		Starting new buried line, and putting in test boxes. Lines from KT to RAMPARTS checked to RAILWAY.	
"	2/2/16		Buried line started out.	
"	3/2/16		Laid new line from C8 to KT in the BEKE which was connected at CULVERT under POSTHORN HOOK RD to a metallic circuit belonging to HAR, which runs through YPRES to RAMPARTS near Left Bde Hqrs. 100 R.A. continued burying new route from LCHW to KS. 15 Cyclists & 25 RA continued digging of new line. Continued digging up 'Pair' in YPRES between LEFT Bde and SALLYPORT. This work being performed by [strikethrough] Brigade Section. Experimenting with wire netting for a Telephone circuit.	
"	4th.		Four armoured Test Boxes taken to be installed on buried route. Line to 129th Field Coy RE from RE dump needed up & replaced by a metallic circuit of D1 cable from YKR direct to 19 Co. The line has been tee-d on to the Cohewan from YKR to RE hump.	
"	5th.		Buried route plugged out more frequently & completed as far as LITTLE GATE. (TRAVERSE) Continued experimenting with wire netting & searching for earths. (TRAVERSE)	

Army Form C. 2118.

WAR DIARY
or
INTELLIGENCE SUMMARY.
(Erase heading not required.)

Place	Date	Hour	Summary of Events and Information	Remarks and references to Appendices
RENINGHELST	6/2/16		Working on LGHW. (Edith Grey Home in the West) route	
"	7th	(Night)	Continued work of relaying LGHW route. Commenced setting up periscope at KS (Kruishoek) for visual.	
"	8th		Commenced overhauling Bahn lines of testing ble. Overhauling lines.	
"	9th		Periscope erected at KS in order that visual can avoid be opened with ZILLEBEKE in the event of telegraph & telephonic wires failing. This proved to be the case on the 14th.	
"	10th		15 Men employed on reopening and deepening portion of route from KS to LGHW.	
"	11th		Ten men parties proceeded out to continue the buried route from KS. This work was performed at night. 5 line ets. installed at Ramparts. Rather slender rest by hostile aeroplane bomb which fell in close proximity to the stables. (GAS ALERT order received Sunder line to Ramparts (YPRES) = RK3. this from 8am to 4pm.	
"	12th		One was kept up during this time by RK13 which was OK to	

Army Form C. 2118.

WAR DIARY
or
INTELLIGENCE SUMMARY.
(Erase heading not required.)

Place	Date	Hour	Summary of Events and Information	Remarks and references to Appendices
RENINGHELST	12th		to	
"	13th		the Goldfish Chateau (GC), and from thence to the RAMPARTS by SV 13. At 8 am RK 14 to ZILLEBEKE was dis, and one in this case was kept up by superimposing on RK 5 & RK 6. At 11 pm the Division received the order to "STAND TO." Priority message was sent to all units. An "S.O.S" message from the 3J Rifle Brigade (17.4.1.B.) sent through to the Heavy ARTILLERY and fire was opened three minutes from the time of receiving gun. Direct flender turned at POPERINGHE.	
"	14th		RK 3. line to RAMPARTS again this, and alternate route to Goldfish Chateau adopted. 6.0 L. wires cut on rail- buried route by LCHW. Very heavy shelling commenced about 3/30 pm & telephones came into both Bgde. Hqrs. telephoned for Dome time. Additional line staff sent out to place cause Hqrs (VxR) to cope with the increased work much heavy shelling. J. "STAND TO" again issued and cancelled. All lines to 17th Bde at ZILLEBEKE. Final one was	

Army Form C. 2118.

WAR DIARY
or
INTELLIGENCE SUMMARY.
(Erase heading not required.)

Place	Date	Hour	Summary of Events and Information	Remarks and references to Appendices
RENINGHELST	14/7/16		Moved from KS (Knochanst) dugout to Brigade & messenger successfully transmitted. Lines resumed working after 3 hr dis.	
"	15th		For some time messages for RT Bde were transmitted through 53rd Division & 149th Bde whose lateral line to RT Bde held up. 76th Bde moved up as Corps Reserve & all telegraph work for them taken via our 17th Brigade. Two additional Infantry Signallers sent to KS. to form a relief for Signal Stn there.	
"	16th		76th Bde at 3.30pm transferred to 51st Bde. 17th Brigade ordered to the Corps reserve. One Battn only being in rest at a time. A small party employed running line from Divl Artillery Sig. Office to another building near by for a new office. Two petrol Lorries sent out in car to repair trestle line near YXR which had suffered from 12.A Tebury message in the Signal Office caused by shell fire during the night. During the remove from the were falling during the first three days; no fatalities.	

WAR DIARY
INTELLIGENCE SUMMARY

Army Form C. 2118.

Place	Date	Hour	Summary of Events and Information	Remarks and references to Appendices
REININGHELST	16/2/16	ctd.		
"	17/2/16		1st day. from 300 to 860 2nd day. " " 300 " 750 3rd day. " " 300 " 600 Party of trainmen sent along trestle route to thoroughly overhaul & strengthen. Small party to ZILLEBEKE Lake to repair armoured cable cut in three places yesterday.	
"	18/2/16		Laid two armoured cables along South edge of ZILLEBEKE Pond to the place where the cable was cut last by point. Ctd. digging up the Pavé in YPRES & improving joints at points where lines had been cut by shell fire during the last few days.	
"	19/2/16		Continued work on reconstructing Trestle Route. Laid 2 armoured cables from MOAT by LILLE GATE (YPRES) onward to approaches to LEFT POLE ROUTE. Continued digging up pavé between those two points. Ad. lines to R.T. Brigade cut at 5 am but line to R.T. group shelling held up & were relayed.	
"	20/2/16		Repairing damage to lines. Ctd. work on TRESTLE route & digging up line.	

Army Form C. 2118.

WAR DIARY
or
INTELLIGENCE SUMMARY.
(Erase heading not required.)

Instructions regarding War Diaries and Intelligence Summaries are contained in F. S. Regs., Part II. and the Staff Manual respectively. Title pages will be prepared in manuscript.

Place	Date	Hour	Summary of Events and Information	Remarks and references to Appendices
BEDINGHELST	21/5/16		Overhauling Trestle Route. Two working parties engaged.	
"	21-6		Finished repairing Trestle Route.	
"	22nd		Two parties at night engaged in pushing on new lines between LILLE GATE and ZILLEBEKE.	
"	23rd		At night 160 men digging in 2 matellen C2 fm ZILLEBEKE	
"	24/16		At night 250 continued work and completed to RAMPARTS (Ypres). Two armoured cables laid from south side of LILLE GATE under the streets of YPRES and YPRES-LYS RIVER & thence from where it emerged from river to New Brigade Hqtrs.	
"	25th		Wiring through Rampart line to YPRES station.	
"	26th		Continued further route thro' CB. to RAMPARTS	
"	27th		Completed line from MOAT to RAMPARTS by laying armoured cable. Made good all joints in L.G.H.W. route.	
"	28th		Dug trench from Trestle Route to YXR in which to substitute wire pair so as to cut out last half mile of Trestle Route	
"	29th		Work on informing lines from R.A. H.Q. to artillery this & anigun lines.	

Army Form C. 2118.

WAR DIARY
— of —
INTELLIGENCE SUMMARY.

No 2 Section 24th Sig Coy R.E.   Appendix No 1.

Place	Date	Hour	Summary of Events and Information	Remarks and references to Appendices
ZILLEBEKE LAKE	1.2.16	5ᵖ	Lines patrolled & maintained. Armoured cable from L. Bn Hqrs to coy Hqrs (Support), & Corps in line, completed, & filled with joint boxes about every 100ˣ. Signals v. good. Cable cut in GRAFTON ST by direct hit on 4ᵗʰ. Alternative air-line run between L & R.l Bn Hqrs, as the overhead wire was only line existing. Visual from CULVERT, by WING HO, to Beautruck by GORDON HO. also back from Bde Hq to test stn K5 at KRUISSTRAAT. Casualties nil.	
"	6.2	1ᵖ	GRAFTON ST & REGENT ST shelled almost every day, rendering armoured cables there unreliable. Lateral armoured line run from L Bn at HALFWAY HO to R Bn of L Bde in WITTEPOORT FM, & tee run from it just S. of MENIN RD to two coy Hqrs in CULVERT. Armoured line started from fwd coys of R Bn. in B85 & C.1 to Plem Hqrs in R7, S. of ZOUAVE WOOD. This much finished.	
"		13ᵖ	Lateral & loop complete, when enemy bombarded Bde front & heavily cutting lines forward from Bns. Armoured cable in C.T.s proved invaluable in heavy shell fire, but held up very well in the often over ground unlikely to be shelled. Body of Bde linesmen went up at dusk 13ᵗʰ to try & put loop front in armoured cable to avoid cutting. Two attempts were made, but on each	

WAR DIARY
INTELLIGENCE SUMMARY

Army Form C. 2118.

Place	Date	Hour	Summary of Events and Information	Remarks and references to Appendices
ZILLEBEKE LAKE	14.2.16		Occasion were prevented by enemy barrage of shell on REGENT ST, but returned 5 AM. Connection with culvert restored by 3RB shine men at about 8AM, but broken almost at once by renewed hostile shelling, which continued without interruption, the most intense being between 3 & 6 PM, when enemy shelled all our work area. Cutting new plan from to Div (R/K 5+6) at about 3·30 P.M. Line to Bttns (3RB + 12 RF) held up all through the bombardment, armoured lateral to WITTEPOORT went during the afts. Wright MSS sent through 149 Bde in R. + 73 Bde m left. Visual with K5 used during night 14/15. Sent up 3 m DS to 146 Bttn + carrier pigeons. Cue re estab to front corp of 1 RF (who relieved 3RB). 12 RF did not keep touch with front corp for any length of time. Confusion everywhere.	
	15		day. Cue re estab with Bn in reserve at CHATEAU BELGE, and with Bde in YPRES (73 ul) on all lines. One Div line R.K. 15, abandoned as too badly damaged. 8 QUEENS Sigs relieved 12 RF about 8 PM, all lines working. 1 N. STAFF Sigs relieved 1 RF nyt 15/17 and 72 Bde coming when 17th, all writhing in Cue, but armoured line to CULVERT	
	16		still dis. 17 Bde section to relieve P.D.&L 148A. HODGE, and returned to WITTEPOORT	

Army Form C. 2118.

WAR DIARY
or
INTELLIGENCE SUMMARY.
(Erase heading not required.)

Place	Date	Hour	Summary of Events and Information	Remarks and references to Appendices
REST CAMP H14A	FEBY 17—21		Section resting and refitting. Lines to Canal patrolled & maintained. Rifles, S.A.A gudelines, &c. inspected.	
"	22		2 NCOs & 4 men went up to ZILLEBEKE LAKE to relieve 4 men of 76,8,+ help them move their office to S.E. corner of YPRES ramparts, owing to heavy shelling of dugouts. 2 9 8 men came to H14A.	
"	25		Men were returned on completion of change of offices. Casualties NIL.	
"	26-29		Lines patrolled.	

8.8.0.17.18.

[signature] Lieut ??? 3/LRE

WAR DIARY
or
INTELLIGENCE SUMMARY.

No. 3 Section 24th Div Sig Coy
Army Form C. 2118.

Sup 72 1 Bt.

Appendix 2

Place	Date	Hour	Summary of Events and Information	Remarks and references to Appendices
YPRES	1.2.16		Lines patrolled and work on new buried cable continued	
	2.2.16		"	
	3.2.16		Lines patrolled. No. 50209 Cpl HOUGHTON. E wounded. Shrapnel. Left forearm	
	4.2.16		Lines patrolled. New buried cable laid a.d.	
	5.2.16		Lines patrolled and necessary improvements made.	
	6.2.16		"	
	7.2.16		"	
	8.2.16		Lines patrolled and shown to linesmen of 73rd IB signal section	
H.14.A.2.4	9.2.16		Handed over to Sigs 73 IB at 6pm. Bde HQ moved 3pm to next over at VLAMERTINGHE H.4.A.24 (Ref 28)	
"	10.2.16		Laid a new area improved and instruments attached to	
"	11.2.16		Lines improved and a technical store room and office	
"	12.2.16		Lines patrolled.	
	13.2.16		Area patrolled. Officer sent for Signallers E. SURREYS from 6pm – 9pm who's section was sent to THE PRINCESS at POPERINGHE	
	14.2.16		Lines patrolled	
	15.2.16		Linesmen sent up to bury lines in ZILLEBEKE area as instruments of both attended to	
I.21.A.2.7	16.2.16		Battn instruments patrolled and attended to them. Took over from Sigs 17.IB at ZILLEBEKE DUGOUTS I 21.A.2.7. (Ref 28) at 6pm. Bde HQ moved ZILLEBEKE Dugout 3pm. Plan of lines attached. Line to HOOGE begun.	
	17.2.16		Work on line for Battn HQ in HALFWAY HOUSE to HOOGE continued	
	18.2.16		Lines patrolled and line to HOOGE continued	
	19.2.16		Lines patrolled and line to HOOGE continued. Bde HQ shelled 11.45pm to 2.a.m. All men Div exch A Div?	
	20.2.16		Lines improved right old trench	
	21.2.16		Walked on line till 5 am. Bde HQ shelled 9.30am to 2 am. Line mended.	
	22.2.16		Line to HOOGE continued. Bde HQ shelled 8.30pm – 10.30pm. Line mended	
	23.2.16		Line to HOOGE from HALFWAY House finished and satisfactory. Battn shelled 12.30pm – 3.30pm. Linesmen mended. Busy	
	24.2.16		line to new Battn HQ continued by Div sigs. I 14 B 2.4 began by No 1 Coy. (Buried line was from NEW HQ to D.R)	
I.14.B.2.4	25.2.16		Buried line to new HQ continued by Div sigs. Got last mail line from HOOGE to CIR (HQ of Coy Right Batt began) Line from NEW HQ to Battn is from old finished. Battn HQ moved I.14B.2.4 at 10.30am. Central line from HOOGE to CIR continued	

WAR DIARY
or
INTELLIGENCE SUMMARY

Army Form C. 2118.

Place	Date	Hour	Summary of Events and Information	Remarks and references to Appendices
Ypres	26.2.16 27.2.16		Enemy patrolled. Line O.10 to Bellewaarde Lake. Enemy patrolled. Line to Yeomanry Post from Halfway House completed. Report opening obtained to East of line to House. On road. Enemy continued work. Sketch of Ypres	
"	28.2.16		Enemy patrolled. Enemy continued water/gas. Shelter 1/2 miles S/DS and up to Zonnebeke Coy HQrs in place of armoured cables for completion of Potijze HQrs C.I.A. line.	
"	29.2.16		Enemy patrolled. Enemy water/gas shelters finished. Officers Mess seeking fitted up. Divn worked out outside the office.	
"	1.3.16.		Enemy patrolled. Certain amount of shelling around HQrs no damage no plane however.	

APPENDIX 3

Army Form C. 2118.

February 1916.   4 Sec. 24 Signal Coy.

WAR DIARY
or
INTELLIGENCE SUMMARY.
Sheet 1.

Place	Date	Hour	Summary of Events and Information	Remarks and references to Appendices
H.14.a Sheet 28.	1. 2.		Maintained communication in the rest area with lines as appendix I.	App.I
	3.		Patrolled lines to Battalions and cut off several "legs off" and reeled them up.	
	4.			
	5.		Lines to Camps A.B.C. broken. Sent up 1 Sgt & 4 linemen to Ramparts to take over.	
	6.			
	7.		Cleared up officer arrest camp.	
	8.		Signors and 4 operators sent at 10 a.m. to take over new headquarters in RAMPARTS. 10 p.m. rest of section left rest camp for RAMPARTS. Lines mended took over from Sigs 72 I.B. at 6 p.m.; Lines to Battn. div. Hq.	
RAMPARTS	8.		7 p.m. Bn. giving wedding lines to left Bath; adv. Hq.	
	9.		div 8 p.m. mended Tam. Jn. Lines here broken by shells. E.W. lines div. to R.E. both near by and everyone except M.R. Tested Visual from Railway wood to M.R	

WAR DIARY
or
INTELLIGENCE SUMMARY

Army Form C. 2118.

Sheet II.

Place	Date	Hour	Summary of Events and Information	Remarks and references to Appendices
YPRES	10		Tested visual from RAILWAY WOOD to MENIN RD.	
	11.		Laid British line from H.Q. adv. right batt. to Halfway House at	
			dawn. Completed 4.30 a.m.	
	12.		Inspected company lines in right bathn. Answers to all very satisfactory. Line to 107 Bde Dis 10.50 p - 12.35am	
	13.		Lines to Z.R. div 4.30 p.m. Telephone operator shot in left hand.	
			Line cut by shell at 11.40am repaired 12 noon. Recons to R.M.A.S. cut	
			25 min repair through our & enemy trenches.	
	14.		107 Bde R.F.A. move H.Q'rs. handed lines to new huts. no 73 Bde lines to left bathn. 18 Bde ord advanced work batn cut by	
			very heavy shelling.	
	15.		Line to bathn in convent YPRES cut. 17 Bde Div. lines advanced went out at night and laid two new lines	
			Right bathn and night bathn advanced H.Q'rs.	

WAR DIARY
or
INTELLIGENCE SUMMARY
(Erase heading not required.)

Army Form C. 2118.

February. Sheet III.

Place	Date	Hour	Summary of Events and Information	Remarks and references to Appendices
YPRES.	16		repaired all lines to MR. apperdix II. Tried XW pair to WBatt Hy and found it not worth repairing beyond Batt Hy.	AGR
	17.		repaired XY line as far as Hellfire Corner and L5 twisted anywayPC.	AGR
	18.		repaired XY line from Hellfirecorner to YprBatt. putting in 1/4 mile of armoured. L5 repaired to PC.	AGR
	19.		XY repaired to within 300 yds of Adv. W. batt. where it becomes untraceable in swamp. repaired E.T. laid new tees of L5 pair down Bellewarde Beek to Adv W. Batt.	AGR
	20.		continued XY with new wire to Adv W. Batt.	AGR
	21.		CD broken in two places in brook. Visual signal from Railway wood to MR tested and lamps found to be out of alignment. 2.1.2.3 to 72 Bde broken.	AGR
	22.		CD repaired. Z.12.3 again broken. tested Visual again unable on account of snow. A Lineman from 76 Bde came up to learn lines.	AGR

Army Form C. 2118.

WAR DIARY
or
INTELLIGENCE SUMMARY

February. Sheet IV.

(Erase heading not required.)

Instructions regarding War Diaries and Intelligence Summaries are contained in F. S. Regs., Part II. and the Staff Manual respectively. Title pages will be prepared in manuscript.

Place	Date	Hour	Summary of Events and Information	Remarks and references to Appendices
YPRES	23		patrolled lines. 2.G.B. Changed position of their Hqrs they shortened our lines to them accordingly	A.G.R.
	24		laid pair of D.3 wires in place of old F.7. which were reeled up.	A.G.R.
	25		handed over to Sign 16.IB. at 6 pm arrived POPERINGHE 11 pm	A.G.R.
POPERINGHE	26		extended existing line from Y. Corps to Bde Hqrs. and tel part to 6th Div.	A.G.R.
	27		laid line to Battalions in Camps A and B.	A.G.R.
	28		laid lines to Battalions in POPERINGHE.	
	29		maintained communication	A. Ritchie v/Capt

WAR DIARY
or
INTELLIGENCE SUMMARY. Sub-Appendix 1

Army Form C. 2118.

(Erase heading not required.)

Place	Date	Hour	Summary of Events and Information	Remarks and references to Appendices

Camp [A]   Camp [C]

Camp [B]

[A/C] H.114.A.

☐ H.21.B.37.

[HQ] H.13.D.55.

Camp [D]

E Camp H.19.B.26.

[YX]

Sketch

Communications of 193rd Div
in Rest Camp

WAR DIARY
or
INTELLIGENCE SUMMARY.

Army Form C. 2118.

Sub-Appendix II

Communications of 73 I.B. at YPRES.
22/2/16.

2 4 Div
Signals

Vol 8
———

Army Form C. 2118.

WAR DIARY
or
INTELLIGENCE SUMMARY. 24th Divl Signal Coy R.E.

(Erase heading not required.)

Instructions regarding War Diaries and Intelligence Summaries are contained in F. S. Regs., Part II. and the Staff Manual respectively. Title pages will be prepared in manuscript.

Place	Date	Hour	Summary of Events and Information	Remarks and references to Appendices
RENINGHELST	1/3/16		12 bays of Trestle Route Alevin down by H.E. Shell. Rem- new stretch H. line taken in to form YXR to T.P.O.P. & casting. beyond LGHW crumped in one cartier in this E.C. (bluish shell.) wires a YXR stragglers of horning over front line from R.H.Q. Two gun lines continued construction of infantry in saml. Continued improving back R.A. lines.	
	2/3/16		Kept of party on R/C YXR leading wires. All Subs lines are now diagrammatic and taped (contin) beyond and pasted (for marking), YXR & and cartr t SXR to Premier - Route YXR to Buffs. new Lech R.A. Lines & myn gun lines.	
	3/3/16		LGHW line cut in 9 places in 250 yards, S.E. of L.A.A. imminent weather so no time to repair.	
	4/3/16		Continued improving back R.A. + myngun lines. & R.A. back on Buffs.	
	5/3/16			

of messages La Prisich Guers A.D.S.S.
14-2-16 ... 365 (any Blizzard)
1-3-16 ... 373
2-3-16 ... 530
3-3-16 ... 243
4-3-16 ... 560

Army Form C. 2118.

WAR DIARY
or
INTELLIGENCE SUMMARY.
(Erase heading not required.)

Place	Date	Hour	Summary of Events and Information	Remarks and references to Appendices
RENINGHELST	6/3/16		Continued digging in gunner line thro' YPRES. New buried cables being laid from YXR to BECQUE.	
	7/3/16		Continued laying new buried route from YXR to BECQUE. D5 line laid from BECQUE to Artillery H'qrs. BELGIAN CHA. Preliminary lines for taking over new Right front (150th I.B.) Laid a length of 2 armoured cables and 2 D5 cables to a junction of LGHW Route going to position of a battery. East of Touth Route stopped at first where line was destroyed by shell fire.	Rebels
	8/3/16		All lines were dis to Right Brigade at ZILLEBEKE at 5.0 p.m. owing to very heavy shelling. All work sent on 50th DIVN to my own lines at 7.6 p.m. Very heavy traffic in men going to line Cyclists could not circul. work for 50th & 50th DIVNS owing to the lines to these divisions being also blocked. Vehicles working to ZR (7th I.B) at 8.0 p.m on a new line (old line RKH) being still (?))	

2353 Wt W2544/1454 250,000 5/15 D.D.&L. A.D.S.S. Forms/C 2118.

Army Form C. 2118.

WAR DIARY
or
INTELLIGENCE SUMMARY.
(Erase heading not required.)

Place	Date	Hour	Summary of Events and Information	Remarks and references to Appendices
RENINGHELST.	10/3/16		Small party at KRUISTRAAT (K5) straightening up (RAH) trench again to ZA and used for summer trench. Later and new line was marked C.	
	11/3/16		Alternative route via GC (GOLDFISH CH.) marked and CPW wood used with good results. One row (R and and mounting to trough and trough constructed of K5 for laying and wiring to trough and new sill-boards and telephone cable made then fire.	
	12/3/16		Small party straightening up at YXR and starting a new trench.	Rentuspe
	13/3/16		All wires checked up to YXR. Small party on O... trench wires. Continued improvement of staging levels.	
	14/3/16			
	15/3/16		Visited back portion of YC 85 + L with regiment men with K5 and C.B. (Comr. of BFC (VE)	
	16/3/16		Long journey round and then returned to K5 to meet	

2353 Wt. W2544/1454 700,000 5/15 D.D & L. A.D.S.S. Forms/C 2118.

Army Form C. 2118.

WAR DIARY
or
INTELLIGENCE SUMMARY.
(Erase heading not required.)

Place	Date	Hour	Summary of Events and Information	Remarks and references to Appendices
RENINGHELST	16/3/16 (contd)		communication with Right Brigade at ZILLEBEKE blown over by shell-fire. Enemy artillery activity in the neighbourhood of K.5., Z.R. line (R.K.4) dig + camp kept up by trenching R.K.4, 5 and 6. Dummy Hooper R.K. 1, 2, 3, + 4 "dumped" and GO trees planted to N neighbourhood of LGHW (= LOCRE ROAD 2 mil S of YPRES) During the day three lorries (Y.C. 2, 5, 6.) were broken in 17 places between K.S. and CANAL by shell-fire and rejoined.	Rollis/r
	17/3/16		Phone lines placed on BECQUE Route.	
	18/3/16 19/3/16		1 N.C.O. + 3 men sent by 3rd Canadian Division to take over Y.X.R., 1 N.C.O. 3 men to take over K.S, & Enever for Burcard lines, while 1 N.C.O. and 3 men were sent to take over lines at "Left" brigade where H.Q. were established in YPRES. 73rd Bde Signals [struck] relieved by 9th Canadian Bde Signals. Signalmaster from 3rd Canadians arrived to take over Signal Office. 7th Bde Signals relieved by 8th Canadian Bde Sig.s at 3.45 p.m.	
	20/3/16			

WAR DIARY or INTELLIGENCE SUMMARY

Army Form C. 2118.

Place	Date	Hour	Summary of Events and Information	Remarks and references to Appendices
RENINGHELST	21/3/16		K.S. Test station staff relieved by 3rd Canadians 12 noon. 17th Bde Signals relieved by 7th Canadian Bde Sig'ls.	
	22/3/16		Company moved by march route from RENINGHEST to FLÊTRE. Billets taken up at FLÊTRE and those previously occupied by 3rd Canadian Divl Signal Coy. Signal Office opened at FLÊTRE, 17th Bde at THIEFPOUCK, 72nd Bde at MT DES CATS, 73rd Bde at METEREN. Artillery at REECKE. Signal Office for 24th Division closed 3 pm at RENINGHEST and re-opened same hour at FLÊTRE. 17th 73rd as usual	3/4/16
FLÊTRE	23/3/16 - 26/3/16	12 noon.	Continuing in 24th Divn & engaged in preparing to take over new lines from relieving 24th Div by 1st Canadian Divn.	
	27/3/16		5 linemen sent to WESTHOFF FARM (command of 1st Canadian Divn) to take over lines.	
	29/3/16		1 N.C.O. and signalmen (1 gun + 4 lines) to WESTH FF Farm to take over office from 1st Canadian Divison	

Army Form C. 2118.

WAR DIARY
INTELLIGENCE SUMMARY.
(Erase heading not required.)

Place	Date	Hour	Summary of Events and Information	Remarks and references to Appendices
FLÊTRE	30/3/16		The Company proceeded by march route from FLÊTRE to ST JANS CAPPEL to relieve 1st Canadian Division. Two cable detachments were sent in under the command of 2 subaltern to WESTHOFF FARM (the advanced HQ). The detachments will provide nothing further until Division have got started.	
ST JANS CAPPEL	31/3/16.		Visited 72nd Bde in continuation of Canadian Corps scheme.	Billets
			The average number of messages dealt with in Brit. Signal Office during month was 420 per day in normal days being about 400 but from 14th to 31st the average number was 600 of which 200 were transmitted. In addition 300 letters a day were dealt with by DRLS. In no single case was a message lost or misdelivered. During the month the scheme for the introduction of	

… Infantry and artillery in fuzzy … [illegible handwritten war diary entry]

Rutledge

No. 45934 Cpl Rutter J.

Appendix I

WAR DIARY
or
INTELLIGENCE SUMMARY

No 2 Section
2n Sig. Coy

Army Form C. 2118.

Place	Date	Hour	Summary of Events and Information	Remarks and references to Appendices
REST CAMP H.4.A.	1 – 8/3	—	Section resting. However went up to 150 Bde in advance.	Military History /HGRE
ZILLEBEKE LAKE	9/3		Took over lines from 150 Bde. 50 Div at 4 p.m. Wires on Trench lines which were not in V good condition.	
"	10/3 – 13/3		Amound cable broken in front line.	
"	13/3		Bde amound cable broken as well as left Batt front line.	
"	15/3		Amound to Coys, owing to heavy shelling left Batt were thei' H.Q. up about 1000 yds. Pole lines extended with amound. Wires wen night.	G.S. Murray
"	16/3		Wireless Shewd out of position near Dd left Bn H.Q.	
"	18/3		When Bde gd took over lines, there were 3 Batt in line; from Div. Sitn owing to heavy sh'y his Batt to the line, the Left Batt H.Q. is un-worked and to the Front cable Rout became the left Batt and the Right Batt remains as after this wise need only small alteration in the lines. Connections made and all correct. 7th Canadian Bde took over lines at 9 p.m. Bde Sailn Marched to H.W.A. Hut 28 xrd Camp.	

WAR DIARY
INTELLIGENCE SUMMARY

Army Form C. 2118.

Place	Date	Hour	Summary of Events and Information	Remarks and references to Appendices
	22/3		Staff at H.Q.A. Sheet 28.	
	23/3		Moved to new road H.Q. Sheet 27 9.35 B.44. Arrived at 11 A.M. via Poperinghe, Abeele, Godewaersvelde and country at new H.Q. at Thieushouk at 5:30 P.M. Office opened at 6 P.M. Branches and phone to Div. at FLETRE. Lines also to each Bath. on Sitting map viz: Sheet 27, MAA, 1st Roy Fus Q.33.D.5.2. 3rd Rifle Bde Q.29.B.9.4. 12 Roy Fus Q.23.A.4.4. 8"Buff. W.S.C.39. Both on lines and unloading Starr sit. Sheet D. Lieut enlisted on landed on to 7th Canadian Bde.	O.S.Manville
THIEUSHOUK	24/3			
	25/3		Section resting & refitting.	
	26–27		Linesmen went up to 2 Canadian Bde to go over lines.	
	28			
T21.D.5.2 (Sheet 28)	30		Rest of Section moved to CZB Hqrs at T21 D.5.2. (Sheet 28 BELGIUM) took over Sig 5 PM, CZB taking over at THIEUSHOUK at 9 AM. Comme by sounder & phone to DIV + YxR. 3 airlines to report centre in PLOEGSTEERT WOOD, + Battle Hq on Hill 63. 3 airlines to each of the 2 Btns in the line one airline to Btn in reserve. Lines to log. Hq. partially buried	H.Lloyd Spencer 1/4/15

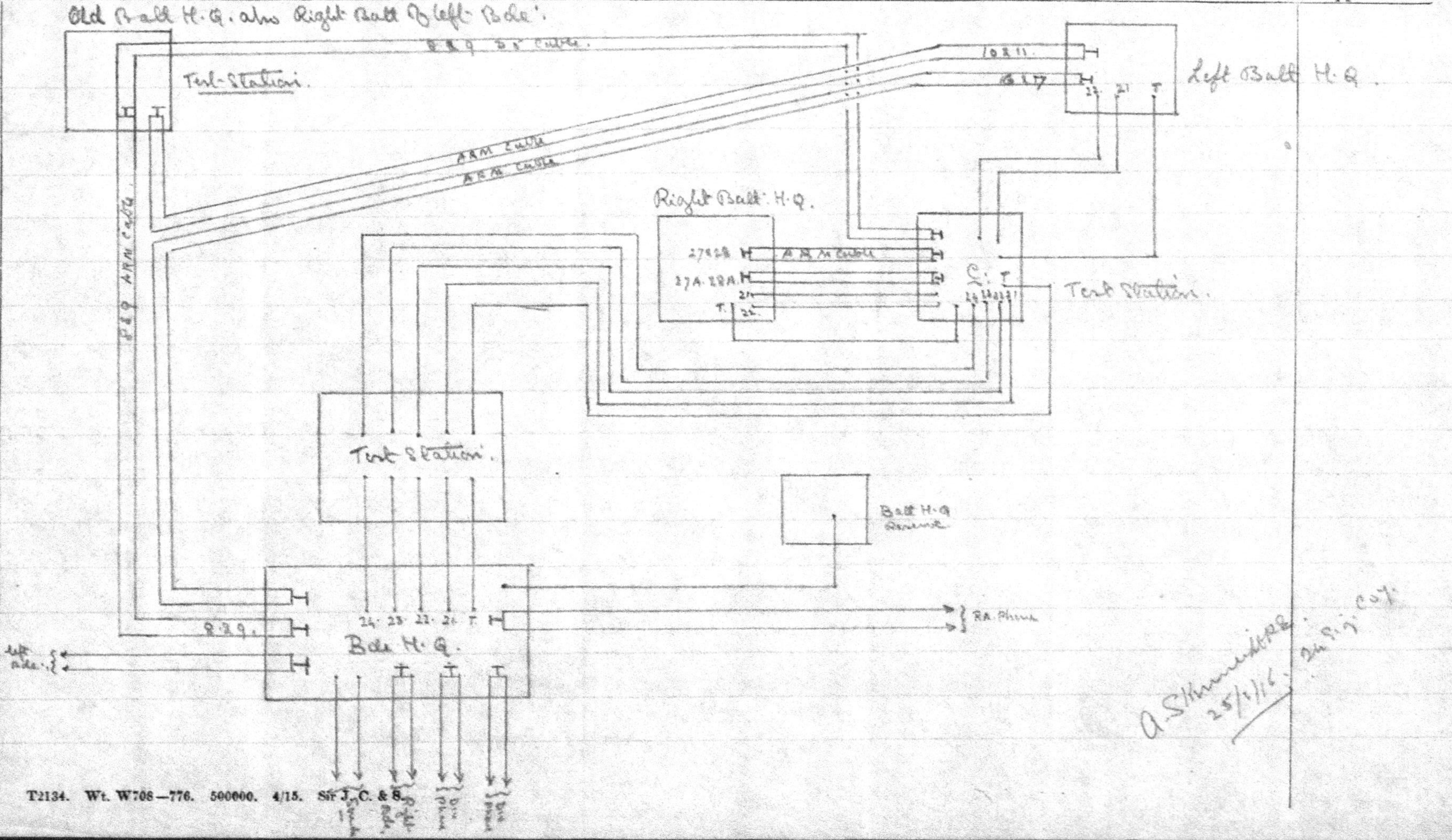

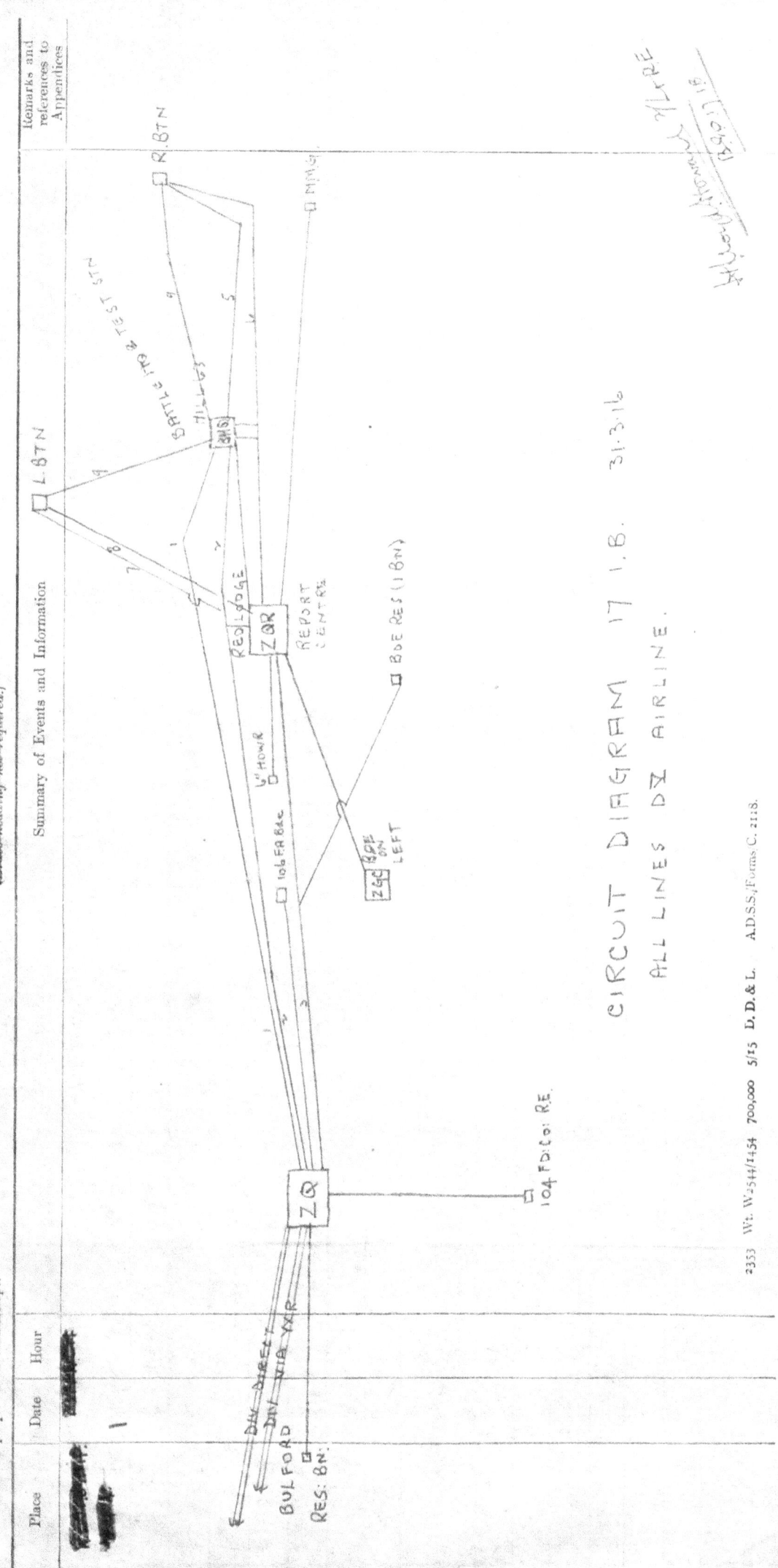

Appendix II

WAR DIARY
or
INTELLIGENCE SUMMARY

Army Form C. 2118.

N°3 Section
2nd L. Dn. L. Signal Co. R.E.

Place	Date	Hour	Summary of Events and Information	Remarks and references to Appendices
Ypres	2.3.16		Lines patrolled return amount of shelling around Hd Qrs no damage done	(officer diagram of line attached)
Ypres	3.3.16		Lines patrolled two ones or air Buzzer phone and one RK s.b, shelling at Yost - Shrap of heavy Zillebeke dugouts —	
Ypres	3.3.16		Lines patrolled and 13JB linesmen instructed in lines tests faulty. P.P. leads into office or RK s.b replaced with D5. also buried to Battns.	
Ypres	4.3.16		Lines patrolled and handed over to 13 JB linesmen — assistance given to RA south armoured cable in Ypres. Handed over to 3JC at 3.30 pm.	
			Hom office opens in Rue de Messines POPERINGHE — Bee nut of action. Rw Head's in Camp A. E Surreys in Camp B. M staffs at Malt factory by POP. 3/6. Queens in Rue de Cimetière, POP. comm to YX via ECO.	
POPERINGHE	5.3.16		Lines patrolled by linesmen to all Battns to learn route	
"	6.3.16		M staffs moved to Rue de Cassell at 5 pm — comm by orderly	
"	7.3.16		Line E Malt Factory recovered and relaid to staffs new H.Q. in Rue de Cassell.	M staff up
"	8.3.16		Line to E.C.D. aid room - linesmen on it but great difficulty experienced in tracing it through P.B.P. comm to YX through P.b. and later through Y.F.	

Army Form C. 2118.

WAR DIARY
or
INTELLIGENCE SUMMARY.
(Erase heading not required.)

Instructions regarding War Diaries and Intelligence Summaries are contained in F. S. Regs., Part II. and the Staff Manual respectively. Title pages will be prepared in manuscript.

Place	Date	Hour	Summary of Events and Information	Remarks and references to Appendices
POPERINGHE	9-3-16		1.30am. Line to ECO put right by cutting out length and replacing. Bde H.Q. moved to H.14.a. Map 28. at 4pm. Sig office handed over E.26.d.1. 3.30pm. Sig office H.14.a. taken over 2.15pm. ement Y X by Oernders. Telephone Battns. Rivets Camp A. E Scileys Camp B. Queens Camp E, N. STAFFS Camp F.	
H.14.A.	10-3-16		Line to Camp A & B. dis. at 7 am. repaired at 8.30 am. Ad linemen on line	
OUDERDOM			till 4pm. removing faults.	
"	11-3-16		Line to Camp D. dis 3pm. OK. 3.50 pm.	
"	12-3-16		Lines patrolled.	
"	13-3-16		Lines laid to 12th & 13th Bde. Machine gun Cos. at H.13.c.3.2.	
"	14-3-16		Lines patrolled — DIVN Sounder line dis. 1.30pm. OK 2.15pm.	
"	15-3-16		Linemen to RAMPARTS. YPRES to learn lines of 13 J.B. in ZILLEBEKE sector.	
"	16-3-16		Relieved 13 J.B. in ZILLEBEKE sector. Headquarters in YPRES RAMPARTS — BR. B.Von Sig H.a.b D.9.a.m.	
YPRES	17-3-16		Relabelling lines in Rampalls. of new system of station calls vg. Bde H.Q. Z.11. Test Stn. at ZILLEBEKE Z.B. Battn. in red at ZILLEBEKE D.y.	

WAR DIARY
or
INTELLIGENCE SUMMARY.
(Erase heading not required.)

Place	Date	Hour	Summary of Events and Information	Remarks and references to Appendices
YPRES	17.3.16		Cont'd.	
"	18.3.16		HALFWAY HOUSE – D10, ZOUAVE WOOD – D5, Battn in Reserve at Belgian Chateau D14. Continued detailing lines – Improving buried line being laid to Zouave Wood – Buried part of line left open 2.11 to 2.13 – Instructing linesmen from 8th Canadian Bde in lines to Bn.	
"	19.3.16		Instructing Canadian linesmen in latest communications etc.	
"	20.3.16		Relieved by 8th Canadian Bde at 3-30 p.m. Took over signals at H14A at 4 p.m.	
H14A	21.3.16		Handed over signals to 17SB. at 1-30 p.m. Moved to new area starting 3 p.m.	
OUDERDOM			Route Reninghelst, Westoutre, Mt Kokereele, Berthen to R.19.d.65, map 27. arriving 7.45 p.m.	
R.19.d.6.5	22.3.16		Established communication with YX at FLETRE at 4 p.m.	
Bn Hd Qrs. Cade-map 27	23.3.16		Chief to Battn by cycle orderly. Overhauling and supplying equipment.	
"	24.3.16		Established communication to Dumps at T.16.d. map 27 who use cyclists to F.1.B.4. Linesmen went to St Sommaire Bel to lines lines.	
"	26.3.16		Resting	

WAR DIARY
or
INTELLIGENCE SUMMARY.
(Erase heading not required.)

Army Form C. 2118.

Place	Date	Hour	Summary of Events and Information	Remarks and references to Appendices
Mareuil	27.3.16		Took over signals in new area at 1.30pm - Whinery Signals not answered till 11 am next day. Head Sig. office at Pil. His Cole until 4pm Easter Sat. to Hurdean Rd.	(Officers appn of War attached)
Bugs Fm.	28.3.16		New Headqrs. at Bugs Farm - N.33 a + b. map 20. Signal taken over by N.33 a + b. map 20. Signal taken over 3pm Switches and fell	
"			Patrolling and testing lines in new area + making lines sig'ed a Red X pieces. Could not use Red X	
"	29.3.16		by shell fire on cable down. Patrolling lines. took 1m to tea 7m from m.u Lef Bn line	
"	30.3.16		Patrolled lines, then repaired line to Left Bott. south for new burial line in main reserve	
"	31.3.16		Lines Patrolled, improving lines with offices from advanced posts.	

31/3/16

G.W. [signature]
O.C. H: 3 Sectn 24 Div
J.S. Co.

Comms 72.1.B.

[Diagram showing communication network with nodes labeled D5, D10, Z8, Z11, 72.1.B, 17.6, Z3, with connecting lines labeled Right Batt, Left Batt, Tuchy R.W. right Batt, Armoured cable to Right Batt right Bn, Batt military, Z8-Z3 line, Z4-D9 line, Z4-D10 line, Z8-D10 line, etc.]

Z.B = Tech STN at original Bde HQ in ZILLEBEKE BUND
72.1.B = new Bde HQ in Ramflex STO vaults S of MENIN GATE

Right Batt: hot armoured cable circuits.
Left Batt: comp ckts in MENIN cellars had bn armoured cable methods of comms ??

10/31/16
[signatures]

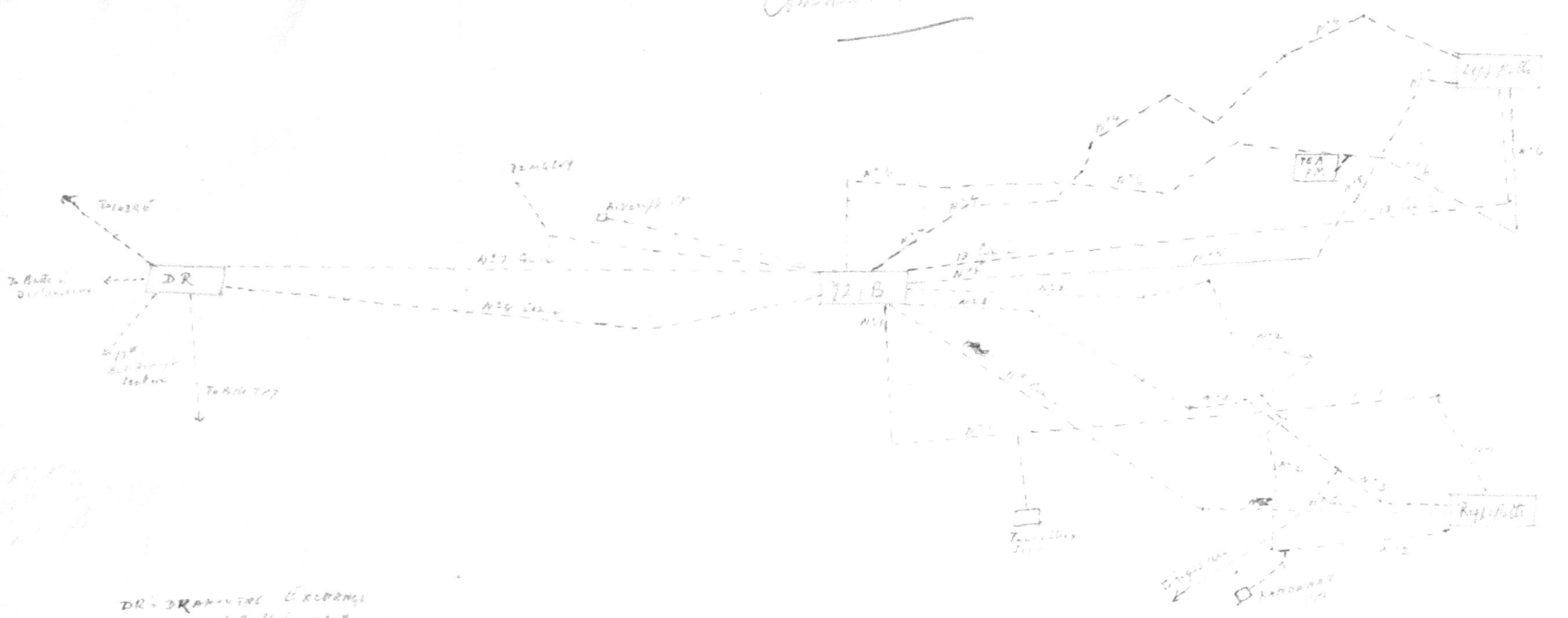

Appendix III

WAR DIARY — 4 Sect. 24 Signal Coy. Army Form C. 2118.
or
INTELLIGENCE SUMMARY. March, 1915. Sheet 1

Place	Date	Hour	Summary of Events and Information	Remarks and references to Appendices
POPERINGHE	1.		Maintained communications with battys and various units of 2nd Troops in POP.	ASR
	2.		Sent up Sgt and 4 men to learn lines in new sector.	ASR
	3.		Line to V Corps and tel pair to 6 Div broken in POP by shell fire and repaired.	ASR
YPRES	4.		At POP 3pm took over on Ramparts at 4pm from Sigs 72.18 Lines as in Appendix 1	ASR
	5.		1 and 2 dis at 7pm. 2,4 and 5 dis at 8pm. RK 5&6 very faint all day. 1 and 2. and 2,4 and 5 repaired by 10pm.	ASR
	6.		Z.1/2. front several tel junk repaired through closely by 11am. Line from ZOUAVE WOOD to R.T. Des Horus.	ASR
	7.		Inspected Tuileries Chimney Zillebeke with view to try establishing lamp station. Impossible to get inside chimney. Lamp could be seen by enemy. RK 5/6 weak between YPRES and Zillebeke Lake.	ASR
	8.		Z.1/2. dis 1pm. repaired 1.20 pm.	
	9.		RK 5/6 required by Div for 17 Bde. RK. 1/2 used to Belgian Chau. RK. 1/2 started from KS tst station to Belgian Chau. GC.13. dis 10:30 am. reason unknown to Sigs ZGC used to Belgian Chau. Line cannot have been broken as GC 14 J/S, running in same trench remained through. RK 3 dis. 8.30 pm.	ASR

Army Form C. 2118. 2

WAR DIARY of 4 Sect. 24 Signal Coy. R.E. Sheet II.
or
INTELLIGENCE SUMMARY March 1916.

(Erase heading not required.)

Instructions regarding War Diaries and Intelligence Summaries are contained in F.S. Regs. Part II. and the Staff Manual respectively. Title pages will be prepared in manuscript.

Place	Date	Hour	Summary of Events and Information	Remarks and references to Appendices
YPRES	10.		Maintained communication.	
	11.		Lines to front coys of left batn cut at 3pm. S/R	
	12.		Maintained communication.	
	13.		Line to Belgian Chau RK 12. cut at 2pm through at 4pm. Z.1.42. dis from 3.30 to 5.15. Brigade issued Ins.t. US at 9pm. Issue of rations.	
	14.			
	15.		Lines to front coys of left batn. cut at 2.20pm. Repairs of cable K12 and 4 lines of S19S. Z9B came into action. Lines reopened all coys except support of right batn cut 3.30pm repaired 8pm. Z.1.42. cut at 3.10pm also T.S. & naers at 4.30pm. Cut again also T.S. at 5.15pm and others.	
	16.		Aerial NCO. about 5th (?) a furthur one taken over from Z9B. wire from Z9B which has gone back into reserve S/R. at noon. NCOs and then from Z9B.	

WAR DIARY

INTELLIGENCE SUMMARY

Army Form C. 2118.

Sheet III
March 19/15.

Place	Date	Hour	Summary of Events and Information	Remarks and references to Appendices
YPRES	16		3.30pm handed over to SIGS. 2GB. 5.30pm arrived at H.14.a.	A.S.R.
H.14.a sheet 28 (B)	17.			
	18.	9.15am.	Sent N.C.O. and 5 men to take over office of 9th Cav. Bde. at Meteren. 12.30pm handed over to 9 Cav. Bde. 6pm. arrived at Meteren (sheet 27) X.17.C.3.3. Communication by wire opened with 5. Cav. Mtd. Rifles. 7. Northamptonshires and 13 Middlesex. by orderly with 129 Fd. Coy. 72 Fd. Amt. and 73 MG. Coy.	A.S.R. A.S.R.
Meteren	19.		73 MG Coy. entered wire from 7 Northamptonshires. 9R.Sussex sent 2nd Lieut R.C. arrived in Bde. area 6pm. Communication with 9 Sx. by wire with 2nd Lieuten by orders. laid line to 2 Lieuten. Sent two men to take over from 2 men of 9th Canadian Brigade in Kemmel defences.	19" A.S.R. A.S.R.
	20.			
	21.		went to H.Q. of 3 Can. Inf. Bde. at T.23.D.6.9 (sheet 28) to arrange relief.	
	22.		Sent N.C.O. and 3 linemen to H.Q. 3 Can. Inf. Bde.	A.S.R.
	23			
	24	10 am.	Sent N.C.O. and 5 men to take over from 3. Can. Inf. Bde. Noon left Meteren. 2pm arrived at T.23.D.6.9. 3pm took over from SIGS. 3 Can. Inf. Bde.	A.S.R.

Army Form C. 2118.

WAR DIARY

4 Sect. 24 Signal Coy. Rifle Brigade.

March 1916. Sheet IV.

(Erase heading not required.)

Instructions regarding War Diaries and Intelligence Summaries are contained in F. S. Regs., Part II. and the Staff Manual respectively. Title pages will be prepared in manuscript.

Place	Date	Hour	Summary of Events and Information	Remarks and references to Appendices
PETITE MUNQUE. FM. Sheet 28. T.23.D.6.9.	25.		Patrolled lines as in appendix III.	A.J.K
	26.		No. 10 dis. and repaired.	A.J.K
	27.		Patrolled lines	A.J.K
	28.			
	29.		No. 2. and No. 12. to Right battn diss. from 7 pm to 10.30 pm.	
	30.		Cut "Tees" out of old battle hqrs and straightened them into new battle hqrs.	
	31.		Lead No. 11 into right battn hqrs. and made metallic pair of 1 and 2 to left battn hqrs.	A.J.K

APPENDIX I.

COMMUNICATIONS OF 73. BDE. in YPRES.
7/3/16.

Diagram showing communications network with nodes: YX, ZP, GC, ZGC, Left Gr Roug, SF, KS (Kruisstraat, Halt in Belgian Chau), TS (Zillebeke Lake), B.W. in Zillebeke Lake Dout, Left Batt., Right Batt., 150 Bde.

Connections labeled: GC 1/5, GC 14/15, RK 1, RK 1/5, RK 5/6, RK 5, Z 5, Z 12, aerial 21, Bde Buried.

Aspitche
YPRES.

Communication of 73rd Inf. Bde.
at X.17.c.33. (sheet 28)

20/3/16

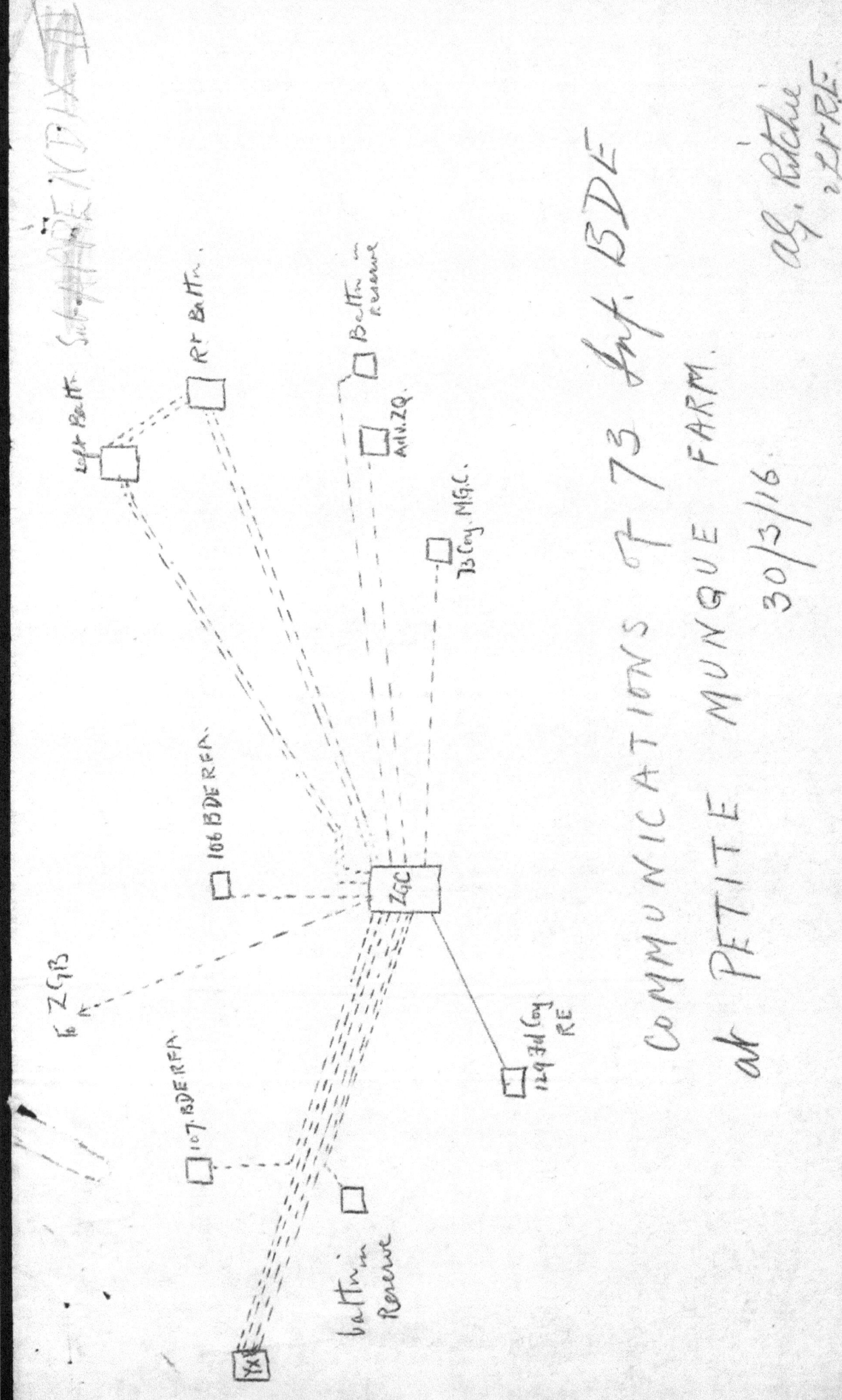

WAR DIARY or INTELLIGENCE SUMMARY

24th Divisional Signal Company

Vol 9

Place	Date	Hour	Summary of Events and Information	Remarks and references to Appendices
ST. JANS CAPPEL	1st Feb.		New telephone lair built, using bad & single line to Regt near ENGLISH FARM to 107th Bde RHA HQ in NEUVE EGLISE. D5 cable used on permanent poles along road. Joined in spare pair (31 and 32) to ENGLISH FARM.	
	2nd Feb.		129th Field Co RE complain of tel. sparking and being to NIEPPE township. We have had spare cable to Regt. 15 line 2 wire ex dining line is with 24th Divnl Arty Office (FX). Line put to 107 brigade in until...	
	3rd Feb.		Well telephone line made to 107th RFA HQ and lines for Ré extension to Regt and Inf 72nd & 73rd Bdes at PETITE MUNQUE (26 and 25) and ... (Fanc ?) also. Contact found in BAILLEUL ... by linesmen.	
	4th Feb.		... and 107th RFA line found OK Niepp broken by shell splinters, lines broken ... well at 4.15 pm. Breaks into DAC DADOS in all cases lineman inpart lines OK cause ... RMA ...	

WAR DIARY
INTELLIGENCE SUMMARY

Place	Date	Hour	Summary of Events and Information	Remarks and references to Appendices
ST JANS CAPPEL	4/1/16		Full charge on 1 and 2 — 27 — 28 (YX – ZGC). DAC and entrance phone lines shown earth out and field new line to DAC new office.	Wathers R/h
	5/1/16		Working party sent out. Visual code arranged with 92nd IB.	
	6/1/16		92nd IB refused lines on all lines 6.30am. Line busy f'shed. Field Phone first. Nine spans broken in field fair fm mile D1 run round shelling area. Lines working 2.30 pm. 103rd Field Co. line broken by shell-fire and repaired.	
	7/1/16		HE bank line said by 2nd Corp's wire invented the line and tested 6 miles proper joint. 92nd IB enquiring when office moving to shelling at 12.30 pm. 92nd IB moved to DRANOUTRE infantry party at 6 PM to divert Soundr line, company completed 11.30 pm Infantry 103rd Field Co Phone Fair for field telephone. 104rd Fd Co HE by 8 mile came into U.U.U.49 by local phone	
	8/1/16		Trouble with enemy from line which is on the continue and seal shelling the 11 am 107th RFA line cleaned.	

Army Form C. 2118.

WAR DIARY
or
INTELLIGENCE SUMMARY
(Erase heading not required.)

Instructions regarding War Diaries and Intelligence Summaries are contained in F. S. Regs., Part II. and the Staff Manual respectively. Title pages will be prepared in manuscript.

Place	Date	Hour	Summary of Events and Information	Remarks and references to Appendices
ST JANS CAPPEL	8th		108th RFA had orders to billet new office and one gun at ??	Wildoote Eglise
	9th 10.30		Fair to 72nd IB. Enemy bomb plane refused (came in later). Aeroplane fell on 72nd IB, 108th RFA and one fell in mile (??) at 9.30 m all lines mis to reper lines and 3 poles broken. Line mending from commencement made one special line to... the second line and for second line repaired again and not 16 J trunk wire to Bus Farm (72nd =3 & 4) running party on to Locomaintin area (New 72nd IB Hg). 20 J wire in line — 72nd IB put in 2 p.m. temp. base in fire, continued line to DRANOUTRE...	
	10th		DAC line again faulty — tested at night — and contact between Y & XZR and Z...	

WAR DIARY
or
INTELLIGENCE SUMMARY
(Erase heading not required.)

Army Form C. 2118.

Place	Date	Hour	Summary of Events and Information	Remarks and references to Appendices
ST-JANS CAPPEL	13th		Runs to DRANOUTRE completed. Telephoned Schoolfair dismantled to their new office.	Rathad Bn
	14th		Phone fair and sounder line continued from eight of new route to 72nd I.B's new office. Considerable trouble with the lead about Signal Office Swan lanes due many to trouble with live on 72nd Bn sound lead due to sheer Kilmed TRANSPORT FARM. Jumper met on 144th and 149th Field C/S lead, which reported in the afternoon. Working party removed just off route up Flete lane District chamber on 72nd I.B land overhead. Only rept. G. Sounder line to 72nd I.B Cyc Infts Hdqrs. Re drawn in phone pair and built two lines from tee-off to BAILLEUL & Y & R to work in this H.Q. fair. Returning 4 wires Brit Signal office	
	16th		Office ¼ to BAILLEUL.	
	17th		All lines tested and rearranged from Y&R. Work continued at BAILLEUL Informing tent phone lines and wiring new Signal Office.	

Army Form C. 2118.

WAR DIARY
or
INTELLIGENCE SUMMARY
(Erase heading not required.)

Place	Date	Hour	Summary of Events and Information	Remarks and references to Appendices
BAILLEUL	18th		Divnl Signal Office and Company billets moved from ST. SYLVS- CAPPEL to BAILLEUL. 7th IB Sommain and 10th FA moved far- ward.	
	19th			
	20th			
	21st			
	22nd		Commenced fitting up new office	

Army Form C. 2118.

WAR DIARY
or
INTELLIGENCE SUMMARY.
(Erase heading not required.)

Instructions regarding War Diaries and Intelligence Summaries are contained in F. S. Regs., Part II. and the Staff Manual respectively. Title pages will be prepared in manuscript.

Place	Date	Hour	Summary of Events and Information	Remarks and references to Appendices
BAILLEUL	23/4/16		New office continued with 2" YXR. Commenced finding H Pole round. Contact cleared between 2 and 6 in morn. Dealt myself.	Bailleul Sqn
	24/4/16		New office completed at YXR and moved into at 11 hrs. All lines OK. Enemy FX (2nd arty FX) put to new office. Cleared bury-wire previous Signal Co camp to new office.	
	25/4/16		Continued burying in H Pole route. Technical School Line broken by wagon near their end. New pole put in 3rd Trench Commenced clearing cable round old office (YXR). Faulty hrs 109A and 106A RGA cleared	
	26/4/16		Continued clearing cable round YXR old office. Lineman sent to 72nd IB to learn lines to BUS FARM. All routes out hauled from YXR.	
	27/4/16		Gas alarm given by 73rd IB at 12.30am. Starting to cancelled at 1.15am. Took over 9th 17th IB from YXR by 73rd. New phone being laid in to YXR Hy. Corps and working 7.27 km. (25+ ab) (BN 1 and 2)	

WAR DIARY or INTELLIGENCE SUMMARY

Army Form C. 2118.

24TH SIGNAL CO.

Place	Date	Hour	Summary of Events and Information	Remarks and references to Appendices
BAILLEUL	27/4/16		Tested lines and fitted up FXR (Divl Sig Brig HQ)	
	28/4/16		Completed running in 4 full-tone to 73rd I.B. lines cleared on YX – ZQ (7th IB) lines and Tatham's School line.	
	29/4/16		Surveyed route for D5 pair from DRANOUTRE to BUS FARM. Running to 72nd IB strong current in my wire stays on each pole. None at IB.	
			and 72nd IB attempted repair	
	30/4/16		YXR, fus affects lines fors 12.30 am 3th ED these hundreds. fuse broke. Aus for nr 12.30 am – seven wire gas humidity by lack in wires. 3rd ED Reg'l station reported times then the Rd St Sig Lne to Divn central station, completed 15 am. 10' PiA wire in all lines 1.30 am. Air gun victim 150 yds offere trying to shell D5 between fuse to BUS FARM. Party laying D5 between fuse to BUS FARM. Another gas alarm at 10 pm but at wind was right.	

Army Form C. 2118.

WAR DIARY
—of—
INTELLIGENCE SUMMARY.
(Erase heading not required.) No 2nd Section ~~Battn~~ Signal Co R.E.

Place	Date	Hour	Summary of Events and Information	Remarks and references to Appendices
SHEET 28 T21D 52	APRIL 1916			
	1 – 2		Lines patrolled & maintained.	
	3 – 4		Wgt. Work begun on burying 2 quads (18th/19th I.R.A.) from Bde Battle Hq at U13d 12 (Sheet 18) to R. Bn Hq at A3H HOUSE in trench 5ft deep. Ground very wet towards end of work.	
	4 – 5		Work continued. I Bn Hq moved from cellar at U13a 57 to about U13d 52. Lines run to them O.K.	
	5 – 6		No work on trench owing to Bn relief. Bde Hqrs moved during 5th to	
PETITE MUNQUE FARM			That occupied by 73 18 at PETITE MUNQUE FM, 73 18 moving to T21d 52. All change of lines except transport completed by 3 P.M.	
	6 – 7		Work on trench continued, 2 IT's led off to R.A. O.P. just N.W. of CHÂLÂ HUTTE. Transport lines completed during 7th.	
"	7 – 8		Work continued. Queen Canvas in rolls about 6ft wide, laid alongside	
	8 – 9		of trench & excavated earth put on it thereby greatly relieving visibility of site of trench when filled in, also helping filling in as men could lift returned edge of canvas & tip earth into trench.	
	9 – 10			
	10 – 11		Work on R Bn line completed, all lines O.K.	
	11 – 12 – 13		Work on I.B. line begun from cellar. 1 Offr 112 R.F. slightly wounded by stray bullet. Bn relief, hence no work on buried line. 12 – 13 No work owing to heavy rain.	
"	13 – 14		Wgt Work continued on very soft ground till hit on 14 – 15. Work in ??	
	14 – 15		150X from Battle Hq, all line O.K. to there. Casualties. 6th I.O.R. wounded by stray fire. 7th I.O.R. evacuated to hospital for operation.	

2353 Wt W2544/1454 700,000 5/15 D.&D. & L. A.D.S.S./Forms/C. 2118.

Army Form C. 2118.

WAR DIARY
INTELLIGENCE SUMMARY
(Erase heading not required.)

Place	Date	Hour	Summary of Events and Information	Remarks and references to Appendices
PETITE MUNQUE FARM	APRIL 1916			
	15-16 nyt		Work begun on burying one grad forward from CELLARS (Bn Hat stn) to meet two buried armoured cables at ORMOND AVENUE (U7d 7.5.) leading to WINTER TRENCH (U8 a 1.1.) On same night a DI metallic pair was run from O.P. at THATCHED COTTAGE (T18 b 8.5.) to O.P. at LE ROSSIGNOL (U13 b 2.7.) with T off into CELLARS. Line O.K. Trench very wet, + av: depth only 3ft.	Hildgtrand. Temple.
"	16-17 "		Work continued back towards CELLARS ending 150' distant. Found half of trench only 4ft or av: owing to wet, remainder good work at 5ft.	
"	17-18 "		No work owing to relief. R.In shelled out of ASH HOUSE, 4 lines were connected through there, + In Sig moved to Bde Battle Hqrs.	
"	18-19 "		No work owing to rain.	
"	19-20 "		Work finished back to CELLARS. Line O.K.	
"	20-21 "		Work finished from point reached on 14/15 nyt, into Bde Battle Hqr. This trench was also used for lines running back from B.B. Hqr past R.A. Bde B. Hqr just our side of the ridge of HILL 63, + contained 5 quads; it branched off from left Bn trench about 200' from B.B.Hqrs.	
"	21-22 "		Work continued back along ridge past BARREL HOUSE, but completely held up by rain at a depth of 3ft, when work was suspended.	

Army Form C. 2118.

WAR DIARY

INTELLIGENCE SUMMARY.
(Erase heading not required.)

Place	Date	Hour	Summary of Events and Information	Remarks and references to Appendices
PETITE MUNQUE FARM	APRIL 1916			
	22-23	nt	No work owing to ground being very wet.	
	23-24	"	" relief	
	24-25	"	Work continued from end of piece abandoned on nyt 21-22. The also had to be left owing to flooding.	
	25-26	nyt	Part of last nit reclaimed + about 100' more done. This way dry.	
	26-27	"	More reclaimed, amounting to about 200' + 50' new trench dug	
	27-28	" 30.	Work on mined crater.	

Army Form C. 2118.

WAR DIARY or INTELLIGENCE SUMMARY.

No 3 Sector 24th Div Sig Coy

(Erase heading not required.)

Place	Date	Hour	Summary of Events and Information	Remarks and references to Appendices
BUS FARM	1-4-16		Patrolled wires in morning. Enemy shelling 5 pm. Sig office moved to Advanced reserve office. Lines 1, 2, 3, 11, to Rt Battn down at 6 pm — through Battn 6-15 pm. All lines OK 7-15 pm. Laying buried route to Left Battn	G.W.J
"	2-4-16		Temporary repairs of lasting U-made permanent. Morning lines walked. Continued buried route to Left Battn.	G.W.J
"	3-4-16		Line 4 to Left Battn dn 6.30 am – 8.C Dranoutre 9-30 am – 11 to Rt Battn 9-40. 2 to Rt Battn 9-40 am. 3 to Rt Battn 9-40 am. All perf sig lt missing Roy –. All other breaks mended. Close to enemy shellfire. S.C. Dranoutre dn at 7.30 pm. B.K. 11-30 pm. Continued Buried route to Left Battn	J.D.J
"	4-4-16		Testing and joining up lengths of quad in buried route. Line – 20-11 to Rt Battn down 2.40 am. to R bn 6.40 by 9.45 am. Called on with buried route	J.J.J
"	5-4-16		Patrolled lines. Line 3 to Rt Bn. dn 3.45 am. I.X. 5.30 pm. Div temporary now 4-10 pm. B.K. 5.45 pm. Continued buried route — Excellent chap	J.J.J
"	6-4-16		Heavy shelling in early morning, wires 11+3 to Rt Battn down 4.55 am R.K. 5.20 am. Bell Phone and sounder lines to dn at 5.45 am. Sounder OK 9 am. Phone 9 am. O.K. 12.30 pm. O.K. 5.30. S.J. to Sig J, C. & S. 5.30 am & 11.40 am. 4 down 10.45 am up 11.42 am. Com to 003 to sec Sud off	J.J.J

6 Attn Signal Co. Appendix April 1916

Army Form C. 2118.

WAR DIARY
or
INTELLIGENCE SUMMARY.
(Erase heading not required.)

Place	Date	Hour	Summary of Events and Information	Remarks and references to Appendices
BUS FARM	7-4-16		Some shelling in morning – moved to Culvert opposite offices heavy shelling took in Bus Farm at 2 p.m. – moved Signal office to DRANOUTRE at tot about keeping communication with Dennis the whole time – not complete 8 p.m. except for new powder line being laid by signal lieutenant this was complete by 11 p.m. and sounder transferred – Bus Farm becoming too noisy.	ASK etc
DRANOUTRE	8-4-16		Line worked – started pointing on Burial & left Bn in Petit Locre – commenced buried lines to S of Right Bn beginning at Bus Farm.	
"	9-4-16		A few shells round Bus Farm in early morning. Lines 24 to Right Bn dis 5½'s arm OK. 10 am 7 to Bell dis 7.30 am OK, 8 wave journey up left Buried line carried on Burial line to Pt Baton.	
"	10-4-16		Very quiet – no line dis in morning. found full earth on by' Bury Tracing came to fault already put in caused by heat of fires fusing insulation on wire – entire buried line continued being to Pt Baton.	
"	11-4-16		Again quiet. Line patrolled – continued Bury to Pt Bn.	

Army Form C. 2118.

WAR DIARY
or
INTELLIGENCE SUMMARY.
(Erase heading not required.)

Instructions regarding War Diaries and Intelligence Summaries are contained in F. S. Regs., Part II. and the Staff Manual respectively. Title pages will be prepared in manuscript.

Place	Date	Hour	Summary of Events and Information	Remarks and references to Appendices
BRANDHOEK	12-4-16		Some shelling this morning 2 & 3 - 11 & Rt Bn dis. A and BK 'noon' smashing joints in buried line to left Bn.	
"	13-4-16		Very quiet in morning, shelling on left Rly in afternoon - no 1 & Rt Bn dis. BK 6 four - working parties in front continued putting up continued buried line to Rt Bn.	
"	14-4-16		Again quiet, finding on line to left Batn - Party of Divisional G.S. started at forward end of Rt Batn line in daylight - no working parties on buried at night - Batn relief at night - 2 coy. coming up mes Rd then in. Divisional Cyclists again in forward end of buried line - continued thro' night in day.	
"	15-4-16		Two daylight parties out putting forward end on Rt Batn line + one from Rt Batn. Stated at night will be bring out Rail from Batn end to Right Batn.	
"	16-4-16		Some shelling early morning 4-6 left Batn dis 1 sapper BK 10am 11 Rt Batn dis. between BK 4 & 3 noon. Continued night & next day and party to DRANOETRE from Batn at night.	
"	17-4-16		Line patrolled. All BK continued being put in. Rt Bn telling men times of news Op	

WAR DIARY
or
INTELLIGENCE SUMMARY.
(Erase heading not required.)

Army Form C. 2118.

Place	Date	Hour	Summary of Events and Information	Remarks and references to Appendices
DRANOUTRE	18-4-16 cont		Moved new Signal office from Bergny R/Batta company lines along	
"	19-4-16		Quiet all day - enemy arp. brigad at L.Bus Farm for fact she took 9/M	
			R/. R.n fired heavily day + night	
"	20-4-16		Heavy shelling round Lapon Farm in morning also Lancashire farm	
			2-3 L.bus to R/ Batta dug-outs. OK 12 noon. Only the Gervis & R/	
			R/. Batta Broy were known to enter at night, continued during and	9/M
			compelled test she an dugout at Rout farm	
"	21-4-16		Moved back the Undigart - (News everything O.K. - Four borders again	9/M
			on R/ Batta luoy	
"	22-4-16		Work on R/ Batta buoy continued	9/M
"	23-4-16		Work on R/. Batta buoy continued	9/M
"	24-4-16		Left Batta Buoy complete to Left Coy. office. Work on right batta buoy continued	9/M
"	25-4-16		Work on R/ Batta buoy continued	9/M
"	26-4-16		Work on R/ Batta buoy continued but no jackies at night.	9/M
"	27-4-16		R/ Batta Buoy from Batta Battle H.Q to Three Coy offices completed. Work on right batta buoy between Batta Battle H.Q and Bus Farm continued	9/M

Army Form C. 2118.

WAR DIARY
or
INTELLIGENCE SUMMARY.
(Erase heading not required.)

Instructions regarding War Diaries and Intelligence Summaries are contained in F. S. Regs., Part II. and the Staff Manual respectively. Title pages will be prepared in manuscript.

Place	Date	Hour	Summary of Events and Information	Remarks and references to Appendices
DRANOUTRE	28.4.16		Work on right batty heavy continued. 200 yds of bury which was earthing near SAPPER FARM relaid. Party arrived with 'boring machine' to force pipes 5ft deep under most on buried line from BUS FARM to DRANOUTRE	
"	29.4.16		Batn Bury completed to Right Batta Battle HQ. Working party at night returned Left Batta Battle HQ. and R.E. FARM. Enemy attacked with gas 12.45 am 30th and reopened the fires.	
"	30.4.16		Enemy attacked with gas 12.45 am and succeeded in entering Trench D4 but were turned out in about 10 minutes. Bde HQ moved to Battle HQ about 2 am. Though to Battle Battle HQ as new front line during the "Stafa" which lasted till 4.30 am. Bde HQ returned to prior HQ DRANOUTRE about 8 am. Following line went D5 to new front line 13, 6pm. 12, 13, 15 Aircraft Fm, lt. 10.5 p.m.	

T2134. Wt. W708—776. 500,000. 4/15. Sir J. C. & S.

Z.R. = Bde Battle HQ.
D.7. = Left Batt. H.Q.
D.3. = Right Batt. H.Q.
C.94. = Kandahar Farm.
(Bde. Res. Batt. H.Q.)
Aircraft Farm. = S Coys of Bde. Res. Batt.
A.A: Antiaircraft Section R.M.A.
Line 1 runs in R. Douve.
A scheme of buried lines is nearing
completion.

Lines 7, 8 & 13 are coaxial Air Lines.

To Bde on Left.
To Bde on Right.

M.G. Coy.
Aircraft Farm.
D.7
D.3
C.94

B.D.E. HQRS.
To 103rd R.E.
To Div Res. Batt.
To Grenade School
Bde Tpr.
To A.A.

Office Diagram of 72nd INF. BDE. COMMN. 18.4.18

Army Form C. 2118.

4 Sec 24 Sig Coy RE.
April 1916. Sheet 1

WAR DIARY or INTELLIGENCE SUMMARY.
(Erase heading not required.)

74TH SIGNAL CO. Appendix II April 1916

Place	Date	Hour	Summary of Events and Information	Remarks and references to Appendices
PETITE MONQUE FM.	1.		Laid lines into Brigade Battle Hqrs.	AGR
T.23.d.6.9. sheet (28)	2.			
	3.		Buried cable 5 ft deep from right Battalion Hqrs to line of new work	AGR
	4.		Buried cable with party of 200 men from left Battn Hqrs. Extended No.1 & 2 backwards position of new Hqrs.	AGR
	5.		Working party extended No.11 along with No.3 of 17 Bde Signals to 17 Brigade Hqrs. Buried cable to culvert over R.DOUVE near night Battn Hqrs	AGR
T.21.d.5.2. (28)	6.		Exchanged Hqrs with 17 Inf. Bde. Joined 1&2 onto 17 Bde Signals Nos 1&2. Joined No.12 onto No.3 of 17 Bde. No.1&2 Dis. at 7.30 pm and repaired at 6.15pm	AGR
	7.		Hqrs extended line from Brigade to 107 Mey Bde. not ?	
	8.		Laid new line to 75 Coy M.G.C. Sealed up Hqrs. old line. Continued Serials	
	9.		Laid out new piece of 1&2 and fixed up pieces and ends. Continued work. Buried line at night	AGR
	10.		Laid new metallic pair to 107 Bde. R.F.A. Continued service	AGR
	11.		Laid out new lateral to 72 I.B. and joined out to 72 Bde latereal. Continued Buried cable	WG

WAR DIARY
or
INTELLIGENCE SUMMARY.

4 Sec. 24 Sig. Coy. R.E. Army Form C. 2118.

Sheet 2. April 1916

Place	Date	Hour	Summary of Events and Information	Remarks and references to Appendices
T.21d.5,2 (28).	12			
	13.		Nos. 2 and 12. Dis 7am to 11am. Continued buried.	AGR.
	14.		No 11. Dis. Continued buried route.	AGR.
	15.		No 2. Dis. Continued buried route, inspected buried lines to right battalion and found them unburied in places.	AGR. AGR.
	16.		No 2. weak. Lateral to ZgB shown. Continued buried.	AGR.
	17.		Nos 11 & 12. Dis.	AGR.
	18.		Buried cable to left Coy of Rt. Battalion.	AGR.
	19.		No. 12. Dis from 7.30 till 11.45 am. 12.11 till 4.5pm. 12 through 4.45pm 1.2.11 Buried cable to right Coy of right battalion.	AGR.
	20.		Through 5.45 pm. Continued buried cable towards Pke battle hqrs. work not completed on account owing to rain and clayey nature of soil. buried line to right Cy of right battalion.	AGR.
	21.		Unable to bury owing to rain.	AGR.
	22.		Lateral to ZgB. Dis 1.45 – 2.30 pm. Buried cable to right Coy of My right battn.	AGR.

Army Form C. 2118.

4 Sec. 24 Signal Coy. R.E.

Sheet III

WAR DIARY
or
INTELLIGENCE SUMMARY.

April 1916

(Erase heading not required.)

Instructions regarding War Diaries and Intelligence Summaries are contained in F. S. Regs. Part II and the Staff Manual respectively. Title pages will be prepared in manuscript.

Place	Date	Hour	Summary of Events and Information	Remarks and references to Appendices
(28) T21d.S.2.	23.		No 2. Div 8-10 am Retired Zq.div 2.25-2.45 pm.	
	24.		Straightened No.1 172.	
	25.		Laid new pair of 11.412.	a.g.r.
	26.		Buried cable at right towards battle hqrs.	a.g.r.
	27.		Labelled all previously unlabelled lines. picked up old No 3 S.f. 1725 and temporary increments along a.g.r.	
			No 3.	
	28.		172. div. Buried Cable towards Battle hqs. went 2 parties of 25 men in day time.	a.g.r.
			Buried artillery cable to left Coy. left batter, at night	
			Buried Cable in day time towards Battle hqs. No. 172. div 10.2.5 am till 12.15 pm	a.g.r.
	29.		Continued burying artillery cable to left Coy left batter.	
	30.		12.30 am gas gas attack on our left batter and brigade on left. all lines severed from Bde Battle hqrs. to batter lines. Lines from battery to brigade through 2.2 am	
			four through one pair of unconnected buried route to our batter. 2.45 am battery of to right batter on No 12. Same left batter hqrs. 4.30 am all joints permanently made over buried route. Lines ofter tied up on N.12 hqrs.	

"Sub-Appendix I.

COMMUNICATIONS OF 73. 24. Bde.   23/4/16

To Batt. on left.

D.16 Left Bn.

D.8 R^T BATT.

Z.6 Bde Battle Hqrs.

D.69 Battⁿ in Reserve.

G.53 How. Batt^y

736 M.G.C.

Z.Q Z.q.

Z.6

107 Bde. R.F.A.

73/How Batt^y

Z.G.C. 2. lt.

12q 3d Co. R.E.

Y.X

K.P Battⁿ in Div^l Reserve.

Sketch APF.

Appendix No 4.

Account of Communications during recent Gas Attack on 24th Division.

2.30 am   30-4-16.

Division to Infantry Brigades and Artillery Brigades.

Communication with Infantry Brigades was never interrupted. The Left and Centre Brigades moved forward to their battle HQ. In the case of Left Brigade all air-lines but one were cut.

Visual communication was established by lamp from high ground near WESTHOF FARM with Left Brigade and also with central station on HILL 63 which could take work for both Centre and Right Infantry Brigades and Centre and Right Artillery Brigades. Test messages were sent both ways.

All communications with Left Artillery Brigade were cut. The HQ. of this Brigade were shelled and all lines cut just outside their office.

72nd Infantry Brigade.

This Brigade had nearly completed a 5 foot deep buried system.
The lines were completed up to battle HQ. of both Battalions and also to some of the Companies in the front line. These lines held throughout in spite of 12 direct hits on cable trenches (mostly 5.9's) The Battalions were in communication with all their companies throughout.

73rd Infantry Brigade.

This Brigade had 5 feet deep buried lines complete from all Coy HQ. to a point about 200 yards from Brigade Battle HQ. Battalions were using their buried lines to Companies but Brigade was still making use of air lines.

All air lines to Battalions were at once cut but by picking up ends of buried route near Brigade Battle HQ., communication was soon established with Battalions.

Battalions were through to their Companies the whole time in spite of numerous direct hits on buried lines.

Visual communication between Brigade and Battalions had been arranged but was not made use of as the Brigade signallers were all out mending the lines.

Right Infantry Brigade.

This Brigade had 5 foot buried lines to both Battalions and to some of the Companies in front line.

All the Companies who had their buried lines completed maintained communication with their Battalions throughout.

The Left Battalion of this Brigade was disconnected from its left company with whom it was communicating by overground wire.

In no case was a 5 foot buried line cut.

Communications within 24th Division area.

Appendix No 5.

[Stamp: 24TH SIGNAL CO. April 1916 R.E.]

Signs.
- ✚   Battalion Battle HQ.
- ⚑   Brigade Battle HQ.
- ▲   Test points at which R.A. will pick up their forward lines.
- ────   Lines already buried 5 feet deep.
- -----   Lines to be buried 5 feet deep.

This scheme provides for the following communications:-

(All lines referred to will be buried 5 feet deep unless otherwise specified.)

A metallic circuit from every Company HQ in front line to its Battalion HQ.

A metallic circuit from each Battalion HQ. in the line to its Brigade Battle HQ.

In addition the following R.A. communications are provided:-

A metallic circuit from all Companies in front line to a point near Brigade HQ. and thence to the Battery covering it.

The lines from Batteries to these Test points have yet to be completed. They will in most cases be short lines and will be dug in 3 feet deep.

When Division is at WESTHOF FARM, communications to Brigades and from R.A. Brigades to C.R.A. will be as follows:-

From Left Inf: Brigade a telephone pair and sounder line buried back 1 mile from Brigade HQ. and thence on air-line.

From Left R.A. Brigade to C.R.A. a telephone pair buried back for 1 mile and thence as air-line. Also an overhead buzzer line.

From Centre and Right Inf: Brigades a separate telephone pair and sounder line buried back to LA PETITE MUNQUE FARM, and thence on air-lines to WESTHOF FARM.

From Right and Centre Artillery Brigades a telephone pair from each, buried to LA PETITE MUNQUE FARM and thence on

air-line. Also a buzzer air-line.

There will be a buried metallic circuit from Artillery Brigades' Battle HQ. to all the Batteries of that Brigade.

When Division is at Battle HQ. on HILL 63, it will have exactly the same communications with its Brigades as at WESTHOF FARM except with the Left Brigade. The communication to this Brigade will run as follows:-

Buried metallic circuits and sounder line to LA PETITE MUNQUE FARM, thence air-line via WESHHOF FARM to a point on NEUVE EGLISE--------DRANCUTRE Road, when it will again become buried to Brigade HQ.

The same applies to the Left Artillery Brigade.

WESTHOF. FARM. (24th Divisional Advd HQ)

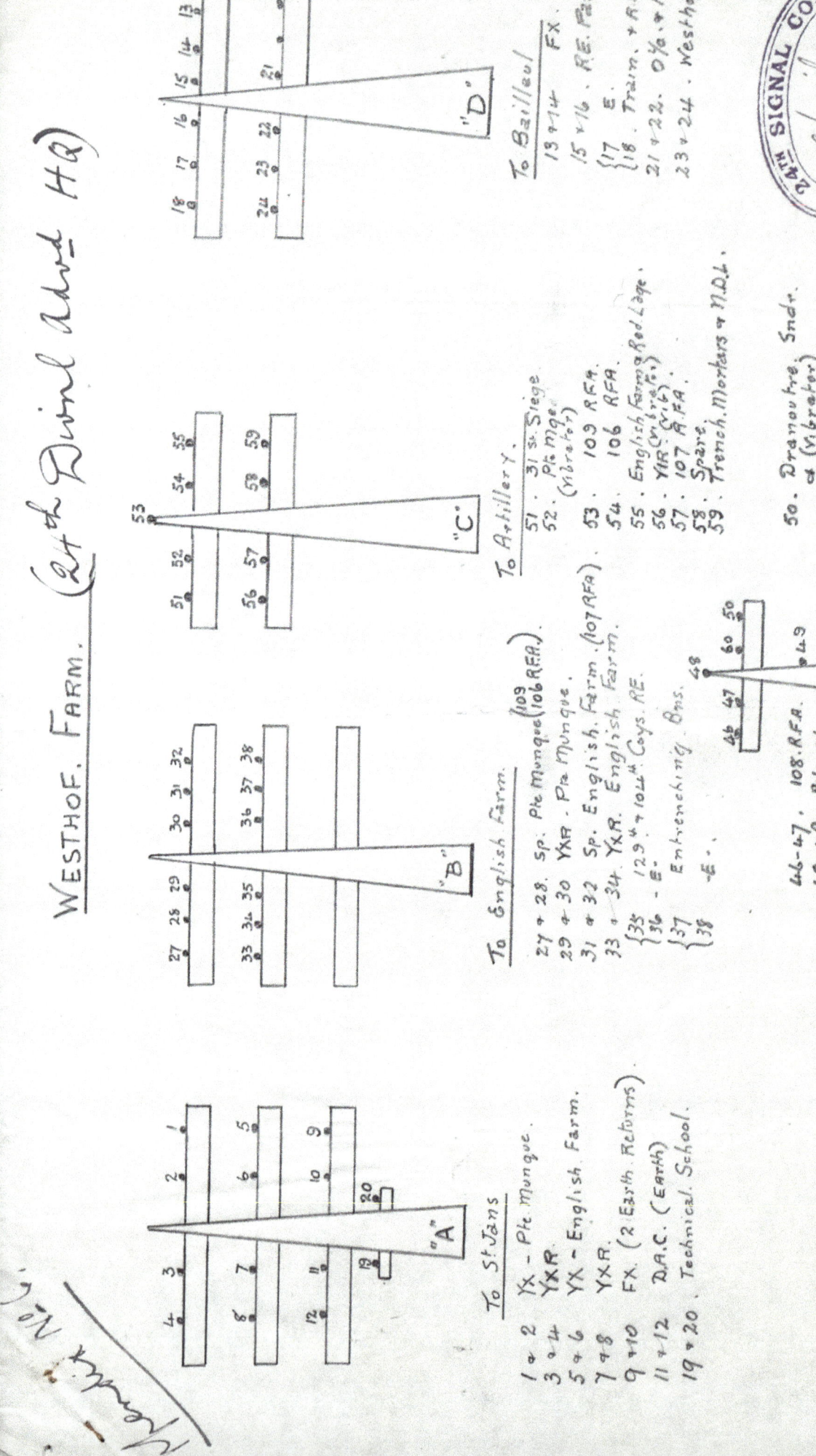

To St Jans
- 1 & 2 YX - Pte Mungue.
- 3 & 4 YxR.
- 5 & 6 YX - English. Farm.
- 7 & 8 YxR.
- 9 & 10 FX. (2: Earth Returns)
- 11 & 12 D.A.C. (Earth)
- 19 & 20 Technical School.

To English Farm.
- 27 & 28. Sp. Pte Mungue (109 RFA)
- 29 & 30 YxR - Pte Mungue.
- 31 & 32 Sp. English Farm. (107 RFA)
- 33 & 34. YxR. English Farm.
- 35 - 12.9 & 104th Coys. R.E.
- 36 - "
- 37 Entrenching Bns.
- 38 " E "

To Artillery.
- 51. 31st Siege
- 52. Pte Mungue (Vibrator)
- 53. 103 RFA.
- 54. 106 RFA.
- 55. English Farm & Red Ldge.
- 56. YxR (Vibrator)
- 57. 107 RFA.
- 58. Spare.
- 59. French. Mortars & N.D.L.

- 46 - 47. 108. R.F.A.
- 48 - 49. Bde at Dranoutre. & 103rd Co. R.E.

- 50. Dranoutre Sndr. at (Vibrator)
- 60. 108 RFA.

To Bailleul
- 13 & 14 FX.
- 15 & 16. RE. Park.
- 17 E.
- 18. Train. & R.M.R.
- 21 & 22. O/C. & A.P.M.
- 23 & 24. Westhof. (Sp)

24th Signal Co. — April 1916

Plug Exchange

1	2	3	4	5	6	7	8	9	10
108	107	109	129	Entg	DAC	FX	RE	TRAIN	OFFICE
RFA.	RFA.	108	104 RE	BNS	DRDOS		PARA.	RM1A	

→ English La Pte
Farm Munque
Nieppe

11	12	13	14	15	16	17	18	19	20
YX	Office	DTAYOMS	OC.	NCO.Ttch			YX	Spare	
		103	RE	West Vch.				Office	
			HFtm.	Ftm. Hov. Troops					

30 RGA

Incoming Terminal Board

[Diagram with numbered terminals 7-28 with labels including YX, INTEN, FX, ORDER, ENTG BNS, RE PARA, TRAIN RM1A, 103 RE, 103 RFA, RSM, etc.]

46 • F6
47 •   •52 •32
       •77
       •62 •26   •36 •35   •37 •38 31
                    CH ORDO ENTG
                              BNS
Sp. to
English La Pte
Farm Munque
Bds

Terminal Board

5	6	7	28
YX	YX	YX	
Office			
33 Engers Sh	29 Pte	30
Farm	Munque

Bde Dramoutre

24TH SIGNAL CO.

D.A.G. 235.

   3rd Echelon.

      Herewith War Diary of the 24th Divisional Signal Company, Royal Engineers, for the month of May 1916.

3/6/16.
                                      A. Skinner Captain,
                                      O.C. 24th Divl Signal Co. R.E.

WAR DIARY

INTELLIGENCE SUMMARY

(Erase heading not required.)

Army Form C. 2118.

May 1916

24th Divisional Signal Company
Royal Engineers

Place	Date	Hour	Summary of Events and Information	Remarks and references to Appendices
BAILLEUL	1/5/16		106th and 107th F.A.B. winter lines were ... Repaired 3.15 p.m. 118th F.A.B. line again ... anything 8.0 p.m. D5 cable put from DRANOUTRE to BUS FARM completed. St Laurent hut by dug-out in 4 places ...	Initials
	2/5/16		having tug placed near route. D5" cable put behind (unreadable) whole front in 3 ... 2 fold hung full on end and hung ... on spread ...	
	3/5/16		107th F.A.B. cable taken over and changed. 11.15 a.m. NIEPPE WIRE - Park lines met with ...	
	4/5/16		Overhauling main tr... main line to NIEPPE line ... faults and running short-ciut. 117th R.F.A. moved to DRANOUTRE. Linemen sent out to make necessary alterations on ... cut in 3 places by shell fire.	

WAR DIARY
INTELLIGENCE SUMMARY

Army Form C. 2118.

Place	Date	Hour	Summary of Events and Information	Remarks and references to Appendices
BAILLEUL	5-5/16		Working party refuring wood line Party in DRANOUTRE line	
		11·15 am	DRANOUTRE being shelled. Tel. I.O. lines cut on the military line refixed and working 12·15 pm. 118th R.F.A. line also cut, refixed and working 1 pm. 12 and 93 telephone lines again cut by shelling line temporary refixed made 5·10 pm. New again cut 7·45 pm. another cut return 8·15 pm. 103rd R.F.A. lines all cut by 11 Civ. lines at	
	6/7/16		morning in DRANOUTRE, refixed 9·15 pm. Three [?] Wiremen 9·30 pm Working Party in DRANOUTRE refixing Wiremen ceased by shell fire Guard 118th R.F.A. Wire & lighting phone lines cut & 6th R.F.A. phone line cut 2·30. 6th Aide from junction pole and lay to telephone hut cut 2·30. 118th R.F.A. own lines	
	7/7/16		on NEUVE-EGLISE — DRANOUTRE road.	
		10·30 am	Temporary repaired and working 11·30 am Contact cleared between Technical School and artillery lines headqrs 118th R.F.A. in lining up new office Returned and out from Y.X.R. refixed all lines O.K.	C.Shumate
	8/7/16		R.E. Park and 103rd Field Co lines changed of early hrs its. 73 am Working Party on NIEPPE line Returning todays which offered to be weak to carry lines. From YR lines his 9·30 am refixed by 11 am.	

Army Form C. 2118.

WAR DIARY
or
INTELLIGENCE SUMMARY.
(Erase heading not required.)

Place	Date	Hour	Summary of Events and Information	Remarks and references to Appendices
BAILLEUL	9/5/16		Watching party sent through 188th R.I.R. lines as known report of several stays had been picked up by Germans	
	10/5/16		149th and 114th field Co. have very heavy gunner were to clear any fruits, skins & refuse to prevent us being on NIEPPE Line, men sent out to sprinkle lingle & Cresote on all dead	
	11/5/16		Lieuts out in all lines. Capt P.T. HENNESSY assumed command of Y.X.R. Trenches handed over to 73rd Bn	
	12/5/16		Nothing of importance. Y.X.R. heavily shelled at Hour 6 & 7 pm. 107th P.F.A. came into B.H.Q.	
	13/5/16		Y.X.R. at 9th & 9.15 heavy reported heavy 7 m.g. and 5 F.A. tried 107 P.F.A. Bring C.Recognoissance of the trenches went on 11th P.F.A	
	14/5/16		enemy shelled the latter rather severely many wounded men at Café Hennessy sent back for were at mount Café Hennessy	
	15/5/16		have refreshed his garrisons sent in as are working party again at DRANOUTRE (2nd Bn)	

Army Form C. 2118.

WAR DIARY
or
INTELLIGENCE SUMMARY.
(Erase heading not required.)

Instructions regarding War Diaries and Intelligence Summaries are contained in F. S. Regs., Part II. and the Staff Manual respectively. Title pages will be prepared in manuscript.

Place	Date	Hour	Summary of Events and Information	Remarks and references to Appendices
BAILLEUL	16	5 P.M.	More earth trouble on 12th and 14th. Field C line. Line patrolled and found to be clear. It was at 13th J.B. central in telephone School and cleared. Telephony party again at 72nd J.B. getting cables	O'Mains
		12 P.M.	Application to Line Branch of 73rd J.B. reported disturbing cable in Bd. condition. 72 and J.B. line strengthened up and wires any pressed. Artillery wires lines wires 5R and 5L cut down by mule. Line near NEUVE EGLISE reported and working OK by Lt McKnight for adept.	
		18 P.M.	Line breakdown sent out. 6 am on R.E. Park line. Found also on NIEPPE Mr James. Lines Z9, 5+14 in contact. Faults cleared and wires probably cabled by heavy shelling on NEUVE EGLISE road. Working party to DRANOUTRE joining cable again	
		19 P.M.	Line run into R.E. Park and BAILLEUL — NEUVE EGLISE and from No 7 and 8 and DAC. Lines testing. Enemy informant found a land stay apparently broken by former had the telephone over the lines in these parts, making several contacts	

Army Form C. 2118.

WAR DIARY
or
INTELLIGENCE SUMMARY.
(Erase heading not required.)

Instructions regarding War Diaries and Intelligence Summaries are contained in F. S. Regs., Part II. and the Staff Manual respectively. Title pages will be prepared in manuscript.

Place	Date	Hour	Summary of Events and Information	Remarks and references to Appendices
BAILLEUL	20/5/16		Watching party continued firing cable at DRANOUTRE. Man sent to mend R.E. post with two by [?] to take through ranges to clear trench timber, for new NEUVE EGLISE line to be put up we are to check. Eng. Bn. sent us 11 men. Examr. found he caused that Lindesten Party[?] had arrived this [?] to [?] to put up Eng. R.E.N. fort	W Stewart
	21/5/16		106th and 110th R.G.A. lines in some[?] cleared [?] [?] 5.45 pm the 2nd Siege[?] [?] front in contact [?] examine found first caused by [?] [?] [?] [?] [?] worked on Coy lines [?] [?] [?]	
	22/5/16		A to B line [?] [?] much interference[?] [?] cut by shell fire. Enemy [?] [?] [?] [?] [?] [?] [?] [?] [?] causing break Suns[?] to en Yx - NX[?] [?] Dac line broken by "L" Sgt [?] [?] [?] [?] 3rd Siege	
	23/5/16		DRANOUTRE work continued. Full am 3rd Siege and [?] [?] [?] [?] [?] [?] [?] 107 Coy R.E. army troops [?] [?] [?] [?] [?] [?] [?] [?]	

WAR DIARY or INTELLIGENCE SUMMARY

Army Form C. 2118.

Place	Date	Hour	Summary of Events and Information	Remarks and references to Appendices
BAILLEUL	24.5.16		Working party to 107th RFA Lutary and trenching D5 cable. 167 Coy RE line continued and finished	
	25.5.16		Working party laying cable from 107th RFA to Hill 63. DAC line lid at noon; anything gone 1pm. Telephone restored in 167 Coy RE	
	26.5.16		Party out on 72nd SB line which had been reported in bad condition, lights strip drawn, lang wires spanning up. 107th RFA lines at Hill 63. 107th RFA work continued R.F.A. work on Hill 63 continued. Route for came air line arranged.	O. Stewart
	27.5.16		NIEPPE line repaired, found to have been trested. Party reported hip trench under shelling in Hill 63.	
	28.5.16		1.30 pm. 116th RIFA buzzer line af trench his shared by Park trenches at 107 AB. RE line patrolled.	
	29.5.16			
	30.5.16		General strengthening of all lines. Party working at the church. Party working at night on Hill 63. Built on line 53 shared.	

Army Form C. 2118.

WAR DIARY
or
INTELLIGENCE SUMMARY.

(Erase heading not required.)

Instructions regarding War Diaries and Intelligence Summaries are contained in F. S. Regs., Part II. and the Staff Manual respectively. Title pages will be prepared in manuscript.

Place	Date	Hour	Summary of Events and Information	Remarks and references to Appendices
BALLEUL	31/5/16		Party at SHRINE Dugout training hard for the attack. Myself found standing all day concrete, yet 18 in mistaped many of the points and him wants done	G Stevens

Appendix I

WAR DIARY
INTELLIGENCE SUMMARY

Army Form C. 2118.

No. 2 Section
24th Divl Sig Co RE

Place	Date	Hour	Summary of Events and Information	Remarks and references to Appendices
PETITE MUNQUE FARM	MAY.			
	1st/2/3rd	Night	Work continued on reclaiming flooded part of trench by BARREL H.Q. & digging on from 10th FA Bde Battle Hq to their Hq T 17 B 17.	
	3-11		Trench continued to T 17 A 19. When RA trench handed off to T 23 B 6.5. T 17 1B trench ctd to T 23 B 8.3. Where lines were temporarily led into tops on airlines.	
	13		Trench begun from RA Battle dugout to join up with one from Y.R. + ZGC Battle dugout. 4 pr (S.R. turns) + 3 pr (D5) used.	
	14		above ctd	
	15		do	
	16		do. also work begun forward from early canadian armoured cable (?) not left coy 9 left Bn) at T 7 B 1.6	
	17-18th		Relief	
	18-19 "		Work ctd towards trench 135, or 70° per night, over WELL RD at trench frame way at T 7 B 6.5. Then straight to where PRINCE ALBERT AV (old C trench) crosses River DOUVE at T 7 B 8.6, along P.AA as far as T 8 A 1.7. then straight across field through gap in hedge at T 8 A 2½ 7½ joining cables laid from trench 135 at T 8 A 1.8	
	19-23			

Army Form C. 2118.

WAR DIARY
INTELLIGENCE SUMMARY.
(Erase heading not required.)

Instructions regarding War Diaries and Intelligence Summaries are contained in F. S. Regs., Part II. and the Staff Manual respectively. Title pages will be prepared in manuscript.

Place	Date	Hour	Summary of Events and Information	Remarks and references to Appendices.
PETITE MUNQUE FARM	MAY			
	24-28		by Btn in left sector refs 22/23 & 23/24. Work now completed, aft 1 night MT for relief on night on 28/29	Xerp 1.1.18 Lieut R
	29-30		Ditch at ASH HOUSE filled up to 70ᵗ where cable to R Bn had been laid in April.	Hindsforwer
	30-31		Work begun for 80ˣ back from back end of Canadian cables (Ra L coy M L Bn) at T 7 C 24.	
	31-1.6.16		work C/a back towards THATCHED COTTAGE — LE ROSSIGNOL RAPD	

Appendix 2.

Army Form C. 2118.

WAR DIARY
or
INTELLIGENCE SUMMARY.
(Erase heading not required.)

No. 3 Section
24th D.W. Sig. Coy. R.E.

Place	Date	Hour	Summary of Events and Information	Remarks and references to Appendices
DRANOUTRE	1.5.16		Buried line between Left Battn HQ and Left Battn. Battle HQ broken 11:30 pm 30th just outside Battle HQ., mended 12:5 am 1st. Enemy shelled area between Bde Battle HQ and DRANOUTRE and broke several air lines.	GPM
"	2.5.16		Line 12 between Bde HQ and Bde Battle HQ Dis 8am OK 9:30am.	GPM
"	3.5.16		Line 13 (semi air line) from Bde Battle HQ to Right Battn Dis 6am OK 10:30am. Joined a right Battn buried line continued	GPM
"	4.5.16		Joining right Battn buried line continued	GPM
"	5.5.16		DRANOUTRE shelled. Nov 7,8,9,12, All lines between Bde HQ and Bde Battle HQ Dis during shelling. Communication with Battns being maintained via 108 RFA for about 50 minutes. Plan jar and Sounder line to Div Dis 11:20 am OK 12:30 p/m. RAA working party on buried line to Coy office of Left Battn.	GPM
"	6.5.16		Working party of 100 by day on bury from Bde Battle HQ to DRANOUTRE, 50 by night for bure to coy office of Left Battn. An air line from Bde Battle HQ to Left Battn Dis 6 p/m, OK 7:30 p/m.	GPM
"	7.5.16		Working party on bury to DRANOUTRE (4 day) party of 50 on Left Battn bry line by Right. No line Dis.	GPM

Army Form C. 2118.

WAR DIARY
or
INTELLIGENCE SUMMARY.
(Erase heading not required.)

Instructions regarding War Diaries and Intelligence Summaries are contained in F. S. Regs., Part II. and the Staff Manual respectively. Title pages will be prepared in manuscript.

Place	Date	Hour	Summary of Events and Information	Remarks and references to Appendices
DRANOUTRE	8.5.16		No working parties owing to relief. No have DIS	G/WW
"	9.5.16		Working party of 50 by day on BUS FM - DRANOUTRE Line. No party at night. No have DIS	G/WW
"	10.5.16		Working party of 50 by day and 50 by night. Line improved and patrolled.	G/WW
"	11.5.16		Working party of 50 by day and 50 by night. Line improved and patrolled.	G/WW
"	12.5.16		Working party of 50 by day and 50 by night.	G/WW
"	13.5.16		Working party of 75 by day and 50 by night. Section dug out for small SG near Bde Battle HQR Chosen.	G/WW
"	14.5.16		Working out disguising buried rods, cables. Working party of 50 in afternoons on buried line from BUS FARM to DRANOUTRE	G/WW
"	15.5.16		Working party 50 by night. Left Battn buried line to C oy.	G/WW
"	16.5.16		Working party 50 by night. Left Battn buried line to C oy.	G/WW
"	17.5.16		Working party 100 tychols BUS FARM - DRANOUTRE bury. Working party C Coy left batln bury - Line to right coy., left batln completed.	G/WW
"	18.5.16		Working party 50 Glasgow Yeomanry BUS FARM - DRANOUTRE bury. Working party left batln to centre coy bury.	G/WW

T/134. Wt. W708-776. 500000. 4/15. Sir J. C. & 9.

Army Form C. 2118.

WAR DIARY
or
INTELLIGENCE SUMMARY.
(Erase heading not required.)

Instructions regarding War Diaries and Intelligence Summaries are contained in F. S. Regs., Part II. and the Staff Manual respectively. Title pages will be prepared in manuscript.

Place	Date	Hour	Summary of Events and Information	Remarks and references to Appendices
DRANOUTRE	19.5.16		Working party 50 Glasgow Yeomanry on BUS FARM – DRANOUTRE hwy. All working parties broken	J.W.
"	20.5.16		Working party 40 on burnt line left halfe to sea the coy which are completed. Working party 20 ants, a BUS FARM – DRANOUTRE hwy	J.W.
"	21.5.16		Working party 50 BUS FARM – DRANOUTRE hwy	J.W.
"	22.5.16		Working party 50 BUS FARM – DRANOUTRE hwy	J.W.
"	23.5.16		R.W. B.W.R H.Q melted about 9.15am – all existing farmed broken. Working party 50 BUS FARM – DRANOUTRE hwy	J.W.
"	24.5.16		Lewis patrolled	J.W.
"	25.5.16		Working party of 50 on BUS FARM – DRANOUTRE buried line	J.W.
"	26.5.16		Working party of 50 on BUS FARM – DRANOUTRE buried line	J.W.
"	27.5.16		Working party of 50 on BUS FARM – DRANOUTRE buried line	J.W.
"	28.5.16		Working party of 50 on BUS FARM – DRANOUTRE buried line	J.W.
"	29.5.16		Neighbourhood of BUS FARM shelled 8am – 11.30am. Working party of 50 on BUS FARM – DRANOUTRE buried line.	J.W.
"	30.5.16		Were a visual signalling dugout on BUS FARM way	J.W.
"	31.5.16		Buried lines between BUS FARM and DRANOUTRE test thru'y Bafanwy. Visual signal finished and P.Cs with transceiver to left Batt. Batt. H.Q. and S.C. + men with Batt. Batt. H.Q. Buried line	

T.134. Wt. W703-776. 500000. 4/15. Sir J. C. & S.

Army Form C. 2118.

WAR DIARY
or
INTELLIGENCE SUMMARY.
(Erase heading not required.)

Instructions regarding War Diaries and Intelligence Summaries are contained in F. S. Regs., Part II. and the Staff Manual respectively. Title pages will be prepared in manuscript.

Place	Date	Hour	Summary of Events and Information	Remarks and references to Appendices
GRANVILLE	31.5.16		Coy. Split up for final journey to Base Camp of 5th Divn H.Q.	

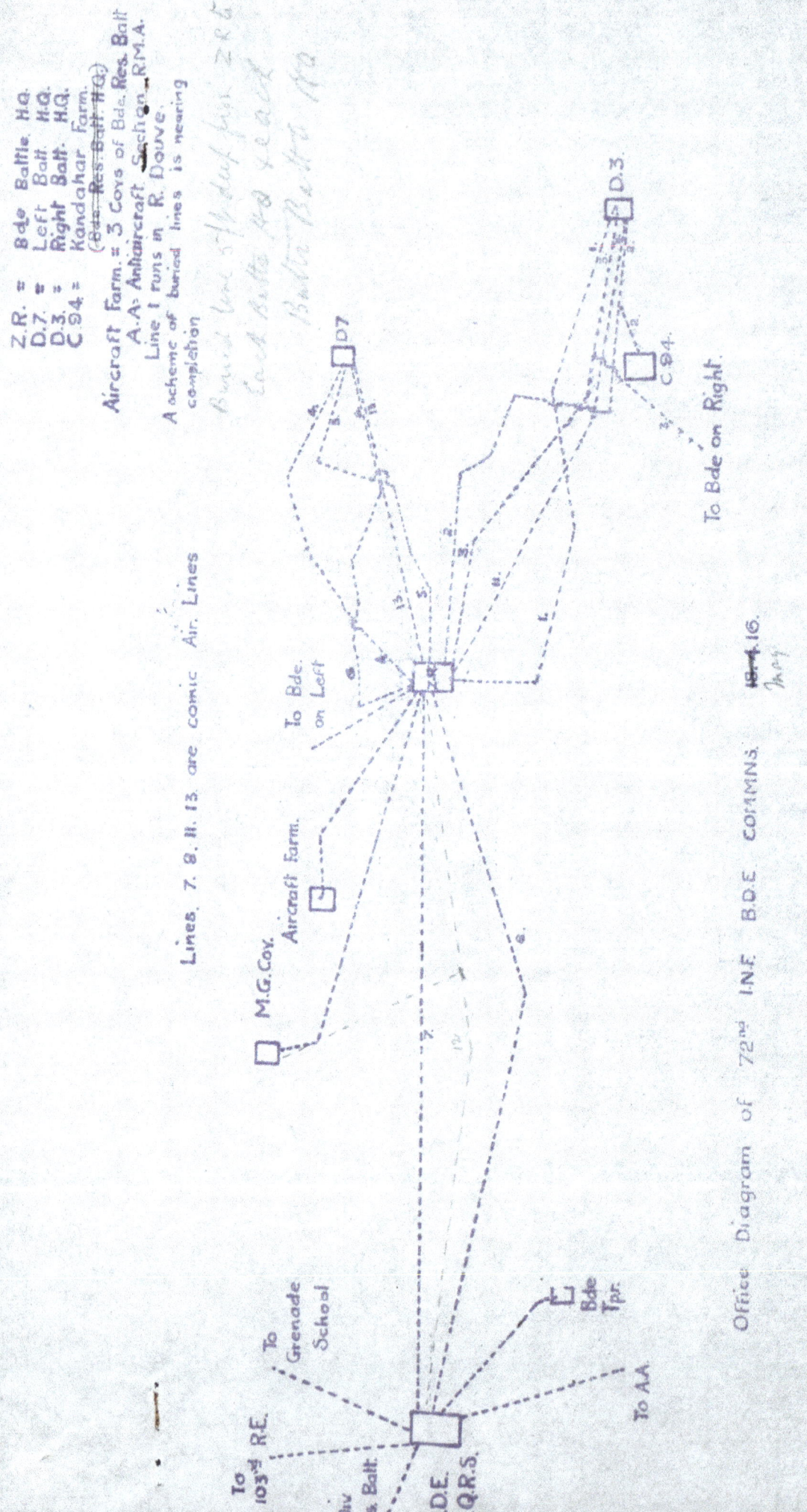

Appendix 3.

4 Sec 24 Signal Coy, R.E.

Sheet I.

May 1916.

WAR DIARY
or
INTELLIGENCE SUMMARY.
(Erase heading not required.)

Army Form C. 2118.

Instructions regarding War Diaries and Intelligence Summaries are contained in F.S. Regs., Part II and the Staff Manual respectively. Title pages will be prepared in manuscript.

Place	Date	Hour	Summary of Events and Information	Remarks and references to Appendices
Sheet 28. T.14.5.2.	1		Continued buried route from Battalion Hqrs to Bde Battle Hqrs in daytime could see.	cep R
	2.		Map two parties of sappers each. finished off buried route right into Bde Battle Hqrs. Nos 5-8 for Artillery. Of the new cables Nos. 1-4 to right batt for Infantry, No 13-18 for Artillery, joined through Nos 3+9 to 11+12 9-12 for Infantry. No 4 in Battle Hqrs, and worked metallic on poled lines 1+2 &c to bff with sail attempt in Battle Hqrs and with ?-butt through Bde Battle Hqrs on buried route to right Battn. through Bde Battle Hqrs and joined through on 1+2 etc	
	3.		Laid new poled pair to Bde Battle Hqrs and repaired by 5.45p.m. 12 wire Buried to right Battn.	
	4.			
	5.		11 dis and repaired poled lines	
	6.		Nos 11 & 12 poled lines lead straight out Bde Battle Hqrs and buried	
	7.		Laid tee at No. 12 to Bath in REDLODGE (R6.) and repaired metallic on 11+12	R
	8.		Patrolled and put up ½ via stays on all poled lines on 2 (?)	

2353 W W2511/1454 700,000 5/15 D.D.&L. A.D.S.S./Forms/C. 2115.

WAR DIARY
or
INTELLIGENCE SUMMARY.

Army Form C. 2118.

May 1916. Sheet II

(Erase heading not required.)

Place	Date	Hour	Summary of Events and Information	Remarks and references to Appendices
Sheet 28. T.2.d.5.2.	9.		Let an extra piece in buried line of Left Coy Rt Batn where it had been uncovered. Telegraphed old communication trench.	2/R.
	10.		Dug in buried lines of Right batn near STINKING FARM.	2/R.
	11.		Fixed up lines in Bde Battle hqrs. Dug in short piece of cable between hqrs near STINKING FM.	2/R.
	12.		Traced out artillery pair from left Bn hqrs to Boyles farm and joined through on buried pair to Coy Stn in C.I.	2/R.
	13.		Placed male marking boards on Bde battle to Batn buried lines and buried lines of Left Batn. Line to 72 Bde div. HQ broke. Handed in our patrol but still in instrce of 72 Bde.	2/R.
	14.		Patrolled airlines, fixed up office of right battalion and free up party in board store.	2/R.
	15.		Buried cable at STINKING FARM. Patrolled lines. Dis leading in Board fixed up and tidied. 107 fine poles straightened. (N.Hants) Bde RFA	WR+F+2/R. 3/R.C Bicycle 4thy B.S.O.
	16.		Completed burial of cable at STINKING FARM. Patrolled lines - Right Company of Right Battalion line - hit Coy 5.9 yesterday - made good	A/R
	17.		Patrolled lines.	A/R

Army Form C. 2118.

Sheet III

WAR DIARY
INTELLIGENCE SUMMARY
(Erase heading not required.)

May, 1916

Instructions regarding War Diaries and Intelligence Summaries are contained in F. S. Regs., Part II. and the Staff Manual respectively. Title pages will be prepared in manuscript.

Place	Date	Hour	Summary of Events and Information	Remarks and references to Appendices
Sheet 28 T21d 5.2	18		Patrolled lines - Ottawa Row and Nos 1 and 2 lines, leading into Battle Dug Out, hit during patrol, damage made good.	M.R.
	19		Patrolled and tested lines. Instructions given to O.C. Sit C.oy of Self Bkn to fire on shell holes where cable exposed.	M.R. M.R. M.R.
	20		Patrolled lines.	M.R.
	21		Patrolled and tested lines.	
	22		Patrolled and tested Lines. Accompanied O.C. Signals on an inspection of the Coy Offices and lines from FLETCHERS FIELD to Brigade, BATTLE HEADQUARTERS. Visual demonstration - BATTALIONS to FLETCHERS FIELD.	
	23		Patrolled lines.	M.R.
	24		Patrolled lines. Contact between 11/12 field lines and one of 2nd line.	M.R.
	25		Patrolled lines. One K Z.P. cut out on their patrol	

WAR DIARY or INTELLIGENCE SUMMARY

Army Form C. 2118.

4 Sec. 24 Div Signal Company, May 1916, sheet N

Place	Date	Hour	Summary of Events and Information	Remarks and references to Appendices
T.21.d.5.2.	26.		Led lines into new concrete dugout of battery left battn	asK
T.26.d/28	27.		patrolled lines.	asK
	28.		Picked up portion of German pair.	asK
	29.		Laid comic airline pair to A Batty 107 Bde RFA. to pick up pair in Battle H.Q.	asK
	30.		Moved route to battery right, coy right battn in trench 136. Led lines into dugout of right coy right battn.	asK
	31.		Line to T3/1. Trouble to Batty dus. aligned lamps from both front coys of left batt on visual stations in Flotsam Field and tested them. Installed digging lines in to right coy Battn for night battn.	

R.G. Ritchie
L.A.B.

COMMUNICATIONS of 73 Inf Bde
at (28) *Harding* T.21.d.5.2.

[Z5] ZQ2.

[F5] 107 Bde R.E.

[Z11] T.M. Batty

[Z14. 2GC]

[YxR]

[KP] Bgn DV Reserve.

[YX]

[D.16] 2/1 Batn

[Z6.]

[D8.] N.F. Pattn.

[D4.] 8 in Bde Reserve.

[ZQ] ZQ.

[1246] R.E.

142 airline
a.d.10
11.d.12 airline
11.d.10
a.d.10
142

Forwardline on all overhead cable lines dotted.

30/5/16.

24th DIVISIONAL SIGNAL COMPANY, R.E.
No. 256
Date 2-7-16

The Officer i/c,

   A.G's Office at the Base.

   Herewith the War Diary of the 24th Divisional Signal Company, Royal Engineers, for the month of June, 1916.

2/7/16.

for G. [signature]
            Captain.
O.C. 24th Divl Signal Co. R.E.

24th Div.
Army Form C. 2118
Signals

WAR DIARY
or
INTELLIGENCE SUMMARY
(Erase heading not required.)

Army Form C. 2118

24th Div. Divisional Signal Co. R.E.
June 1916

Place	Date	Hour	Summary of Events and Information	Remarks and references to Appendices
BAILLEUL	1/6/16		Patrol sent out on arty. route where enemy branches were causing eighth earth. 72nd SB lines reported stuck across NEUVE EGLISE road. Runner sent out to straighten them up. Party hanging wire on HILL 63 for artillery.	Vol.
	2/6/16		Work continued in SHRINE dugout (HILL 63) fixing up lines to groups etc. Party sent on Arty Round changing insulators and installing lines. 106 RFA and HQ 72nd Inf. Brigade taken over. Line from ENGLISH FARM to HQ 72 Inf. Bgde. having fallen in, owing 7 pm. 72 Inf. Bgde. Bn. now use YXR signal office.	

O/C 24th Signal Co. Capt. Peskett.

WAR DIARY or INTELLIGENCE SUMMARY

Army Form C. 2118.

Place	Date	Hour	Summary of Events and Information	Remarks and references to Appendices
BAILLEUL	3/11		SHRINE dugout work continued. D5 four men from lateral route to YXR and bridges on 108th RFA line making communication from DRANOUTRE to HILL 63. Trouble experienced thro' Construction Party of L Signals crossing our lines unspotting contacts.	
	4/11	8 am	Earth fault on 51st Batty line caused by hm.	
		11 am	Contact on 17th FB line found to be caused by dirty	
			line crossing Trench Route.	
		7.30pm	Withdrew junk to HILL 63.	
	5/11		Work continued on SHRINE dugout. Swingel made for communication to Dickerbusch	
			Enemy Battn lines cleared. Faults on 72nd FB and very faulty on 155 Army Batty. Batty. 7.40 pm Party to	
			HILL 63 for work there.	
	6/11		Bad cont'd on YX - YXR route cleared also fault on 72nd FB line. SHRINE dugout work continued.	
	7/11		3 extra lines built on twelve route from ENGLISH FARM. (73rd FB) to 12th FB. 5pm. 72nd FB lines cut by	

O/C 2nd Signal Co.
Capt.

WAR DIARY
or
INTELLIGENCE SUMMARY

Army Form C. 2118.

Place	Date	Hour	Summary of Events and Information	Remarks and references to Appendices
BAILLEUL	7th (contd).		Shell fire on NEUVE-EGLISE — DRANOUTRE road about midway. Fires temporarily put through for the night. D5 Coy (Sgn) now from FXR to infantry lines of 155 Heavy Batty and front Naval Station to their Batty HQ in NEUVE EGLISE giving communication down from Wagon lines to HQ.	
	9 p.m.		Working party out strengthening 72nd FB lines which had been weakened by shell fire. Big Bertha has again been and knocked one out to retain it. Switching party to 73rd F.B. to extend 8 line air-formed route across the road to Toy hill. Pack rump running to 17th FB.	
	10 p.m.		Cable section carrying from Second Army to — new cut by our cable actions for improving W relay Heavy Signal company.	
	11 p.m.		7.30 pm. Nightly wiring party leaves for HILL 63. New humour from Second Army on shower treated and practice SHRINE dugout-account continued. All lines O.K.	

WAR DIARY or INTELLIGENCE SUMMARY

Army Form C. 2118.

(Erase heading not required.)

Place	Date	Hour	Summary of Events and Information	Remarks and references to Appendices
BAILLEUL	12/4/16	8.30 a.m.	One of our cable sections leaves for training at Second Army Signal Camp under Lieut. W.H. WILKINSON. R.E. Engineer lines patrolled and several lines restored. SHRINE dugout enlarged.	
	13/4/16		All lines O.K. except Armentières Buttoin which sheared entries. Enemy lines found covered by tunnel of Bn. Very heavy mine falling all day.	
	14/4/16		Telephones removed from R.E. Dump NIEPPE, and further telegraph wire R.E. Dump had shown had no use by, nothing at work night to midnight.	
	15/4/16		R.E. Dump line, all O.K. DAC line very slack, party of 3 out on it, straining up and staying.	Bullecourt O/C 24th Signal Co.
	16/4/16		SHRINE dugout still being worked up. ANZAC lines heavy shown over lines	
	17/4/16		Working party working on lines running up HILL 63. ANZAC's accompany our Enemy patrolling lines.	

WAR DIARY or INTELLIGENCE SUMMARY.

Army Form C. 2118.

(Erase heading not required.)

Instructions regarding War Diaries and Intelligence Summaries are contained in F. S. Regs., Part II and the Staff Manual respectively. Title pages will be prepared in manuscript.

Place	Date	Hour	Summary of Events and Information	Remarks and references to Appendices
BAILLEUL	17/7/16	12·5 a.m.	Gas alarm given 12·45 a.m. 'Stand to' ordered. Gas cable company ready at YXR in case of enemy firing under bombardment.	
		2·30 a.m.	'Stand to' cancelled. All lines O.K. during heavy bombardment and rifle & machine gun fire. 7·15 a.m. Bombardment started with increased vigour by Bosche and reply by our own forces. 7 & 8 Coys down to H. Says (mug guard). 7·30 a.m. Reported wires of Coy Switch in many places to have been cut — 300 yards from Billets by shell fire. 7·31 a.m. Bombardment of F 17 reported to 41st DSC. Report sent on by 41st Div. Sig. to 24 Div. Sig. 2·10 p.m. 17·10 p.m. Enemy raid on 17 R.B.'s and returned 2·15 a.m. Bullets fired by snipers in no mans land.	
	19/7/16		Enemy machine gun fire on our standing patrol of 1 N.C.O. and 3 men fating B2 LICRE follows D5. No 5 near 17a J3 Cache (for base road)	O/C 24th Signal Coy

2353 Wt. W2544/1454 700,000 5/15 D. D. & L. A.D.S.S. Forms/C.2118.

Army Form C. 2118.

WAR DIARY
or
INTELLIGENCE SUMMARY.
(Erase heading not required.)

Instructions regarding War Diaries and Intelligence Summaries are contained in F. S. Regs., Part II. and the Staff Manual respectively. Title pages will be prepared in manuscript.

Place	Date	Hour	Summary of Events and Information	Remarks and references to Appendices
BAILLEUL	20/11		Working party laying cable in Reserve trench between 17th JB and 7th ANZAC Brigade. 5pm party to 3rd Bdge Butchery and found all quiet. 7th ANZAC Bde. DRANOUTRE. Working party to lay lines near HILL 63, and install Party in reserve trenches between 17th JB and 7th ANZACS.	
	21/11		NIEPPE. lines labelled.	
	22/11		Inst the Rend Giblins. KEMMEL and SCHERPENBERG reconn'd by working party of 4 men. 106 R.F.A. Schuler lines aus 12 men. Full found outside office of 106 R. 3-15 pm VX - 72nd JB somewhere in contact with N° 50 line. 11 am gas alert on. 11.45 am gas alert off.	M/Larks O.C. 24th Signal Co.
	23/11	10 to 12	JJ D5 cable being buried be let down gradient -- ENGLISH FARM and LA PETITE MUNQUE.	
	24/11	1.30 pm	Exty. Button line dug. Burying began 2.30 pm. 5 pm	
			107th R.F.A.	
	25/11		Burial party on 72nd JB line returned, having nil work experienced. Burial party on 72nd JB line returned, having nil work experienced. Burial to DRANOUTRE and BUS FARM.	

Army Form C. 2118.

WAR DIARY
or
INTELLIGENCE SUMMARY

(Erase heading not required.)

Instructions regarding War Diaries and Intelligence Summaries are contained in F. S. Regs., Part II. and the Staff Manual respectively. Title pages will be prepared in manuscript.

Place	Date	Hour	Summary of Events and Information	Remarks and references to Appendices
BAILLEUL	25/6/16	8.45 p.m	72nd FB relieved the No. 11 section for the night. Scout Army still within "N" return, nos. having completed to-morrow yesterday.	
	26/6/16	8.15 am	107th R.E. A living faulty. 10.30am hrs hanging No. 17 office.	
		10 am	72nd FB found No. 69 O.K. signals are found near MUD FARM. 5 fm Visual Station from sunset hrs 5 and 6 on Junction O/c to Balloon Commander.	
	27/6/16		Between NEUVE ÉGLISE and DRANOUTRE working party on buried wires at- LA PETITE MUNQUE FARM.	Pechaudu
	28/6/16		Lines No. 27 T 28, 29 T 30, 61 T 65 changed by TRIPLE to twisted, everything O.K. on completion of change.	
	29/6/16		Buried route and additional T junction made with iron markers. Working party on buried route near	
	30/6/16		ANTI- AIRCRAFT FARM. 74th FB cleared on R.E. Park lines and Trestle rout lines overhauled.	

Army Form C. 2118.

WAR DIARY

Appendix I

INTELLIGENCE SUMMARY

(Erase heading not required)

No 2 Section, 24th Divl Sigl Coy R.E.

Place	Date	Hour	Summary of Events and Information	Remarks and references to Appendices
PETITE MUNQUE FARM. T.23.d.8.9. SHEET 28	JUNE 1916			
	1/2 nyt		Line from trench 135 continued back towards VILLA HOUSE, uphill parallel to ORMOND TRENCH at about v7.2.2, 2"D Twin" put in as well as 2 ironbound "J"s	Attd appd transmd Signl
	2/3 nyt		No party owing to relief	
	3/4 "		" " " " " " artillery shoot	
	4 – 9 nyt		Work continued on same line in direction of VILLA HOUSE to hedge about 80ˣ N of road, then leaving 4' left on to N side of road about 120ˣ W 57 CELLARS	
	10/11 & 11/12		No parties owing to relief &c.	
	12/13 nyt		Trench abandoned just short of road at depth of 3'½" owing to heavy rain	
	13/14 "		No work owing to rain. During this fortnight the offices at the CELLARS was properly fitted up with leading in board + meter each.	
	14/15 "		Work begun on Tee from L Coy lines of R bn, at top of QUEBEC AV: on E of MESSINES – PLOEGSTEERT road + parallel to it, towards ADVANCED EST: this was reached on 2nd night, + trench then crossed SUBSIDIARY LINE between road + only way. Here the L Coy lines were laid into and thence to G.P. twins brought back past J. (U.14.c. 6.5 Sheet 28 Belgium.)	

BACK EST: across PROWSE PT road + MASTED HQ to new tn dugouts in locality J. (U.14.c. 6.5 SHEET 28 BELGIUM.)

T./134. Wt. W708–776. 500000. 4/15. Sir J.C.&S.

Army Form C. 2118.

WAR DIARY
INTELLIGENCE SUMMARY.
(Erase heading not required.)

Instructions regarding War Diaries and Intelligence Summaries are contained in F.S. Regs., Part II. and the Staff Manual respectively. Title pages will be prepared in manuscript.

Place	Date	Hour	Summary of Events and Information	Remarks and references to Appendices
PETITE MUNQUE FARM T23.d.89.(Sheet 28)	JUNE 1916 19/20 Nyt		Trench reclaimed & deepened that was begun on Nyt 12/13 & line brought through gap & down road on N side towards OB (CELLARS)	Lieut. R.E.
	20/21		line ctd for 70° but abandoned owing to large amount of water & a lot of things falling in.	
	21/22		line dug down to road avoiding mount and finished into old cable trench just N. of OB. lines to L Coy jointed up & tested OK.	Hd. Qrs. phones. Lieut. R.E.
	22/23		Various bits cleaned up. Inverness of 2 ANZAC BDE attached for last 2 days & taken over all lines.	
X17c.43.	23		Sup ZQ handed over to AZ8 at 5 PM and moved into rest area at X17c.43. (sheet 27 Belgium) lines to be already laid, so were used. Came with YX through	
	24-26		ECO. Section resting & refitting. Stores, harness, rifles, eqpt. & gas helmets inspected	
LOCRE	27-30		Bde hqrs & 2 bns (1 & 12 RF) moved to LOCRE relieving 15o I.B. (50 Div) came to YX through exch: into LOCRE. to Z9c direct, also YEK. 2 Buffs + 3 RB in touch by cable from YX, 1 & 12 RF by orderly from ZQ. Inverness sent to DRANOUTRE to take over lines from ZQB to their battle Hq, at Bus FM, thence to their L bn, lateral to ZQc & their battle Hq to ZQc & Q bn.	

T2134. Wt. W708—776. 500000. 4/15. Sir J. C. & S.

Appendix 2

Army Form C. 2118.

24th DIVISIONAL
SIGNAL COMPANY,
R.E.

WAR DIARY
or
INTELLIGENCE SUMMARY.
(Erase heading not required.)

No 3 Section
24th Div Sig Coy R.E.

Place	Date	Hour	Summary of Events and Information	Remarks and references to Appendices
Branafs.	1/6/16		Work on communication for left by office of right Batts in D2	full
	2/6/16		Visual from trench D2 to Obs. O.P. on Hill 63 arranged. Liaison between Coy. office in D2 and right and left coys arranged	full
	3/6/16		Liaison from Right Batt. HQ to left Batt. of Right Bde laid. Visual Augent Test in on 5 ft steps tony to Bde Battle HQ	full
	4/6/16		Minor enterprise from D2 trench at 12.30 am. Visual and other methods of communication successful. No line D1s	full full
	5/6/16		Work on right Batts. buried wire - fitting up leading-in board in right Batt. Battle HQ	full
	5/6/16		Work on right Batts Battle HQ fitting's completed. Visual circuit strengthened	full
	7/6/16		Visual dugout strengthened. Party of 60 on new line between left Batts HQ and R.E. Farm.	full
	8/6/16		Party of 60 on buried line between left Batts Batts HQrs R.E.Farm — work completed. Fault on Z5 - Z8 road. located and put OK. D span from Dranoute to Bus Farm picked up	full full
	9/6/16		Line 3 between Bus Farm and Dranoutre noted up. Luser land N between Bus Farm and right Batts reeled up	full

WAR DIARY
or
INTELLIGENCE SUMMARY.
(Erase heading not required.)

Army Form C. 2118.

Place	Date	Hour	Summary of Events and Information	Remarks and references to Appendices
Dranoutre	10.6.16		Line 6 between Bus Farm and Left Batt. reeled up. Line 7 between DRANOUTRE and Bus Farm reeled up.	
	11.6.16		Putting through left Batt. Armed Line and attaching to subway board in left Batt. Bath. H.Q. cabined, Line 12 improved.	
	12.6.16		Line patrolled and improved. Reeling up airline commenced.	
	13.6.16		New airline to M.G. Coy from Dranoutre started. Reeling up old airline continued.	
	14.6.16		Airline to M.G. Coy completed. Line from Bus Farm to Aircraft Farm improved, airlines reeled up.	
	15.6.16		Work on Line 12 continued. Test put in against enemy of Red Line. Diagram showing route. Completing all jointing on buried routes. Line patrolled and improved.	
	16.6.16		Gas attack by enemy 1.20 a.m. All lines held throughout except around A Coy. H.Q. which went D/S half hour. Got through to their Coy.'s throughout. Also Bath B—	
	17.6.16		Red Rear H.Q. Not completed. Received 1.5 more yards of Cable by Divisional Signal Section.	

Army Form C. 2118.

WAR DIARY
or
INTELLIGENCE SUMMARY.
(Erase heading not required.)

Instructions regarding War Diaries and Intelligence Summaries are contained in F. S. Regs., Part II. and the Staff Manual respectively. Title pages will be prepared in manuscript.

Place	Date	Hour	Summary of Events and Information	Remarks and references to Appendices
BRANDHOEK	17.6.16		During Artillery duel of our Bns we suffered 2 O.R. wounded	78/1
	18.6.16		Buried Pass C. Stanghan - 9am - Kestbitz	9/1
	20.6.16		Line Snowden, Break road, Stanghan, Wieltze & road Facing Hock	9/1
	21.6.16		Working party of 150 on West Yuill between the Left Bn & Rifle Bde HQ and right Cyl R Bn	9/1
			Battle HQrs. Reconnoitring line & continued	
	22.6.16		Indians reconstituted	9/1
	23.6.16		Line 12" reconstructed	9/1
	24.6.16		Line 12 reconnoitred and weak posts in Dilago A – Bas Farm - buried posts Strengthened	9/1
	25.6.16		7pm Bn Farm to Ancoeff Farm contains to Arctic Farm and Jumps to Wieltze furnished by D	9/1
			Draws to Contact K Arctic Farm and battled bn 7 line to Suomens at 1.30am Farm brig bmh	9/1
			Hq Rpt, Lines 26-22 & 7.B Load Officers performances Referee Kermardells mainly Farm and	9/1
			the C. Cy. took parts in Bn Farm - Down in trays of implanted. Run strengthen near Delvage 1st Bn Farm	9/1
	26.6.16		Left to told as brigadiers and found successful	9/1
	27.6.16		Lieut HE Fuller Reith in Rifle Reserve came from Arctic Farm to Ancoeff Farm every 10	9/1
			every Stealing	
	28.6.16		Was a before proceeded by of against every offer to Front D.2 11:30pm Athenaum	9/1

2353 Wt. W5344/1434 700,000 5/15 D,D,&L. A.D.S.S./Forms/C. 2118.

Army Form C. 2118.

WAR DIARY
or
INTELLIGENCE SUMMARY.
(Erase heading not required.)

Place	Date	Hour	Summary of Events and Information	Remarks and references to Appendices

Instructions regarding War Diaries and Intelligence Summaries are contained in F. S. Regs., Part II. and the Staff Manual respectively. Title pages will be prepared in manuscript.

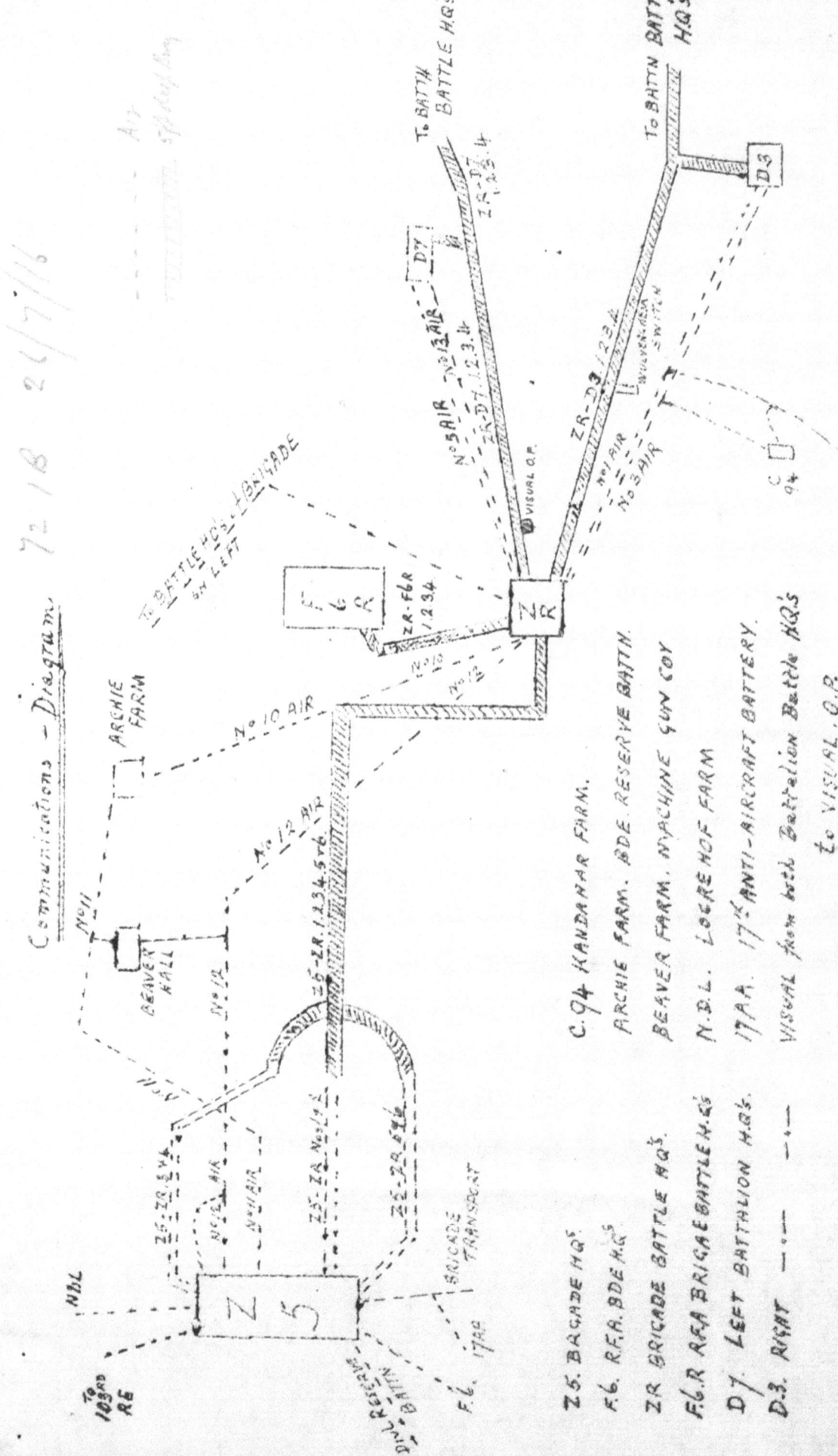

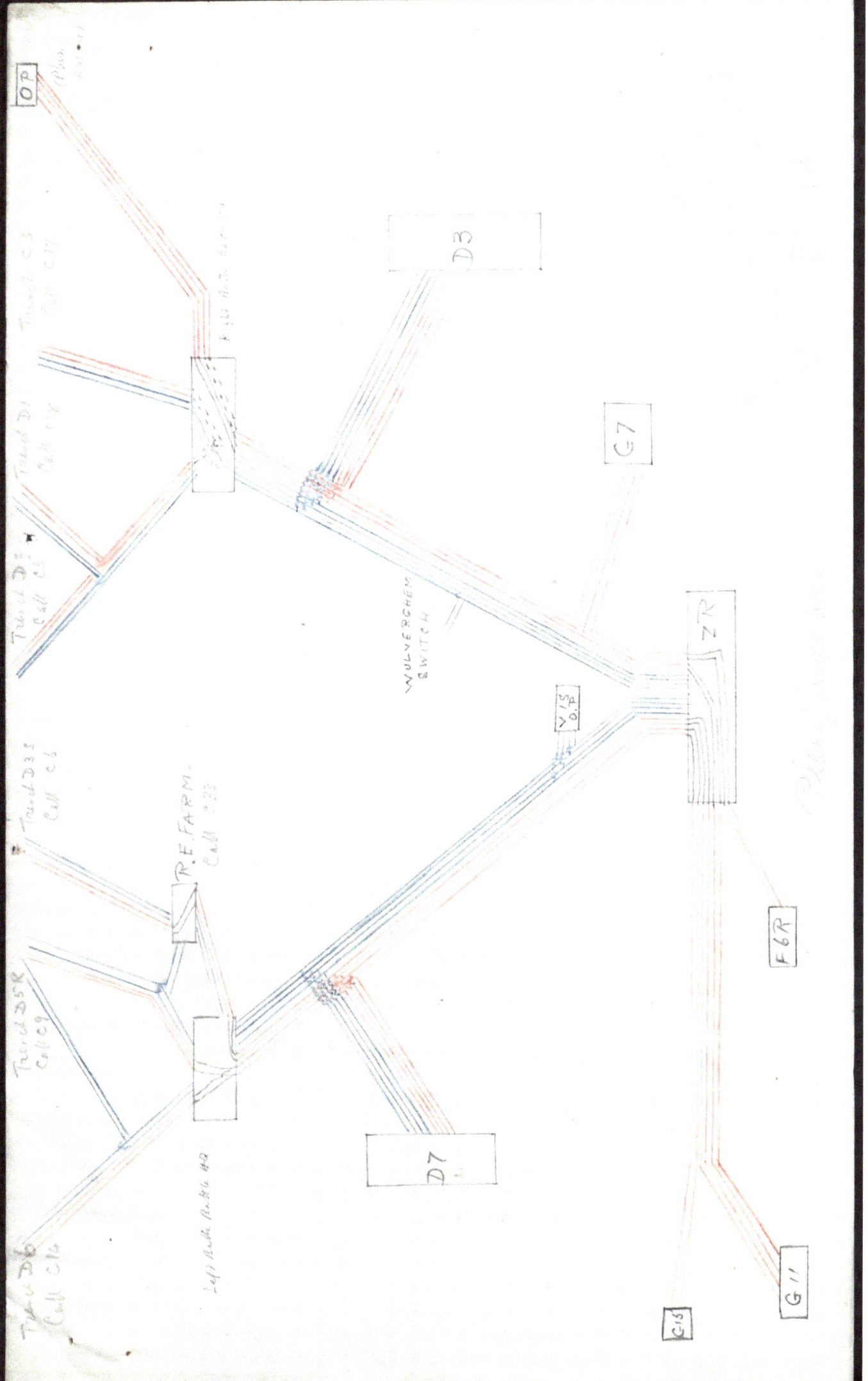

APPENDIX VI. No 3 Sect. 24th Div'l Sig. Co.

COMMUNICATIONS. 72/B

From BUS FARM DUGOUTS (N.33.d.2½.1½.) Brigade Battle Headquarters.

    To Right Battalion.   4 Lines buried 5 feet deep.
        ST. QUENTIN.   (ZR - D.3. Nos. 1.2.3. & 4.)

                            Airlines.
                            No.1.   D.5. cable in R.DOUVE.
                            No.3.   D.5. cable poled.

    To Right Battalion   4 Lines buried 5 feet deep.
       Battle H.Q's.   (ZR - D.3. Nos. 1.2.3 & 4.)
       (T.6.a.2.3.)

    To Left Battalion.   4 Lines buried 5 feet deep.
       COOKER FARM.   (ZR - D.7. Nos. 1.2.3 & 4.)

                            Airlines.
                            No.5.   D.5. cable in ditches.
                            No.13. Comic air line.

    To Left Battalion.   4 Lines buried 5 feet deep.
       Battle H.Q's.   (ZR - D.7. Nos. 1.2.3 & 4.)
       (N.35.d.7.8.)

    To R.F.A. Brigade.   4 Lines buried 5 feet deep.
       Battle H.Q's.   (ZR - F.6.R. Nos. 1.2.3 & 4.)
       (N.33.d.2.2½.)

    To KANDAHAR FARM.   D.5. cable, teed in on Air line 1.
       (T.10.d.5.8.)   D.5. cable, teed in on Air line 3.
    (1 Coy. of Battalion in Brigade Reserve).

    To ARCHIE FARM.   D.1. cable on poles. (No. 10)
       (N.32.b.1.4½.)
       (Battalion in Brigade Reserve.)

    To Brigade H.Q's.   D.5. cable,.
       on right.   teed in on Air line 1.

    To Battle H.Q's.   D.5. cable in ditches and poled.
       Brigade on left.

    To Visual Signalling Teed in on 5 feet deep bury.
       Dugout on BUS   (Z.5. - D.7. Nos. 1.2.3 & 4.)
       FARM RIDGE.(N.33.d.7.3½.)

    To WULVERGHEM SWITCH. Teed in on 5 feet deep bury.
       (T.4.b.5.1.)   (ZR - D.3. Nos. 1 & 2).
    (Position to which Company of Battalion in Brigade
      Reserve moves from Kandahar Farm in case of attack)

    To BEAVER HALL.   Teed in on Air line 12.
       (N.31.a.9.5.)
       (Brigade Machine Gun Company.)

VISUAL SIGNALLING to Dugout on BUS FARM Ridge. (N.33.d.7.3½.)

    From Left Battalion Battle Headquarters.
    From S.P.4. (80 yards from Right Battalion Battle H.Q'S.)

VISUAL SIGNALLING to Divisional Visual Signalling Dugout
                  on Hill 63.

    From Trench D.2.

~~APPENDIX VI~~ (Continued).

From BRIGADE HEADQUARTERS, DRANOUTRE.

To BUS FARM DUGOUTS (N.33.d.2½.1½.)
    BRIGADE BATTLE HEADQUARTERS.

        6 Lines buried 5 feet deep.
        (Z.5. - ZR. Nos. 1.2.3.4.5 & 6.)

Airline.

No.12. D.5. cable on poles.
(This line is looped at M.36.d.10.4.
and enters DRANOUTRE by 2 seperate
routes).

To ARCHIE FARM.(N.32.b.1.4½.) (Battalion in Brigade Reserve.)	Airline No. 11. D.1. on poles and hedges.
To BEAVER HALL.(N.31.a.9.5.) (Brigade Machine Gun Company).	Teed in on Airline 11. Teed in on Airline 12.
To R.F.A. Brigade.	D.1. Air.
To Battalion in Divisional Reserve. DRANOUTRE.	D.1. Air.
To LOCREHOF FARM. (M.29.d.4.4.) (12th Sherwood Foresters)	D.1. Air.
To Brigade Transport.	D.5. on trees.
To 103rd Field Company R.E.	D.5. Air. Phone Pair.
To 17th Anti-Aircraft Battery.	D.5. Air.
Observation Post. KEMMEL.	D.5. Air. (Under patrol of Corps Signals).

APPENDIX VI. (Continued).

From Left Battalion Forward.

Battalion Headquarters -

    To Battle Headquarters.   2 wires buried 5 feet deep.
                                        D.5. cable in ditches.

    To Right Battalion of   Metallic pair
      Brigade on Left.

Battalion Battle Headquarters.-

    To R.E.FARM.(Coy. in
              support).   4 Lines buried 5 feet deep.
    To D.6.   2 Lines buried 5 feet deep.
    To D.5.R.   2 "   "   " " "
    To D.3.S.   2 "   "   " " "
    To D.4.S. (spare
              station).   Tee off 2 lines buried 5
                                feet deep.

The four offices in the front line are linked up by a lateral metallic pair of D.1. cable which is tested 3 times daily and only used in great emergency.
There is also a lateral metallic pair of D.1. cable between the right Company office of this Battalion and left company office of battalion on the right.

VISUAL SIGNALLING.

    To Battalion Headquarters from S.P.7.
                                         CHESHIRE LANE
                                         R.E.FARM.

From Right Battalion Forward.

Battalion Headquarters -

    To Battle Headquarters.   2 Lines buried 5 feet deep.
                                        D.5. cable in a stream.

    To S.P.4.   D.5. cable in a stream.

    To Left Battalion of   Armoured twin in a stream.
      Brigade on right.

Battalion Battle Headquarters -

    To S.P.4.   D.1. metallic pair in
                                disused trench.
    To D.2.   2 Lines buried 5 feet deep.
    To D.1.   2 Lines buried 5 feet deep.
    To C.3.   2 Lines buried 5 feet deep.

The three offices in the front line are linked up by a lateral metallic pair of D.1. cable which is tested 3 times daily and only used in great emergency.
There is also a lateral metallic pair of D.1. cable between the left company office of this battalion and right company office of battalion on the left.

VISUAL SIGNALLING.

    From D.2. to Divisional Visual Dugout on Hill 63.
    From D.2. to Battalion Headquarters.

Appendix 3

WAR DIARY or INTELLIGENCE SUMMARY. Army Form C. 2118.

of 4 Sec. 24th Signal Coy. R.E. June 1916.

Sheet 1

Place	Date	Hour	Summary of Events and Information	Remarks and references to Appendices
(B) T.21.d.5.2.	1.		Patrolled lines.	a.g.x
	2.		Patrolled lines, 11 & 12 dis and repaired	a.g.c
	3.		Patrolled lines, put new leading in battn. hqrs.	a.g.c
	4.		Buried cable into new dugout in right coy left Battn.	a.g.R
	5.		Finished Hq going up cable from new dugout in 142 (right coy dugout) to buried cable bracket Left hqrs.	a.g.R
	6.		Buried cables into new dugout in Hqrs end (reffy. coy. right battn.)	a.g.R
	7.		Buried lines from battn. hqrs to brigade battle hqrs. and also coy. left near RATION FARM. Continued burying cables from new dugout in right 142. Coy.	a.g.R
	8.		Patrolled lines.	
	9.		Aligned and fixed poles from Visual Station to Elletches Field.	a.g.
	10.		Patrolled lines. Buried piece of cable left uncovered on west Battn. lines to coy.	a.g.
	11.		Deepened portion of buried line from Brigade to Br. battn coy.	a.g.c

Army Form C. 2118.

WAR DIARY or INTELLIGENCE SUMMARY.

See 24 Signal Coy R.E.
June 1916.
Sheet II.

(Erase heading not required.)

Instructions regarding War Diaries and Intelligence Summaries are contained in F.S. Regs., Part II. and the Staff Manual respectively. Title pages will be prepared in manuscript.

Place	Date	Hour	Summary of Events and Information	Remarks and references to Appendices
(28) T.21.d.5.2.	12.		Deepened portion of cable buried from right batt. to right Coy. wires 2th station	a.S.R.
			HANBURY AVENUE.	a.S.R.
	13.		Joined through extra pair from left batt's Hqrs to left Coy.	
	14.		Patrolled lines.	a.S.R.
	15.		Patrolled lines. 2/Cpl. Orven A. to England on receiving a commission.	a.S.R.
	16.		Sent N.C.O. and 1 lineman to 150 Bde to learn lines. Made joint on buried cable leading to Strand M.G.	a.S.R.
	17.	12.30 a.m.	Enemy put H.E. gas main front, all telephone lines in brigade area left unused from from	
			left Battery to Imbro Terrace (Cayenne reserve). Quiet again at 3 a.m. Nos. 7 & 10 airlines did at 9.30 a.m.	
			Two linemen set out to repair 9 & 10, one killed and one wounded. 10 a.m. 1 & 2 airlines and 7 & 8 A.R.	
			lines broken 10.30 a.m. 9 & 10 repaired. 7 pm handed over to Sigs. 7th Australian Brigade	a.S.R.
ST. JANS CAPPEL	18		9.35 pm arrived at ST JANS CAPPEL having left three men with 7th Australian Brigade	
			maintain communication with unit from ST JANS CAPPEL separately. Handed to 50th Brigade	
			Reconnoitred lines in area about B Coy took over by 73 Bde.	a.S.R.
	19.		Sent two linemen to 150 Inf Bde to learn lines.	a.S.R.
	20.		Sent signal and orderlies to 150 Bde at 2pm. Left ST JANS CAPPEL at 3pm took over from S141	
LENNEL RIEL	21.		150 Bde at 10.30pm	a.S.R.
L.3) N.30.d.2.a.	22.		Laid new pair to 251st Bde R.F.A. Patrolled lines.	a.S.R.
			Patrolled lines.	a.S.R.
	23.		Remark:	a.S.R.

Army Form C. 2118.

WAR DIARY (4 Sec. 2nd Signal Coy. RE)
or
INTELLIGENCE SUMMARY. June 1916 Sheet II.

(Erase heading not required.)

Place	Date	Hour	Summary of Events and Information	Remarks and references to Appendices
KEMMEL HILL	24.		Remade joint at our Battle Hqs of Left Battalion. Found buried pair straight through from SP.10 to Brigade Hqs and thence on field cable pair direct through to F.19 (251st Bde R.F.A). Found through buried pair direct from Z.12 Brigade Hqrs to D.17 CH₂ leg of Right Battalion at Lindenhoek Crossroads to converge up 251 Bde R.F.A. with new battery Remade joints in junction box op right intermed. lines.	
	25.		Cat out test joint between brigade and Test Station. Remade joint and tested. Testers arranged that Lyft. 150 Pde could talk direct to Right Coy of 2nd Battalion from position which faster from his brigade made raids on German opposite our front. RE	
	26.		Laid line to T/M Battery from Battalion in Kemmel Shelters.	
	27.		Laid Tee If No.3 to Brigade Transport. Line to Dismounted Battalion at [illegible] cut and repaired. Reconnoitred route for new buried line from Right Battery to LINDENHOEK and DRANOUTRE.	
	28.		Patrolled lines. Finished burying cable from Zone ad SOMERFM BAHS out Z.12 on buried route from Right Battalion to DRANOUTRE Hqtrs exc't route via Jean [illegible]	
	29.		Laid pair from Left Battalion of VIERSTRAAT. Jct / Contact Right Batt. on E. of DRANOUTRE. Started burying cable from Right Battalion to DRANOUTRE.	
	30.			

COMMUNICATIONS of 73 Inf Bde

at (28) T.21.d.5.2.

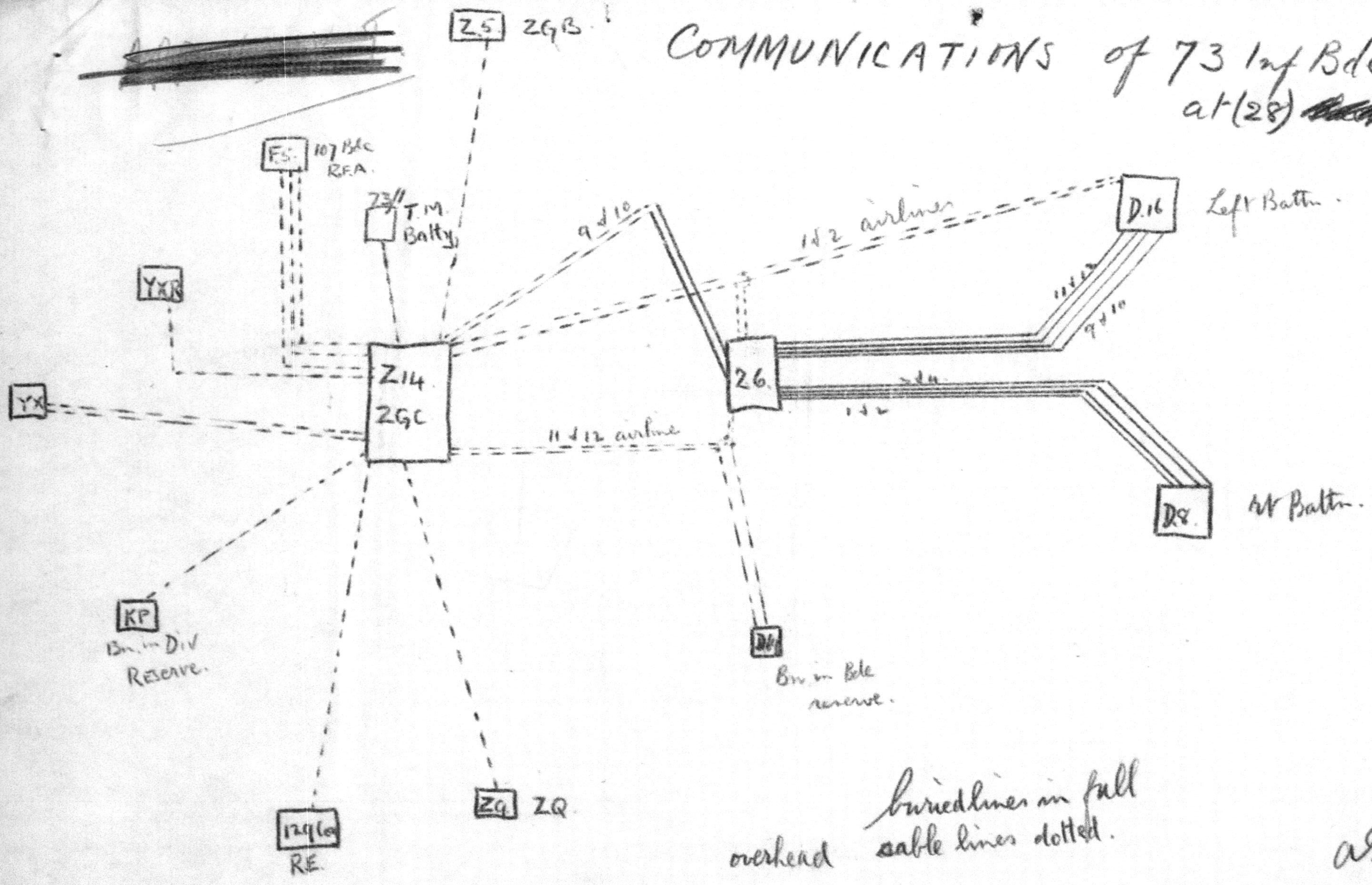
Z.5 ZGB
F.S. 107 Bde RFA
T.M. Batty
YXR
YX
Z14 ZGC
9 & 10
1 & 2 airlines
D.16 Left Battn.
11 & 12
9 & 10
26.
1 & 2
11 & 12 airline
D.8. Rt Battn.
KP Bn in Div Reserve.
Bn in Bde reserve.
129 Co RE.
ZQ ZQ

buried lines in full
overhead cable lines dotted.

A. G. Ritchie
Lt. RE.

30/5/16.

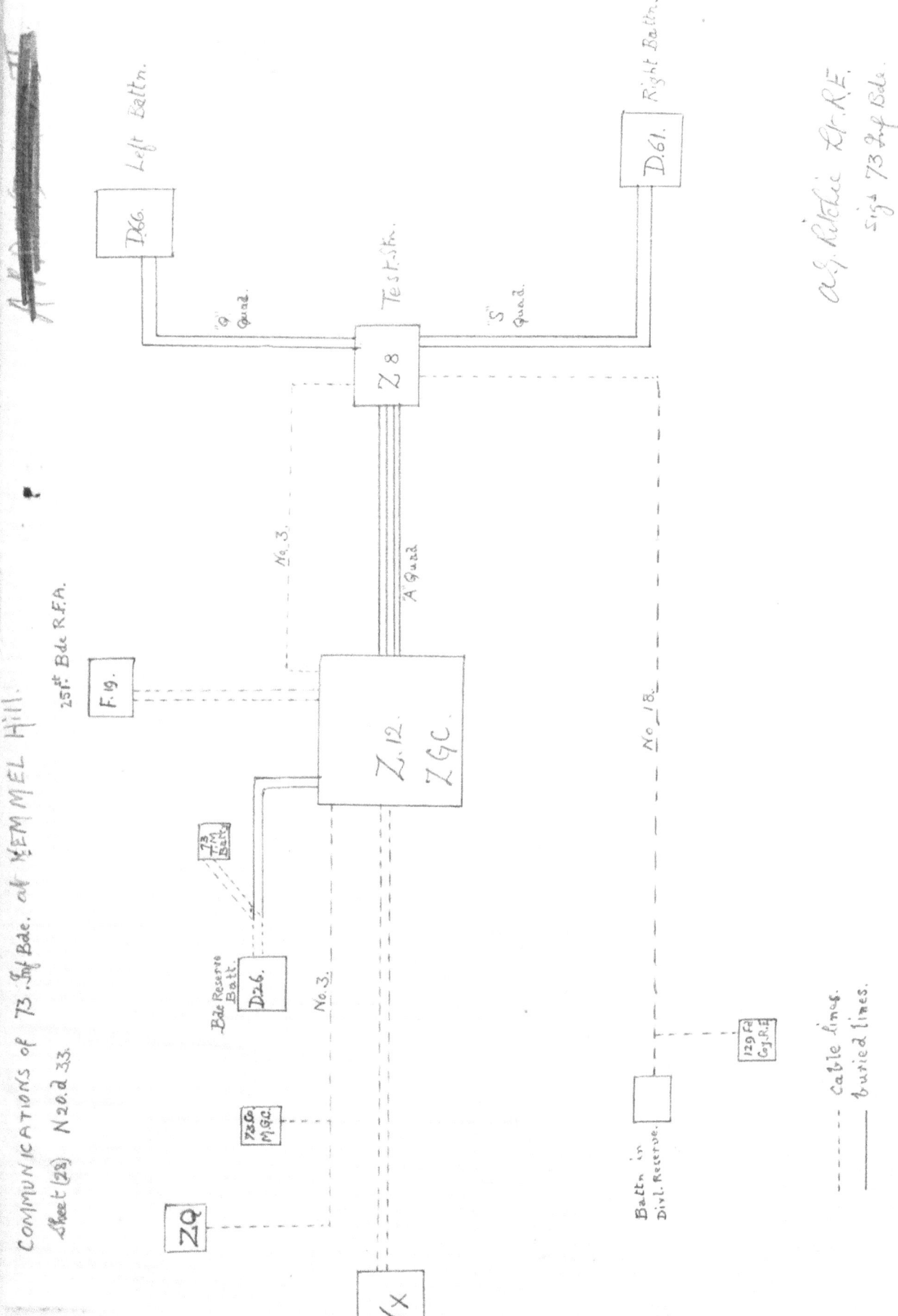

WAR DIARY
INTELLIGENCE SUMMARY

24th Division Signals
Vol 12

24th DIVISIONAL SIGNAL COMPANY, R.E.

Place	Date	Hour	Summary of Events and Information	Remarks
BAILLEUL	1/7/16		Taken over entirety of R.E. park and 7th ANZAC lines returned	
"	2/7/16		Commenced laying up new signal office at LOCRE	
"	3/7/16		Arthur Bung Stot at LOCRE. The two cable detachments start of WESTHOF FARM move to CONVENT LOCRE to the ground at the Convent	Bolton
"	4/7/16		New Signal Office at LOCRE. Some wires charging over from Pack Hut telephone to CONVENT at here. Just had from Signal Office arranged the CONVENT to new signal office. Infantry working parties on duty	
LOCRE	5/7/16		Work of laying up new signal office continued. Artillery and Inf. office being connected up to Exchange. Working parties 200 extra per day on laying cables. One HM 2 day and 300 to night.	

Army Form C. 2118.

WAR DIARY
or
INTELLIGENCE SUMMARY.
(Erase heading not required.)

Instructions regarding War Diaries and Intelligence Summaries are contained in F. S. Regs., Part II. and the Staff Manual respectively. Title pages will be prepared in manuscript.

Place	Date	Hour	Summary of Events and Information	Remarks and references to Appendices
LOCRE	19/10		*[illegible handwritten entries]*	

WAR DIARY
or
INTELLIGENCE SUMMARY

Army Form C. 2118.

Place	Date	Hour	Summary of Events and Information	Remarks and references to Appendices
BAILLEUL	1/4/16		Exchange R.E. Branch from our Div. into Eng. Branch. DRANOUTRE (7 to 46) Rond Elysee	
"			formerly used by company occupied by 73rd R.E. in addition to NEUVE EGLISE	
	12/4/16		Company to NEUVE EGLISE. BAILLEUL — WESTHOF now Westhof Fm	
			Camp used by...	
			BAILLEUL 6 to 40 NIEUWE EGLISE... 73rd R.E. Billet	
			BAILLEUL... DRANOUTRE	
			and LOCRE... LOCRE and CONVENT	
	13/4/16		BETHUNE...	
			LOCRE... KEMMEL...	
			NAC E (9th 73rd (13 46))	
			Sub FARM – LINDENHOEK	Ryanl
	14/4/16			
"			TO KEMMEL village	

Army Form C. 2118.

WAR DIARY
or
INTELLIGENCE SUMMARY.
(Erase heading not required.)

Instructions regarding War Diaries and Intelligence Summaries are contained in F. S. Regs., Part II. and the Staff Manual respectively. Title pages will be prepared in manuscript.

Place	Date	Hour	Summary of Events and Information	Remarks and references to Appendices
BAILEUL	15/7/16		LINDENHOEK noted over...	
	16/7/16			
LONG OFFICER	2/1/16			

2353 Wt. W3544/1454 700,000 5/15 D. D. & L. A.D.S.S. Forms/C 2118.

WAR DIARY
or
INTELLIGENCE SUMMARY

(Erase heading not required.)

Army Form C. 2118.

Place	Date	Hour	Summary of Events and Information	Remarks and references to Appendices
ST JANS CAPPEL	22/7/16 to 24/7/16		entrainment. Usual apathy cleared, commenced for taking up new equipment and turning out new men. Settled personnel turned in setting up of infants etc. General reviewing of all equipment, stores and equipment.	
	25/7/16		Company marched from ST JANS CAPPEL 12.30 pm to ST JANS CAPPEL STN 1.30 pm and entrained in ½ hour.	
			Entrained via BAILLEUL STN HAZEBROUCK — LILLERS — DOULLENS — AMIENS to LONGUEAU STN arriving there 1.15 am 26-7-16.	
			Army detained, travelled by march out to CAVILLON via AMIENS and PONT DE METZ. Halted 2 hours at latter place for breakfast. Arrived CAVILLON 11.30 am. Communication established with brigade and utility.	
CAVILLON	26/7/16			
	27/7/16 28/7/16 29/7/16		Company engaged in changing up in and getting usual equipment, schemes work. Brigades carried out kind out applied training exercises round CAVILLON.	

WAR DIARY
INTELLIGENCE SUMMARY

Army Form C. 2118.

Place	Date	Hour	Summary of Events and Information	Remarks and references to Appendices
CAVILLON	30/7/16		Another travel scheme brought into force in the morning and afternoon. The company proceeded that morning to CAVILLON.	
CORBIE	31/7/16	11-20 a.m (30-7-16)	and proceeded to CORBIE on AMIENS arriving at 11 am (31-7-16) and billeted at CORBIE. 12 men in the 1st Corps Signal Office. Communications established with Bdes and artillery.	

Army Form C. 2118.

WAR DIARY
or
INTELLIGENCE SUMMARY.
(Erase heading not required.)

24th DIVISIONAL SIGNAL COMPANY, R.E.

No. .... Date ....

Appendix No I

No 1 Section

Place	Date	Hour	Summary of Events and Information	Remarks and references to Appendices
DRANOUTRE	JULY 1916			
	1		Sigr ZQ relieved earlier.	
	2-3	night	Sigr ZGB 3.30 PM. Bus FM relieved Sigr ZQ. Work continued on trench begun by Sigr ZGC (where R ln became L) from our Lm Htrs, NEWPORT DUGOUTS, back towards BUS FM — LINDENHOEK road to meet line being dug from DRANOUTRE, over S. slope of KEMMEL hill, towards Fauw road. 12 prs put in. Work did till night of	
	6-7		when end of new leading track was reached, when digging began from above mentioned road towards fwd end of cable. Then line was put through on	
	7		Work then began fwd from a point about 100° WNW of NEWPORT DUGOUTS heading for FM D'ITOINE (N29 C19) & got about 250° to lay box hedge NNE of dugouts. Small party (12-20) worked on back part of line near the road finishing 6ft	
	9-14		On 11th DRANOUTRE was shelled with 11 rounds of 5.9" one of which dropped somewhere near to Yx for a short time	Hostile artillery 2/7/18

Army Form C. 2118.

WAR DIARY
or
INTELLIGENCE SUMMARY
(Erase heading not required)

Place	Date	Hour	Summary of Events and Information	Remarks and references to Appendices
DRANOUTRE	JULY 15–18		Work ctd. forward on trench from NEWPORT DUGOUTS going about due N from Iex hedge (see index 7th inst) & crossing REGENT ST just short of SPY FM (COESTEKER); thence eastwards (put on N. side of R. St.) line had got 600–700x when on	
	19		Bde was relieved by 151 I.B. Their sap had come up early & went over all lines which were handed over O/C above 1 pm. 17 I.B. to LOCRE. Casualties nil.	
	20		Section resting & refitting.	
	21		Bde moved to new area on BAILLEUL–METEREN ROAD. (square X 17 shurr7).	
	22–23		Section inspected. All equipt, rifles, gasmasks, haversacks & refitted	
	24–25		Left 1 AM. entrained at BAILLEUL, dep 10.20 AM. arr LONGUEAU nr AMIENS 7.30 PM. marched through AMIENS westward, halting just outside for tea 9.30 PM. March ctd 10.30 & Section arrived REINCOURT, about 18 miles from LONGUEAU, at 5.30 AM. Rested for rest of day.	

WAR DIARY
or
INTELLIGENCE SUMMARY.
(Erase heading not required.)

Army Form C. 2118.

Place	Date	Hour	Summary of Events and Information	Remarks and references to Appendices
RIENCOURT	JULY 26-30		Entirely given to visual ai; horn 9-12:30 scheme am 2-4 p.m. Lewis reading. 9-10 pm Lamp reading. Rifles & p.o. Which inspected & some minor deficiencies made up.	
	31		Left 6:30, & marched to PICQUIGNY. Entraining there. Left 10:30 am. Train through AMIENS & detrained at MERICOURT-L'ABBAYE. rested the first hour past, & then marched to BOIS des TAILLES on BRAY S/S road.	

WAR DIARY or INTELLIGENCE SUMMARY

Army Form C.-2118.

No 3 Section
24th Div Sig Co, R.E.
Appendix No II

Place	Date	Hour	Summary of Events and Information	Remarks and references to Appendices
BRANDHOEK	1/7/16		Dranoutre shelled 8.45 am and 3 pm. Handed over to Sigs 17 & 18 3.30 pm and repaired at their old office at LOCRE at the same hour.	GW
	2/7/16		(System of communication handed over unaltered)	GW
LOCRE	3/7/16		Overhauled and repaired stores. Regimental signallers arrived to sent on DE KLERK for overhauling.	GW
"	4/7/16		Buried lines from Locre Convent Messhouse unfinished. New line from Brigade to Kemmel camp.	GW
"	5/7/16		Forgiveto office but Tee set made	
"	6/7/16		Overhauled Buzzer instruments.	S.7.16
"	7/7/16		(continued) work on convent – Kemmel Berg	S.7.16
"	8/7/16		Putting in Test Box on Berry	S.7.16
"	9/7/16		(continued) work on Test box.	S.7.16
"	10/7/16		Relieved 2nd Australian Bde & 7th Australian Bde at 4 pm along office at LOCRE at 6 pm – QUEENS D16/N9(14) N STAFFS D8 (result) E SURREYS D6 9(Regt Hs) in line. R.M. KENT in reserve in KORTE PIP HUTS –	S.7.16
Englebmeer	9/7/16		Setting lines – trying to put a pair through in being to PETIT PLOEG MUNQUE. Overhauling existing communications	S.7.16
	10/7/16			S.7.16
	11/7/16		Found pair in Pk Bury that could not get communications over Stinking farm & 25 Surveys topped Stinking farm to Battalion. Rd Bde. being to get communications over Stinking farm	S.7.16

Army Form C. 2118.

WAR DIARY
or
INTELLIGENCE SUMMARY
(Erase heading not required.)

Instructions regarding War Diaries and Intelligence Summaries are contained in F.S. Regs., Part II. and the Staff Manual respectively. Title Pages will be prepared in manuscript.

Place	Date	Hour	Summary of Events and Information	Remarks and references to Appendices
English 2	2.7.16		Rain in P.M. bury joined up to fosse on French to Arty Dugout - pair	S.7.H.
"	13.7.16		D' lain from dugout to RED LODGE - D69. giving good results	S.7.H.
			Laid pair to 13 JB A 9 - 2 CC.	S.7.H.
"	14.7.16		Buried 2 pairs from end of P.M. bury to Sig office - pair to D69.	S.7.H.
			1 pair 629. going a good line to Theo Bae.	
"	15.2.16		cutting out spare lines from German pole at Sig office -	S.7.H.
			Repaired office	
"	16.7.16		7.9 - 106 Bought A - moved anti position close to English Farm - Laid	S.3.H.
			pair to Them office	S.7.H.
"	17.7.16		Bee Visual dugout moved and lamp positions verified	S.7.H.
"	18.7.16		Overhauling and cutting out nonworking wires round office	S.7.H.
"	19.7.16		Inst Bae on the lines in this area	S.7.H.
"			Instructing Linemen from 59th DB Linemen - Relieved by Sig Sgt	
"	20.7.16		Continued instruction of 59 WB Linemen - Relieved by Sig Sgt	S.7.H.
			O.B. at 4 p.m. Moved to Mont. an Cats office opened at 6 p.m	
Mont An	21.7.16		Commission to 9th by Dullophone. 30 mins to Balun. all communication	S.7.H.
Cats			to DR	
			Overhauling stores and training in Visual Signalling	S.7.H.
"	22.7.16		Training in Visual Signalling (continued)	S.7.H.

WAR DIARY
or
INTELLIGENCE SUMMARY

Army Form C. 2118.

(Erase heading not required.)

Place	Date	Hour	Summary of Events and Information	Remarks and references to Appendices
Mol. Mr. Cat.	23.7.16		(Continued) training in visual signalling	S.7.H.
	26.7.16		Moved off from Mol-de-Cab at 1.30am proceeding to BAILLEUL station entraining there for LONGUEAU 2 miles SE of AMIENS arriving there at 8pm. moving off from the station at 8.45pm en route to LISSY. Stopped for night at DREUIL VRAMPENS, horses being led forward.	S.7.H.
	27.7.16		Moved off at 8 a.m. arriving at new HQ at 12.30 pm at LISSY (less horses) on CHATEAU at LISSY at 12.30 am. Establishing communication with GX. by DUE phone.	S.7.H.
LISSY.	28.7.16		Training in visual signalling	S.7.H.
	27.7.16		Continued training in visual signalling.	S.7.H.
"	28.7.16		Training - Visual Scheme with Signals Yt.	S.7.H.
"	29.7.16		Training - Visual scheme with Divisional Signals	S.7.H.
"	30.7.16		Training - Visual scheme with Divisional Signals	S.7.H.
"	31.7.16		Left LISSY at 10am marching to AILLY sur SOMME entraining there at 6pm for MERICOURT arriving (+ MORLANCOURT) marching to MORLANCOURT arriving at 9.30pm S.7. McKenzie 2/Lt att 6pm for MERICOURT. comd. LYX na YCER. 1/c Sigd 7A YS	

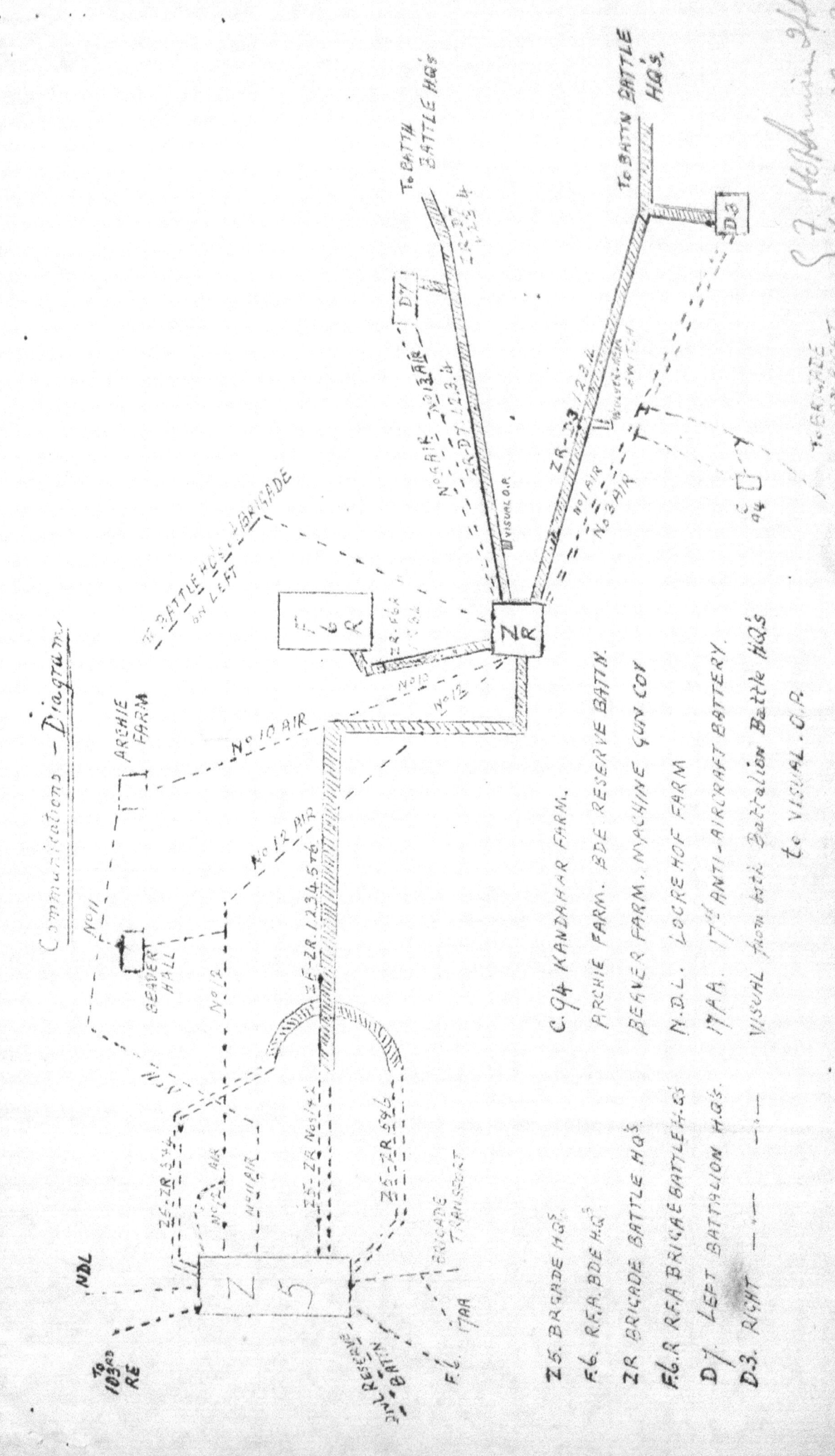

Appendix No. III
July 1916
Sheet - I

M.A.H. Mutton (?)

WAR DIARY or INTELLIGENCE SUMMARY

Army Form C. 2118.

24th DIVISIONAL SIGNAL COMPANY, R.E.

Place	Date	Hour	Summary of Events and Information	Remarks and references to Appendices
KENNEL HILL Sheet 28 M.20.d.33	1.		Buried cable with working party of 130 men and 2 carts from Newport Dugout to DRANOUTRE. Telephonic communication as in Appendix I. NEWPORT DUGOUTS taken over by 1st & 9th R.B.	
	2.		Continued burying cable from NEWPORT DUGOUTS with working party of 200 men. Erected temporary Bn. train to FORT SASKATCHEWAN from Bn. Battalion H.Qrs. at LA POLKA. Left position & moved to FORT SASKATCHEWAN. R/S.L.R. batt. H.Qrs. at LA POLKA.	S.M. A.P. ?
	3.		Patrolled lines.	A.P.
	4.		Patrolled lines. Started burying route of 12 pairs from FORT SASKATCHEWAN forward	A.P.
	5.		Continued with working party of 200 men. Burying forward from SASKATCHEWAN	N.C.
	6.		Continued burying cable forward from FORT SASKATCHEWAN with working party 200 men	B.G.R.
	7.		Patrolled lines.	
	8.		Put through airline No 18 from 73 Coy M.G.C. to LOCRE. Sent N.C.O's men & officers to over Wire and killed. Army Signals 72 Bde.	
	9.		Moved to LOCRE. 12.30 am. Airline handed over to Signals 150 & 151st.	A.P.
	10.		Arranged direct communication between front line and 150 Bde H.Qrs. at N20d 39. Examined lines.	
	11.		Sent 12 men at 3 pm. to new H.Qrs. Put through pair from end of ALOUETTE buried route to new H.Qrs. Put through line from new H.Qrs. to BULFORD CAMP	
T.21.d.2.10	12.		Moved at 9.30 am from LOCRE to T.21.d.2.10. Picked up signal cable pair from 17?/2nd R.E.G. Troops. Bulford Camp line laid in to 73 Coy M.G.C. Two new frameworks from T.F. Signals & ...	
	13.		Fault on pair to 24 Div found and corrected. Patrolled ...	A.P.
	14.		Put through pair to battalion and JRENOTRE. Laid in pair from BULFORD to M.R.W. Coy of 72 Sussex Rgt.	
	15.		Laid pair to end of ALOUETTE BURIED ROUTE and put through another pair to DUG (right H.Qr.)	

Army Form C. 2118.

Sheet II

WAR DIARY
or
INTELLIGENCE SUMMARY.
(Erase heading not required.)

Instructions regarding War Diaries and Intelligence Summaries are contained in F.S. Regs., Part II and the Staff Manual respectively. Title pages will be prepared in manuscript.

Place	Date	Hour	Summary of Events and Information	Remarks and references to Appendices
T.21A 2.10	16		Patrolled lines.	afr
	17		Laid pair to TEST. Point just West of NEUVE-EGLISE — ROMARIN ROAD on the WESTHOF — KEMMEL buried route. And joined the pair through to the Almette buried route and D.16.	afr
	18		Battalion jamming buzzer in trench D.3.	afr
	19		Installed jamming buzzer in trench C.2.	afr
	20		Handed over to Signals 161st Bde. and moved at 7pm to THIEUSHOUCK	afr
THIEUSHOUCK	21		Maintained Communication by orderly.	afr
	22		Section inspected by O.C. Signal Coy. Watched demonstration of liaison between infantry and aircraft	afr
	23		Practised visual signalling with shutters.	
	24		Passed 8 a.m. examined at GODEWAERSVELDE at 8:40 a.m. Reached SALEUX 8:45 p.m. marched to MOLLIENS-VIDAME.	afr
MOLLIENS-VIDAME	25		Arrived at MOLLIENS-VIDAME at 2 a.m. Maintained communication by orderly with units of the brigade	afr
	26		129 Fuery Bde, 73 Field Ambl and 12 Sherwood Foresters. Established visual communication with 96 Royal Sussex Brigade section and 95 Sussex and proving one transmitting station.	afr
	27		Maintained visual communication and gt Sussex. practise message sending and strength.	afr
	28		Visual Scheme with 24 Div Signals, 72 Bde, signallers of 7 Northumptons and 13 Middlesex	afr
	29		Visual scheme with Div. Signals and 72 Bde. Practised with Lieut. Raynor from T.E.	afr
	30		Visual scheme with Div Signals. Maintain platoon of section and hygiene preceded by road at 4pm	afr
	31		Dismounted man provided by Kan. to YAUX-SUR-SOMME arriving there at 7pm. Mounted portion of section marched to VAUX at 5pm.	

A.J. Wilkes Lt. R.E.

2353 Wt. W2344/1454 709,000 5/15 D. D. & L. A.D.S.S./Forms/C. 2118.

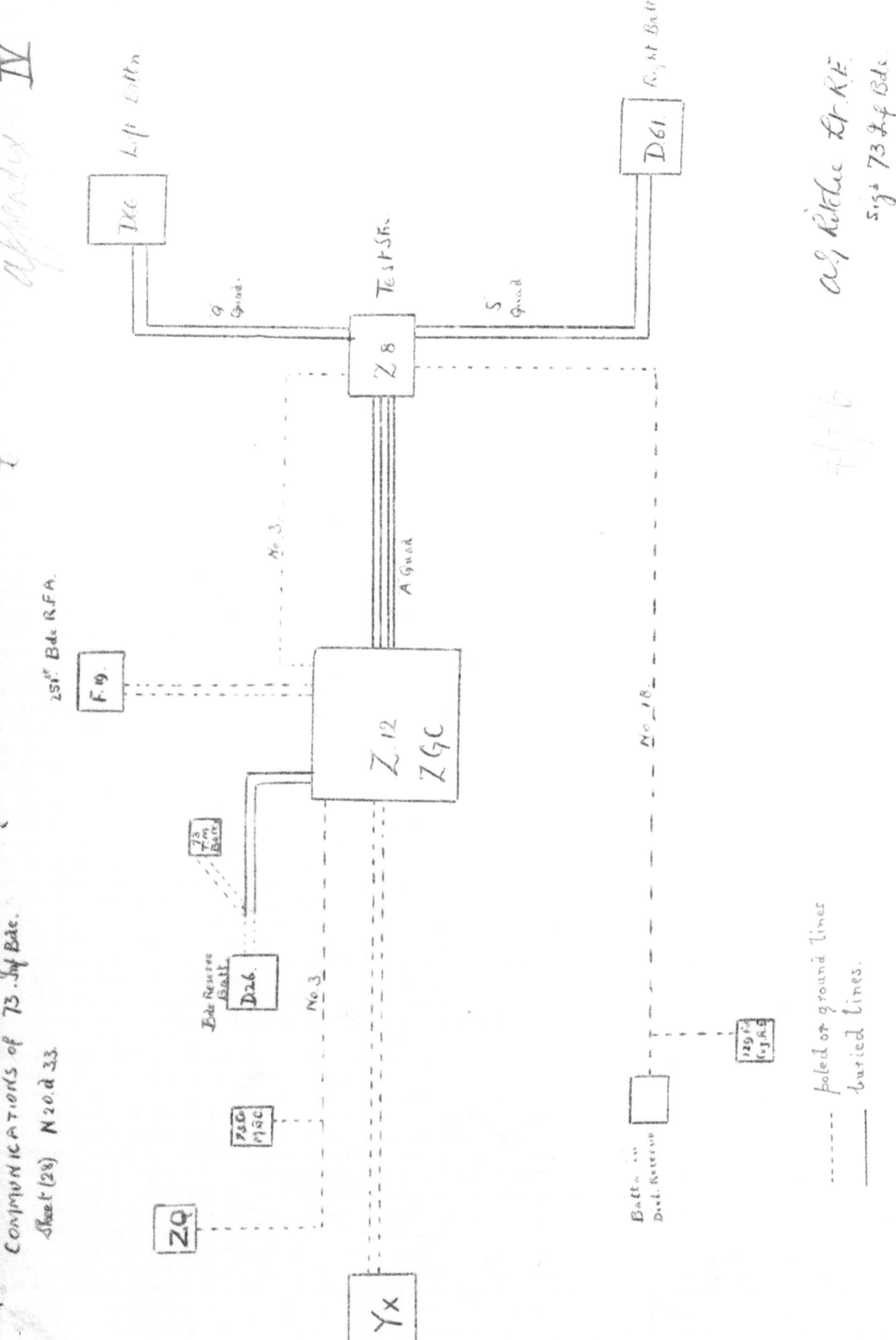

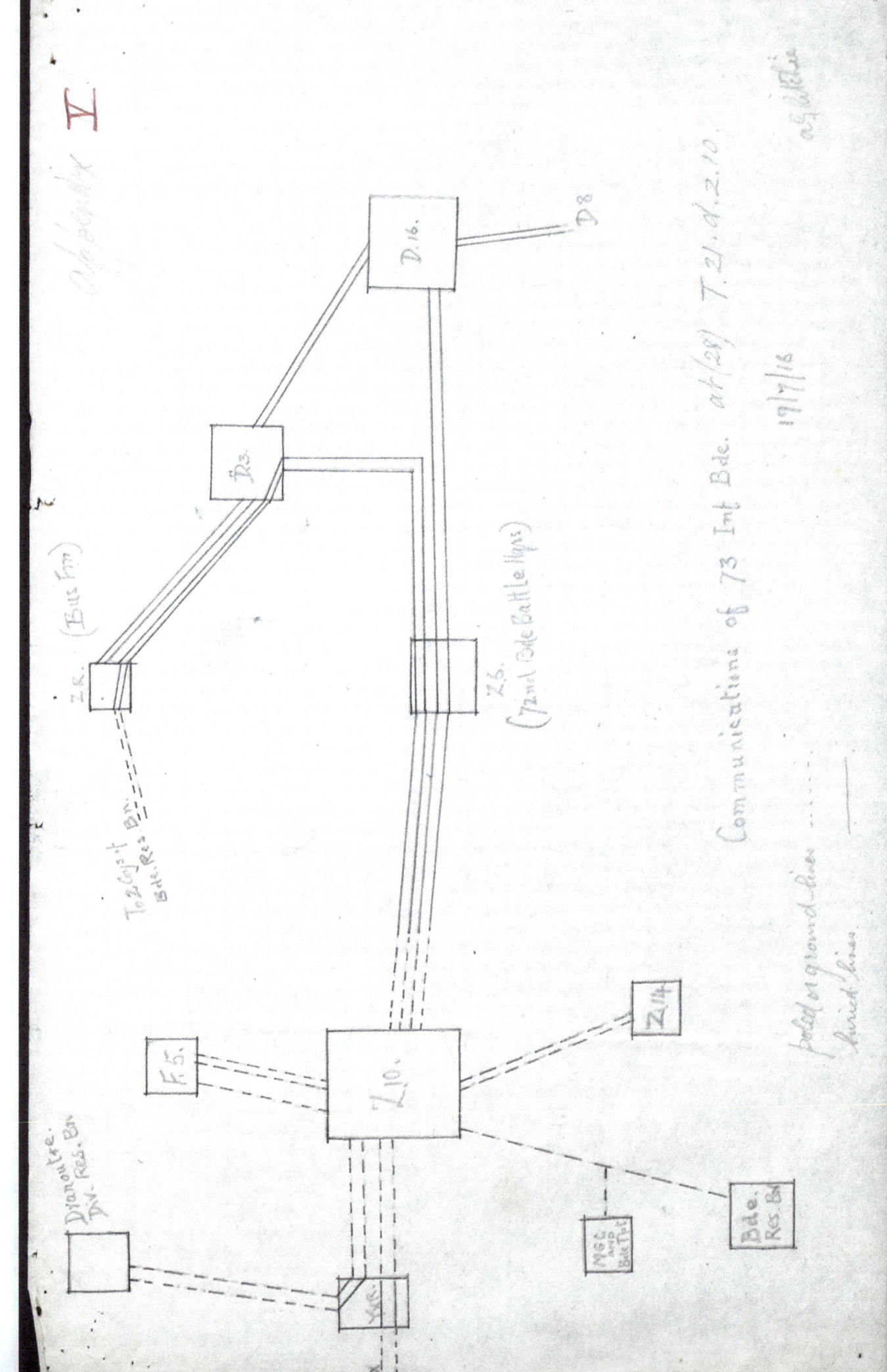

24th Divisional Engineers

24th DIVISION SIGNAL COMPANY R. E.

AUGUST 1916

Headquarters
24th Division

Herewith the War Diary of this company for August 1916.

R S Taylor.
Capt
OC Signals, 24th Division

> 24th DIVISIONAL
> SIGNAL COMPANY,
> R.E.
> 11-9-16.

forwarded to
Q 24th
5/16
R M M...
Capt

Army Form C. 2118.

Signals

WAR DIARY
or
INTELLIGENCE SUMMARY.
(Erase heading not required.)

VOL 13

Place	Date	Hour	Summary of Events and Information	Remarks and references to Appendices
	August 1916		24th Divisional Signal Coy	
CORBIE	1/8/16		Company still had charge of Signal Communication to the ... CITADEL signals relief made at 11am	M. Murphy Capt
CORBIE	2/8/16	3pm	Signal ... CITADEL in early ... moved to CITADEL ... march ... CITADEL 11pm	
CITADEL. 3/8/16 (F.21.a.8.8 BRAY - FRICOURT road)			H for company moved by march-route to FORKED TREE (L.2.a.8.8. BRAY - ALBERT road) arriving ... via FORKED TREE ...	

WAR DIARY
INTELLIGENCE SUMMARY

Army Form C. 2118.

(Erase heading not required.)

Place	Date	Hour	Summary of Events and Information	Remarks and references to Appendices
FORKED TREE	4/9/16		Visual camps commenced erected and visual signalling classes re-commenced	
"	5/9/16		Visual training continued. Permanent airline erected from CITADEL to Othonne in place of a very bad D5 line.	
"	6/9/16		CITADEL – FORKED TREE line repaired in places where badly worn. Visual signalling continued in camp.	
"	7/9/16		Party of 8 N.C.O.s & 10 Linemen sent to reconnoitre 2nd Division lines. CITADEL – Othonne line continued to Bronne Town.	
"	8/9/16	7.15 am	Company marched by march route to CITADEL to relieve 2nd Division Signals. Parties sent out during morning to take over 2nd Division lines. HQ at MINDEN POST exchange at CARNOY and COPSE B, and visual station near COPSE B. 6pm that cancelled and visual parties return to CITADEL	

WAR DIARY
INTELLIGENCE SUMMARY

Army Form C. 2118.

(Erase heading not required.)

Place	Date	Hour	Summary of Events and Information	Remarks and references to Appendices
CITADEL	9/8/16		Parties of Signers of infantry drummers reported starting sent out to BILLON COPSE to view 55th Division front. Signals during afternoon man stps were run out and relief parties laid on to receive incoming Signals at MINDEN POST ANNOY COPSE 3	
"	10/8/16		10 hrs. Relief of 2nd Division completed. Battn. HQ. with Sec. A. at CITADEL. Company HQ. with Sec. B. at MINDEN POST.	
"	11/8/16		and Signal office between the 2 points	
"	12/8/16		Work on lines between Bn. HQ. and companies continued. Visual stn. (flags) at CARNOY	
"	13/8/16		to HQ 5th Div (D.H.Q.)	
"	14/8/16		Two cable lines TRONES (CRATERS)	

WAR DIARY

INTELLIGENCE SUMMARY

Army Form C. 2118.

Place	Date	Hour	Summary of Events and Information	Remarks and references to Appendices
CITADEL	15/8/16		Commenced laying approved tram from 17th FD to new position selected for their HQ, i.e. DUMMY TRENCH, halfway between BERNAFAY and TRONES wood. Lorries laid by round about route via GUN PITS to avoid shelled area.	
"	16/8/16		Heavy rain in the C.T's intact, continued and completed. Single D5 line also run by same route.	
"	17/8/16		Anchored junction from MINDEN POST to pick up armoured pair and D5 line. Lateral line built between DUMMY TRENCH and BRIQUETERIE via LEINSTER ALLEY. Single line south from CRATERS to BRIQUETERIE via MONTAUBAN. During the day Sapper (73rd) Lineman slightly wounded and one R.S.M. Lineman with 17th FD badly wounded.	Capt [initials]
"	18/8/16		Test of lateral line between (?) taken up to GUN PITS. Sgt. SEVILLE and 4 men sent to GUN PITS to act as Test Station. NCO and 4 men (SHERWOOD FORESTERS) sent to GUN PITS to establish visual between 17th FD and GUN PITS	

Army Form C. 2118.

WAR DIARY
or
INTELLIGENCE SUMMARY.
(Erase heading not required.)

Instructions regarding War Diaries and Intelligence Summaries are contained in F. S. Regs., Part II. and the Staff Manual respectively. Title pages will be prepared in manuscript.

Place	Date	Hour	Summary of Events and Information	Remarks and references to Appendices
CITADEL	18/8/16		Arrangements made to show a/c Rifle Bde HQ. and CORNISH ALLEY and 17th JB in DUMMY TRENCH. My several higher GS.IT Sec. No results obtained. Enemy owing to number of each circuits in use in neighbourhood. 24th Division reported W. and S. of GUILLEMONT and suspected of repairs. Fine to BLUE WOOD. Enemy locators made use of between BAZENTIN & BAQUETERIE in PERONNE AVENUE.	(A.W.W.F.)
"	19/8/16		Work on circuits carried on.	
"	20/8/16		— ditto —	
"	21/8/16		Loop line (DC) " DUMMY TRENCH obtained a green wire.	
"	22/8/16		GUN PITS. Distances and information (13th JD) slightly altered. Wires near CITADEL	

WAR DIARY
INTELLIGENCE SUMMARY

(Erase heading not required.)

Place	Date	Hour	Summary of Events and Information	Remarks and references to Appendices
CITADEL	23/6/16		7am. Company relieved by 20th Division Signals. Personnel at outskirts thought in and conducted by route march to FORKED TREE into camp previously supplied them.	
FORKED TREE	24/6/16		Company resting and cleaning up.	
	25/6/16		Company moved by route march to BUIRE (Sheet 62.D)	
BUIRE	26/6/16		[sketch map showing BUIRE, LANCRE, etc., ref. Sh. 62 D.29.c] Company resting, cleaning equipment, vehicles etc getting ready for the trenches.	
"	27/6/16		" " " " " "	
"	28/6/16		" " " " " "	
"	29/6/16		Preparations made for relieving 14th and 33rd Divisional Signal Coys.	
"	30/6/16		Relief parties sent to FRICOURT (Regt Hd) POMMIER REDOUBT (exchange) and MONTAUBAN (Brigade Station)	
"	31/7/16		10th our from 33rd and 14th Divisions at 10 am. Lines to FRICOURT set at 5:30 pm by Relief party moving one part of my party through. Relief finished from FRICOURT [illegible] Company moved to camp at E 11 central ALBERT–BRAY rd.	

LINES between INFANTRY BDES & Minden Post 24th Signals.
22nd August 1916.

G.Pts = Gun Pits.
PG = Carnoy Ex.
DT = Dummy Trench
BRIG = Briqueterie
TB = Talus Bois
CB = Copse B
YxR = 24th Sigs. Hd.

Army Form C. 2118.

WAR DIARY
or
INTELLIGENCE SUMMARY.

No. 2 Section   Appendix No 1.

Instructions regarding War Diaries and Intelligence Summaries are contained in F.S. Regs., Part II. and the Staff Manual respectively. Title pages will be prepared in manuscript.

Place	Date	Hour	Summary of Events and Information	Remarks and references to Appendices
SAND PIT E.18.d.5.3. (Sheet 62d France)	AUGUST 1916 1 – 7		Section doing visual training, morning and afternoon, using venetian shutter, Watson fan & helio. Lamps at night. Also practice with contact patrol aeroplane, which were not very successful. Deficiencies in stores made good.	SS 7/1 17.1.18.
	8		Section moved up to a hyp "near" CRATERS" in old German 2nd line at A3 Coy. (sheet 62 c)	Lloyd Jones
	9		Relieved Sig Lt 18 at A8 & 29 (62.c). Their lines up to BERNAFAY WOOD, via MONTAUBAN, had been reconnoitred 2 days before.	
	10 – 16		Lines patrolled & maintained by div linesmen as far as Rest Stn 1M at SE corner of MONTAUBAN and to stn at gun-pits S22 c 93 (57c) QAR which was shared with IM on L.I; & by one between 2 Rear Stns on to res tm Hqrs NW Corner of BERNAFAY WOOD. One rabbit-netting route from Bde to BERNAFAY, and heavily laddered route between QAR + IM held fairly well. One on from B.W practically hopeless at first as there were no trenches to speak of through TRONES WOOD and not much beyond. One with 1M in line at WATERLOT FM S.18 + 24 (57c) by runners, with

WAR DIARY
INTELLIGENCE SUMMARY.
(Erase heading not required.)

Army Form C. 2118.

Place	Date	Hour	Summary of Events and Information	Remarks and references to Appendices
"CRATERS" A8b 2.9. (b 2 c)	August 16th	10-16 oct	relay post at QAR. Also by pigeons, which gave very fair times. Visual tried from W.Fm to Stn at S27, 22 and to QAR, but no success, owing chiefly to haze & mist. Wires from a point a little SE of MONTAUBAN on the road, worked on to bde; also from Bde to. adv din stn in OXFORD COPSE, & to 34 FA Bde. a little N of that on ridge overlooking CARNOY & W of it. Q office at CARNOY (BRICK ALLEY) with direct line from Bde. & working to Div through trenches in CARNOY. Signal officer moved to hyper & lyddite dugouts + line properly laid in etc. Line run to QAR on NW side of MONTAUBAN which held very well. A soldered GI line was run from Res Bn through TRONES WOOD to night coy & H in line via NEW TRENCH about 600' E of the wood & then up trench T 27 to WATERLOT Fm. This last bit held fairly well, left otherwise was practically always dis owing to constant shelling of TRONES ws.	
	17/8/16	Nft	Bde and hqs in DUMMY TRENCH about S23 & B4 nearly finished. Div lines run in from LONGUEVAL ALLEY & Line from QAR but not	

WAR DIARY of INTELLIGENCE SUMMARY.

Army Form C. 2118.

Place	Date	Hour	Summary of Events and Information	Remarks and references to Appendices
DUMMY TRENCH	August 1916 17th		14 Div trench numbering NG through S23c.18 (where a T trench was dug on nyt 15/16) to "A" line S23c.65 where lines taken down trench, across LONGUEVAL ALLEY & into Hqrs.) to S23c.16 where lines turned R into CT from CRUCIFIX ALLEY to LONGUEVAL ALLEY. Popped into E. side of trench, along trench, across L.A at S.18 C.31 & into visual dugout about 70x beyond. An armoured gun was turned, of which 1 r.am straight through, & the other from QAR to the T. down to DUMMY TRENCH & back on to dugout in WATERLOT Fm, about 5 men from tn by t. the nearest point to which line could be efficiently maintained. O.D. Twin warren toward along DUMMY TRENCH, forming LEINSTER AV just W of TRONES WD at S23d.53, through the new trench in the wood & up to R in hqrs at junction of NEW TR & CORNISH ALLEY about S24c.96. An armoured tn was run from here N up NEW TR & the CT to the t tn SE of W.Fm about S24b.26	
	18		This was all complete by 10am 18th when Bde Hq moved in	

WAR DIARY
or
INTELLIGENCE SUMMARY.
(Erase heading not required.)

Army Form C. 2118.

Place	Date	Hour	Summary of Events and Information	Remarks and references to Appendices
DUMMY TRENCH	AUGUST 1916 18		All lines held up to zero time for our attack & trenches as well, speaking to eat on heavy junk food.	
	18/19 M		time cut up by working parties, but OK by about 4 am 19th. Lateral to Brigstone 72, 73, 75 is thrown in HUNTER AV only.	
	21		di once, on 19th. Line that duty shell for 10 minutes during further attack on 21st. Line to dugout in W. Fm held very well (not not needed, as I was always through via the R.m.	
	22		Relieved by Sig 61 I.B. Bde to HAPPY VALLEY, L3 central (b2A) Rel 25th waiting & refitting.	
	25		Bde moved to D12A & E7C (b2A) just So of AMIENS-ALBERT Rd.	
	26 + 30		Section resting & refitting. 28-31 course on South Inducation Sets at New Can Sir D4ouRS for Bde, Bn sig.	
	31		Bde moved to F8C57-(b2d) CASUALTIES 2 OR wounded SICK	

Army Form C. 2118.

24th DIVISIONAL SIGNAL COMPANY.

Instructions regarding War Diaries and Intelligence Summaries are contained in F.S. Regs., Part II. and the Staff Manual respectively. Title Pages will be prepared in manuscript.

WAR DIARY
or
INTELLIGENCE SUMMARY
(Erase heading not required.)

Appendix No 2 — War Diary No 2 Section

Place	Date	Hour	Summary of Events and Information	Remarks and references to Appendices
MORLANCOURT	1-8-16		Closed office at this place at 1 p.m. Moving to new H.Q. arriving 8-9 p.m.	S.J.R.
E.18.d.4.0	2-8-16		New position E.18.d.4.0 - Ref. map sheet 62D. Training in visual signalling	S.J.R.
"	3-8-16		Training in visual signalling	S.J.R.
"	4-8-16		Training in " "	S.J.R.
"	5-8-16		Training in " "	S.J.R.
"	6-8-16		Training in " "	S.J.R.
"	7-8-16		Training in " "	S.J.R.
"	8-8-16		Training in " "	S.J.R.
"	9-8-16		Training in " "	S.J.R.
"	10-8-16		Moved to new area. Posts H.Q. on Chalk Pit Cannery. A.9.c.8.8 Ref. map S.J.R. with advanced H.Q. at BRIQUETERIE in old German Regimental Battle H.Q. Dugouts. took over signals from 166 Inf Bde at 8 p.m. also stores at Sand pit a/-. 7 am - handing over to 186 Inf Bde. Two Battns in Line with H.Q. in SUNKEN ROAD - S.30.C. Ref 57.C. — GUSERE on Right. N. STAFFS in support at BRIQUETERIE. A.H. 6.9.M. Signal Office &c at Relay Post in trench at - A.6.a.43. - & S.J.R. Ex. Line by enemy shrapnel. Com- & com- munications to Battns. This system from R.J.R. at Post R.J.	S.J.R.

WAR DIARY
or
INTELLIGENCE SUMMARY

Army Form C. 2118.

War Diary N° 3 Section

Place	Date	Hour	Summary of Events and Information	Remarks and references to Appendices
CHALK PIT	11.8.16		Picked up lines forward from BRIDGEPIT to (such as S end of ROSEWOOD and got 2 working pairs, came to [illeg] extd by afternoon	S.7.A.
"	12.8.16		Laid pair D's aver 8m. ground from [illeg] TRAFALGAR & back to [illeg] 3 30 O.R.s opening signal station at [illeg] places at GROVE TOWN [illeg] [illeg] as the and connecting up at switchboard. [illeg] returns particularly heavy. Station of [illeg] [illeg] a [illeg] [illeg] [illeg] [illeg] [illeg] [illeg] No.1 and Relay No.1 [illeg] [illeg] [illeg] [illeg] [illeg] [illeg] [illeg] [illeg] to HQ at 6 a.m being [illeg] [illeg]. Commenced laying insulated armoured cable [illeg] relay point from RJR.	S.7.A.
"	13.8.16		Completed laddered row of 6 ins insulated should laying armoured cable route in to pr cable trench to Sunken Road Int. on end of row No.3 to [illeg] No.5 trench. Laying pair from mth cable & laddering.	S.7.A.
"	14.8.16		[illeg] [illeg] armoured cable I Relay [illeg] [illeg] [illeg] [illeg]	S.7.A.
"	15.8.16		[illeg] of armoured cable [illeg] [illeg] [illeg] [illeg] [illeg] all [illeg] [illeg] [illeg] [illeg]	S.7.A.
"	16.8.16		attack. 1 section of line down round [illeg] [illeg] [illeg] [illeg]. Bolton laying ladder from N°2 Relay to final 6 JVR and then to the Signal Office in Sunken road.	S.7.A.

WAR DIARY
or
INTELLIGENCE SUMMARY

Army Form C. 2118.

War Diary No 3 Section

Place	Date	Hour	Summary of Events and Information	Remarks and references to Appendices
BRIQUETERIE	17.9.16		All Coys paraded and opened when necessary to ensure and inform infantry when lodged south to advance with the front of Sunken Rd. Wounded at 4 yds intervals here. I.T Sgt maintained working at 'C' at both HQrs in company in No 5 Relay and report all through enemy bombardment of first our company trenches + then ag 1st line & relay. Visual & SS not necessary aux & switchboard in PB. Can be seen never from anywhere. Shells (western) would make necessary one hour & 3 ford Pelway. NFH 10 very bad damage and Coys had met batty. 1 throught headq'rs use to signals B,J,B at 4.30 am morning to ctd BM HQ at CHALK PIT moving to CRATERS A.2.d.5.2. at 12.30pm am on arrival 6 YK by one of Bath of morning	S.J.H. S.J.H. S.J.H.
CRATERS	19.9.16 20.9.16		Duty same. Became signals B.6 & two of Division became again. No 4 Section at A24.c.91. 3 relay posts established in LEINSTER AVENUE, one in TRONES line through LEINSTER AVENUE being relaible. Signals to B to land doubled and from Biggr. A24.c.91. WOOD and one at either edge of BERNAFAY WOOD.	S.J.H. S.J.H.

WAR DIARY or INTELLIGENCE SUMMARY

Army Form C. 2118.

(Erase heading not required.)

Place	Date	Hour	Summary of Events and Information	Remarks and references to Appendices

WAR DIARY
or
INTELLIGENCE SUMMARY

Army Form C. 2118.

War Diary. No 3 Section

(Erase heading not required.)

Place	Date	Hour	Summary of Events and Information	Remarks and references to Appendices
RIBEMONT.	31.9.16		Closed Sig office at 10.15 am. Bde moving to camp at Frécourt going on to POMIERES REDOUBT and taking over signals from Sig. 143rd Bde at 8pm. Communications to Battns via Relay Posts at M.T. (Montauban) 2 pairs to this from here to M.R. (Gunpits). 2 pairs and 2 loops to this office — from here to 2 F. 2 pairs to this office — from here to RT. Batt. Found lines and LB by trench tool. All these posts have numbers of runners in case wires go. L.B. having V.b. having also wires to M.T. Bde on Right comm. via M.T. — direct line to Bde on Right.	S.7.H. S.7.H.
POMIERES REDOUBT.	31.9.16		Overhauling forward lines and testing same.	S.7. Hoffmeister Lieutt. O/C Signals attd. Inf Bde.

WAR DIARY
INTELLIGENCE SUMMARY

Army Form C. 2118

No. H Section
24th Div Sig Co. R.E.
Appendix No. 2.
Sheet 1.

Place	Date	Hour	Summary of Events and Information	Remarks and references to Appendices
VAUX-SUR-SOMME.	1.		Maintained communication with 2 Limbers, 7 NORTHANTS, 129 Fd Coy RE, 17 Coy ASC, 24 Divl Supply Col, 73 Fd Amb and 73 Trench Mortar Battery by orderly, with 9th R Sussex and 13 Middlesex through 24 Div.	A.S.R.
	2.		Watched demonstration by No 9 Sqdn RFC of liaison between aeroplanes and infantry. Left VAUX at 5.20 pm. Arrived HAPPY VALLEY at 6 pm.	A.S.R.
HAPPY VALLEY. Sheet 62D. F27.C.28.	3.		Maintained communication with the units of the brigade by orderly.	A.S.R.
	4.		Scheme practicing communicating with two battalions from brigade by aeroplane and visual. Demonstration of an aeroplane communicating with two battalions in attack.	A.S.R.
	5.		Practised Visual Signalling.	
	6.		An aeroplane gave a demonstration with parties of Infantry representing two battalions in attack.	A.S.R.
	7.		Scheme communication being maintained between two battalions in the brigade by wire and visual.	A.S.R.
	8.		Moved at 2.30 pm to CITADEL AREA, Sheet 62D F22a.	A.S.R.
62D. F22a.	9.		Maintained communication with the units of the brigade by orderly. Went to the 166th & 24th Bde at TALUS BOISE to reconnoitre communication. Relief of 166 Bde by 73 Bde cancelled.	A.S.R.
	10.		Practised Visual.	A.S.R.

Army Form C. 2118.

WAR DIARY
or
INTELLIGENCE SUMMARY.
(Erase heading not required.)

Sheet. 2.

Place	Date	Hour	Summary of Events and Information	Remarks and references to Appendices
62D. F.22.a.	11.		Practiced visual, maintained communication by orderly.	A.S.R.
	12.		Practiced visual.	A.S.R.
	13.		Tested over communications of 72 Bde with a view to subsequent relief.	A.S.R
	14.			
	15.		Endeavour to reconnoitre line of 72 Bde.	A.S.R.
	16.		Left CITADEL AREA at 9pm to take over from Sigs 72 Bde. Relief orders cancelled returned to CITADEL at midnight.	A.S.R
	17.		Left F.22.a. at 3.30 p.m. ONE O.R. wounded.	A.S.R.
BRIQUETERIE.	18.		Took gp over Sigs 72.Bde. at 7am. During the attack on 18th Cable communication was maintained as far as No.2 Relay post and forward of that by Runner. Visual communication was used from the left of the objective to left Battalion Hqrs.	A.S.R.
	19.		Repaired lines to battalion hqrs. Cable laid from to left Battn hqrs from No.2. Relay post. 5pm line to left Batt dis. Communication from No.2 post forward by Runner. Front of night	A.S.R
			Batt. handed over to 35th Div. at midnight.	
	20.		Laid line via BERNAFAY WOOD on LEINSTER ALLEY to E edge of TROYES WOOD (S.24 C???) where personal forman RELAY POSTS till 21st. Moved to CRATERS A.8.b.29. Sigs.72.Bde established a RUNNER RELAY POST. Handed over to Sigs 72.Bde. at 4pm. leaving	A.S.R.
62.E. A.8.b.4p.	21.		maintained communication by orderly.	A.S.R.
	22.		Left CRATERS at noon for SANDPIT AREA 62d. E.24.a.88.	A.S.R.
62d. E.24.a.8a.	23.		maintained communication by orderly.	
	24.		Practiced visual.	A.S.R.
	25.		Moved at 5pm to E.18.b.	A.S.R.

WAR DIARY
INTELLIGENCE SUMMARY

Army Form C. 2118.

Sheet 3

(Erase heading not required)

Place	Date	Hour	Summary of Events and Information	Remarks and references to Appendices
62.D. E.16.6.	26		Maintained communication by visual.	OfR
	27		1 OR reinforcement joined.	OfR
	28		Practiced visual. Sent 2 ORs to assist in matter of newly fitted power buzzer and AMPLIFIER.	OfR
	29.		Sent up to reconnoitre communications of 98th Brigade.	
	30.		Moved at 5pm from E.16.b. arrived POZIERES REDOUBT 6pm. Took over from Sigs 98 Bde at 8pm. Communication as in APPENDIX #1. Wild Runner relay post and TEST STATION at 57C. S.2.d.6.5. and Test station at S.16.d.4.00. Lines to Battalion very weak from 2nd Test Station. Messages had to be transmitted.	OfR
POZIERES REDOUBT. 6.C. A.1.B.63.	31.		Established enemies' STATION in CHARLTON TRENCH and direct to Brigade. Line to Battalion died and repaired. Lines from 19th & 21st Test Station died 5pm, repaired 5.45pm. M.R.I. from Bde to No 1 Test Stn died 9am, repaired 11am, died 4·30pm, repaired 5·45pm.	OfR
				OfR & Sigs OfR

Communication handed over by
Sigs 98 Bde. to Sigs 73 Bde.
30/8/16.

- Support Batt.
- Right Battn
- Left Battn
- support Battn

Test Station
S.16.d.04.

Test Station
S.21.d.65.

MR1
Q1

73 Bde

Arty Test Stn.
72 Bde.
YXR

Aychluli ZONE

Royal Engineers

24th Division

24th DIVISIONAL SIGNAL COMPANY

SEPTEMBER 1916

WAR DIARY
INTELLIGENCE SUMMARY

Army Form C. 2118.

September 1916

Place	Date	Hour	Summary of Events and Information	Remarks and references to Appendices

48th Divisional Signal Company

E.11 central — 1/9/16. Communication maintained the whole time with Brigades by telegraph & telephone. Intermediate attempts notes being made when any faults on lines.

BRAY–ALBERT road.
2/9/16. — Ditto —
3/9/16. — Ditto —
4/9/16.
11h.55 a.m. Large C.R.E. left on this command route from BR⇥
ALBERT road ½ mile from them with 13th/18th Th heavy shell fire
YX to H.Q. of same
YX to C.O. right flank
1800 — Cable YX to G YXR there
was later referred during the Germans
but O.R. outside in collection

O/C 24th Signal Coy
A.G. Manning

WAR DIARY
or
INTELLIGENCE SUMMARY.

(Erase heading not required.)

Army Form C. 2118.

Place	Date	Hour	Summary of Events and Information	Remarks and references to Appendices
Ellicourt	5-7-16		Return to Duty & joined unit in field. Have had to give [up?] Car due to usual [?] fault caused by driving high speed [?] replaced by [?] Ford Car.	
"	6-7-16	7am	[?] movement of 33rd Division [?] met by march route DERNANCOURT – MEAULTE – BONNAY – CORBIE & LONGPRÉ.	
LONGPRÉ	7-7-16		Company [?] FLIXECOURT & AILLY LE HAUT CLOCHER [?] [?] [?] 2-6 pm. [?] 41st Division taken over [?] School and ammunition obtained and [?] [?] KONG and moved [?] [?] [?] [?] [?] [?] [?] [?] [?] [?] [?] [?] going when [?] [?] [?] AILLY LE HAUT CLOCHER in [?] [?] [?] [?]	

Army Form C. 2118.

WAR DIARY
or
INTELLIGENCE SUMMARY.
(Erase heading not required.)

Place	Date	Hour	Summary of Events and Information	Remarks and references to Appendices
AILLY LE HAUT CLOCHER (Somme)	8th		Company in rest. General Signal Company training, comparing infantry and heavy and light artillery. All the [illegible] instruction in [illegible] reading. Other [illegible] [illegible] [illegible] at the [illegible]. A Sergeant signalling school was instituted for the most intelligent N.C.O.'s in the Company. During the afternoon I made an expedition by motor to the environs of AILLY [illegible] [illegible] [illegible] [illegible] infantry of about 40 men to AULT and ST-VALERY SUR-SOMME for a period of two [illegible].	
	10th	7-8 am	[illegible] by motor [illegible] AILLY LE HAUT CLOCHER and LONG to LONGPRÉ STN for entrainment. 10 am [illegible] [illegible] small [illegible] [illegible] and [illegible] instruments and staff [illegible] [illegible] [illegible] [illegible] cyclists [illegible] [illegible] [illegible] [illegible] [illegible] [illegible] cycles by road to	A Shinning [illegible] Signal [illegible]
BRAY				

WAR DIARY
or
INTELLIGENCE SUMMARY.

Army Form C. 2118.

(Erase heading not required.)

Place	Date	Hour	Summary of Events and Information	Remarks and references to Appendices
LONGPRÉ STN	19th		Company arrived LONGPRÉ at 2:00 am from [illegible] [illegible] and [illegible] from [illegible] Being relieved [illegible] only set off for the whole day. Half formed and detailed via FLIXECOURT — DOULLENS — [illegible] to FOUQUEREUIL STN via BETHUNE. Some slight [illegible] and [illegible] en route. 1:45 am arrived [illegible] to BRUAY. Ready to move off at 5:30	
	20th		Arrived BRUAY 3:15 am and [illegible] went [illegible] 24 RUE DE LARGILLIÈRE. [illegible] were found in [illegible] RUE DE LA GARE. A very wet night and men rather in resting.	

2353 Wt. W2544/1454 700,000 5/15 D. D. & L. A.D.S.S. Forms/C.2118.

Army Form C. 2118.

WAR DIARY
or
INTELLIGENCE-SUMMARY.
(Erase heading not required.)

Instructions regarding War Diaries and Intelligence Summaries are contained in F.S. Regs., Part II. and the Staff Manual respectively. Title pages will be prepared in manuscript.

Place	Date	Hour	Summary of Events and Information	Remarks and references to Appendices
BRUAY (Rue de Sains)	21/4/16		Arrived at 9th Divisional area. Reported to O.C. 9th Div. who made us get in touch with people in CAMBLAIN L'ABBÉ for instruct. Have something when the Company arrived. Before on the Div Signals there. Equipment overhauled. Clearly indicated that Armoured Motor M.G. Section normally by DR whilst we were there in Signal Office Could not get instruct of work in Signal Office Could as Bn Signalling Officers of 9th Div were having to do it all. Take orders from the ones in BRUAY	
	25/4/16		Asked only if for permission (remain in BRUAY and leave one Signal sent to CAMBLAIN L'ABBÉ for relief of the Divl Signal Officer there on Returning any 12.35 from.	
		10 am	Signal Office full. Z BRUAY	
CAMBLAIN L'ABBÉ	26/4/16		CAMBLAIN L'ABBÉ Same hour. Billets taken over from [illegible] of 9th Div. Sig. Coy	

2353 Wt. W2544/1454 700,000 5/15 D. D. & L. A.D.S.S. Forms/C 2118.

Army Form C. 2118.

WAR DIARY
or
INTELLIGENCE SUMMARY.
(Erase heading not required.)

Instructions regarding War Diaries and Intelligence Summaries are contained in F.S. Regs. Part II and the Staff Manual respectively. Title pages will be prepared in manuscript.

Place	Date	Hour	Summary of Events and Information	Remarks and references to Appendices
CAMBLAIN L'ABBE	27th	6.30	[illegible handwritten entry referencing SOMME, 23rd, Lt. HENNESSY 2nd R.I.F.]	

Appendix No 1.

Army Form C. 2118.

WAR DIARY
INTELLIGENCE SUMMARY. No 2 Section, 24th Div. Sig. Coy. R.E.

Place	Date	Hour	Summary of Events and Information	Remarks and references to Appendices
REST CAMP F8C78 (FRANCE 62A)	SEPTEMBER 1918. 1st		Sec. of NCOs + operators to man visual stn to 73 IB hqrs at POMMIER'S REDOUBT (A16 b 3 FRANCE 62c)	
	2nd		Relieved Sigs 73 IB at P. REDOUBT. Came with present bn by various types of cable, in ofd ETS, with 2 Kerr stns YY at S21 d 69 (FR.57c) and AB at GREEN DUMP about S16 central (do), enroute; to CARLTON TRENCH about S16 bd (do). Visual from P.R. to CARLTON TR, + from there also to ft about S26 d 84. Also by pigeon.	H. Westhope Lt 4 Sgs 17 IB
	4th nght		Laid new DVI brn from AB to YY, greatly improving speaking. Relieved by 165 IB. To rest camp F8C78 as above.	
	4/5 nght 5th (K 6)		To Camp Ben Munches Bres (FR 62d) E7C 33. Entrained EDGEHILL E19 d 55 (do) to LONGPRÉ via AMIENS. Marched to GORENFLOS (Square A.5. LENS no.11, 1:100,000) arr 1 am 7th.	
	7 — 13		Section resting + refitting. All stores inspected, cleaned, + deficiencies made good. Rifle + foot drill. Div on line, was by orderly.	
	13 — 16		Section on 3 days leave to St VALERY SUR SOMME.	
	17 — 18		At GORENFLOS.	

WAR DIARY

INTELLIGENCE SUMMARY

Army Form C. 2118.

Place	Date	Hour	Summary of Events and Information	Remarks and references to Appendices
	SEPTEMBER 1916.			
GORENFLOS	19		Section marched to PONT REMY (ABBEVILLE no 14; 1:100,000)[K9]. Entrained there for PERNES (H11; 36b France) via ABBEVILLE, detrained PERNES & billeted in town. Came with Div via IV Corps, Div by orders.	
			Party went by bus to Hqrs 27 IB at Chateau D'ACQ. (W30 L25) (do) to look round the new line.	
PERNES	21		at PERNES	
	22		Section marched to RUITZ, via BRUAY, at K19 c (do) by convoy.	
	23		" " CHATEAU de la HAIE (no lch) W12 central	
	24		(do), rel South African Bde of 9th Div. All Bns on mine; Section relieved 27 IB sig at CHATEAU D'ACQ. Report centre at CABARET ROUGE (S13 d 75. 7 36 c) line patrols ordered; air patrol (trunk line) fwd to C.R.	
	25			
	26-30		Lines patrolled, maintained, & double[d]. [trunk forward tbm.] Casualties: 3 sick; reinforcements arrived fr France.	

WAR DIARY
INTELLIGENCE SUMMARY

No 3 Section 24th Sig Coy
R.E. (Winter No 2)

Place	Date	Hour	Summary of Events and Information	Remarks and references to Appendices
Guinemont Redoubt	1-9-16		Heavy shelling in region of ZZ and MR all night of 31/1st. Large number of gas shells. Lines between MR and ZZ being hit and broken in 8 places. Shells and in 3 places between MR & MT. communication meanwhile by Vis and runners.	S.7.H.
"	2-9-16		Left Batta. moved its H.Q. to right of Longueval. R/- Batta. reoccupying dugouts in S. came W. edge of Delville Wood. R/- Batta. being about 350 yds apart; R/- Batta. timber to two H.Qrs. Line laid from ZZ laying pair to Left Batta. for lateral comn. Line laid from L. Batta. across open with good results. Visual from L. Batta. to L. Batta. by daylight lamp and Dar. This pt. to not fr with ratio M.T. by daylight lamp and Dar. This pt. to get Vis Zphus. in case of emergency as R/- Batta. unable to get Vis Zphus.	S.7.H.
"	3-9-16		Infantry attack on Guich. Lines though all timed.	S.7.H.
"	4-9-16		Further attack by infantry lines still good.	S.7.H.
"	5-9-16		Instructed Signals 166 Infy Bde in communications in this area and	

WAR DIARY No. 3 Section 24th (Signal) Coy R.E.

Army Form C. 2118.

INTELLIGENCE SUMMARY

(Erase heading not required.)

Place	Date	Hour	Summary of Events and Information	Remarks and references to Appendices
Pommiers Redoubt	5/9/16		(cont'd) handed over signals to them at 9.15 p.m. Section moved off to camp at D.A.D.S. region of Fricourt.	S.7.R.
D.A.D.S. (Fricourt)	6/9/16		Bde H.Q. left this camp, moving to camp # N. of DERNANCOURT on ALBERT—AMIENS road, opening office at 3pm. All communication by orderly.	S.7.R.
(Dernancourt)	7.9.16		Closed office at 10 am. Section moving off to EDGE HILL Stn. (by Dernancourt) entraining at 1 a.m. for LONGPRÉ arriving there at 6.45 p.m — marched from there to Bde H.Q. and billets in Chateau Bois d'Abbey on ABBEVILLE—ST RIQUIER road, about 5 kilos from the former town. arriving at 11.45 pm.	S.7.R.
Bois d'ABBEY	8.9.16		Communication to DIV. and all units by M.A. and orderly.	S.7.R.
"	9.9.16		Posting. Can through to DIV. at 7.30 a.m.	S.7.R.
"	10.9.16		Training – Rifle drill etc. – overhauling, repairing and cleaning instruments	S.7.R.
"	11.9.16		Training – Rifle drill.	S.7.R.
"	12.9.16		Training – 2 hours march	S.7.R.

WAR DIARY
or
INTELLIGENCE SUMMARY

(Erase heading not required.)

Army Form C. 2118.

Instructions regarding War Diaries and Intelligence Summaries are contained in F.S. Regs, Part II. and the Staff Manual respectively. Title Pages will be prepared in manuscript.

Place	Date	Hour	Summary of Events and Information	Remarks and references to Appendices
BOIS DL ABBEY	13-9-16		Party of 8 N.C.O.'s men started on 4 days holiday by seaside at AULT. remainder carried on training and overhauling instruments etc.	S.7.H.
"	14-9-16		Training - Visual Signalling	S.7.H.
"	15-9-16		Training - Visual Signalling	S.7.H.
"	16-9-16		Training Vis. Signalling	S.7.H.
"	17-9-16		Training Visual Signalling	S.7.H.
"	18-9-16		Training Visual Signalling	S.7.H.
"	19-9-16		Training Visual Signalling	S.7.H.
"			Closed Signal office at 6.30pm at BRIAS marching to VALDHOUN - a Rest area - advanced at 9.a.m. marching to ABBEVILLE this entraining there	S.7.H.
VALDHOUN	20-9-16		Came to DIV. by D.R. and to Battns by orderly.	S.7.H.
"	21-9-16		Resting.	S.7.H.
"	22-9-16		Resting.	S.7.H.
"			Overhauling equipment and signalling stores	
"	23-9-16		Training in Visual Signalling	
"	24-9-16		Closed Sig office at 9 am Marching to new area at RUITZ arriving at 1.30 p.m. Came to Div. by D.R. Battns by orderly.	S.7.H.
RUITZ	25-9-16		Resting.	S.7.H.
	26-9-16		Closed office at 8 am marching to DIVL. RESERVE at - Chateau de la Jdare - W.R.C. 9.G.(Ref Sheet 36B. Battns in area - Queens. AMBLAIN d. l. ABBE. N. STAFFS " " " " M.G. Coy " " " "	

Army Form C. 2118.

No. 3 Section
2nd S.S. Coy R.E.

WAR DIARY
or
INTELLIGENCE SUMMARY
(Erase heading not required.)

Instructions regarding War Diaries and Intelligence Summaries are contained in F. S. Regs., Part II. and the Staff Manual respectively. Title Pages will be prepared in manuscript.

Place	Date	Hour	Summary of Events and Information	Remarks and references to Appendices
	26.9.16.	(Contd)	T.W.Keats - Govy. Servins - E.Surpeys - Estree.Cauchie - 12 J.M.B/y. Govy Servins	S.7.A.
Chateau de la Haie	27.9.16.		Comms to Div. by wire also to Battns and M.G. Coy -	S.7.A.
	28.9.16.		Resting	S.7.A.
	29.9.16.		Resting	S.7.A.
	30.9.16.		Resting and overhauling equipment. Reconnoitring lines in Right Bde area - advance party of linesmen went in for instruction in same.	S.7.A.

2449 Wt. W14957/Mgo 750,000 1/16 J.B.C. & A. Forms/C.2118/12.

Appendix No 3.

WAR DIARY
of
A Sec. 24 Signal Coy. R.E.
for the Month of
SEPTEMBER 1916.

Army Form C. 2118.

WAR DIARY
or
INTELLIGENCE SUMMARY.
(Erase heading not required.)

Sheet 1.

Place	Date	Hour	Summary of Events and Information	Remarks and references to Appendices
POMMIERS REDOUBT. 62C. A.1.B.63.	1.		Laid new line (B3 pair) from MR (Test Sta.) of 72nd Bde on nights 1st & 11th Tour Stations. Work over.	APPENDIX I.
	2.		YN2 (from Bde on night) to MONTAUBAN and YN.S (buried pair) from MONTAUBAN to MR. This forms our new line to YY. Relaid lines from YY Test Station to AG Test Station. Lines from MB to Bn. H.Q. repaired. Q.I. din 2:15 pm till 3:20 pm. MR.1. din 8:30 am till 9:45 am. Bn to Left Coy. through again at 7 pm. Sgt S in charge of YY party. Relieved by Sig 17 Bde. at 8 pm. Left POMMIERS REDOUBT at 11 pm, moved to F.S.C. (62d). Left 4 linesmen with sigs 17 Bde till 3 a.m. Laid 3 Iron lines to sigs 72 Bde.	A.S.R. A.S.R. B.L.R.
F.S.C. (62d).	3.		Communicated with battalion by orderly and c/o 17 Bde. Laid wire to transport lines.	A.S.R.
	4.		This battalion with 17th Bde. Communication with other units by orderly.	A.S.R.
DERNANCOURT.	5.		one sapper moved at 10 a.m. to DERNANCOURT. one sapper previously wounded returned. maintained communication by orderly	A.S.R.
	6.		Dismounted portion of section entrained at 6 a.m. other proceeded to LONGPRÉ marched from LONGPRÉ to VAUCHELLES-LES-DOMART. Transport moved by road at 8 a.m. to LONGPRÉ near AMIENS.	A.R.
VAUCHELLES-DOMART.	7.		LONGPRÉ to VAUCHELLES-LES-DOMART. Transport moved from LONGPRÉ to VAUCHELLES-LES-DOMART. maintained communication by orderly.	A.R.
	8.		Laid wires to the four battalions communicated with 73 MG Coy and 73 Fd Amb by orderly.	A.R.
	9. 10.		practised visual signalling with those men not employed in maintaining communication	A.S.R.

Army Form C. 2118.

WAR DIARY
or
INTELLIGENCE SUMMARY.
(Erase heading not required.)

Sheet II.

Place	Date	Hour	Summary of Events and Information	Remarks and references to Appendices
VAUCHELLES-LES-DOMART.	11		1 OR. reinforcement joined.	AJR
	12		practised visually with those men not otherwise employed.	AJR
	13			
	14			
	15.		1 Sgt. reported evacuated to England.	AJR
	16.		Twenty OR of the section to the Seaside, but recalled later in the day.	AJR
	17.			
	18.		1 Sgt. joined section from Base Signal depot. Picked up all lines laid out to the battalions.	AJR
	19.		Moved at 8 a.m. Entrained at LONGPRÉ at 9.30 a.m. arrived FOUQUEREUIL STA. at 7 p.m. arrived	AJR
MARLES-LES-MINES.	20.		MARLES-LES-MINES. at 10 p.m.	AJR
	21.		Maintained communication by orderly.	AJR
			Bde hqrs moved at 10 a.m. to RUITZ.	
	22.		Moved to CHAU DE' LA HAIE sent N.C.O. and 5 linemen to learn lines of 1st S.A. Bde. one 2nd	AJR
	23.		Cpl. to England on being granted a commission.	
			moved from CHAU DE LA HAIE at 4pm 10 OR. to advanced Bde hqrs remainder of section to new	AJR
			hqrs. took over 3.50pm from Sigs 1st South African Infantry Brigade. Lines as in appendix II	
VILLERS-AU-BOIS	24.		Patrolled lines. All communication forward of Bde hqrs by full telephone met overlay, 1 N.C.O.	AJR
			joined section.	
	25.		Patrolled lines.	
	26.		Laid new pair from Signal office to Bde office. DC.g. from BBR to IM Packstation broken by a direct hit on Com. Trench. 1 OR. to hospital.	AJR

Army Form C. 2118.

Sheet III.

WAR DIARY
or
INTELLIGENCE SUMMARY.
(Erase heading not required.)

Instructions regarding War Diaries and Intelligence Summaries are contained in F. S. Regs., Part II. and the Staff Manual respectively. Title pages will be prepared in manuscript.

Place	Date	Hour	Summary of Events and Information	Remarks and references to Appendices
VILLERS-AU-BOIS.	27.		Laid new line from Bde to Bde transport.	S/R.
	28.		Patrolled lines. Remade all joints on buried line from VILLERS to point 'G'.	S/R.
	29.		Patrolled lines. Remade all joints on buried line from point 'G' forward.	S/R.
	30.		Patrolled lines.	S/R.

APPENDIX IV

COMMUNICATIONS of 73 I.Bde. at POMMIERS REDOUBT.

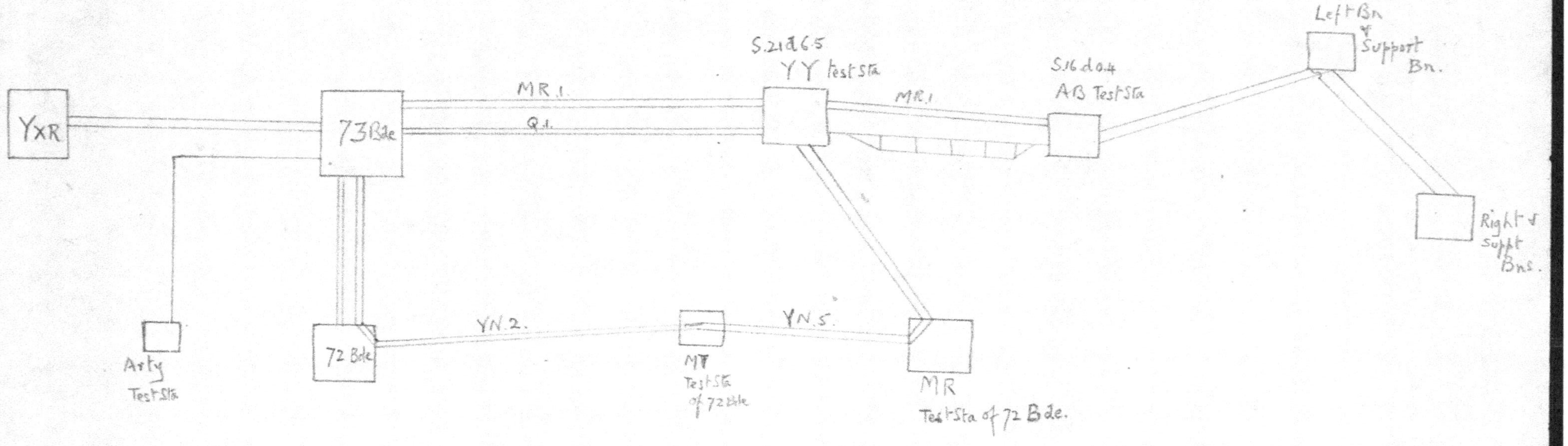

YxR
73 Bde
MR.1.
Q.1.
S.21d6.5
YY Test Sta
MR.1
S.16d0.4
AB Test Sta
Left Bn & Support Bn.
Right & Suppt Bns.
Arty Test Sta
72 Bde
YN.2.
MT Test Sta of 72 Bde
YN.5.
MR
Test Sta of 72 Bde.

a f Ritchie Lt. Sigs 73 Bde
2/9/16.

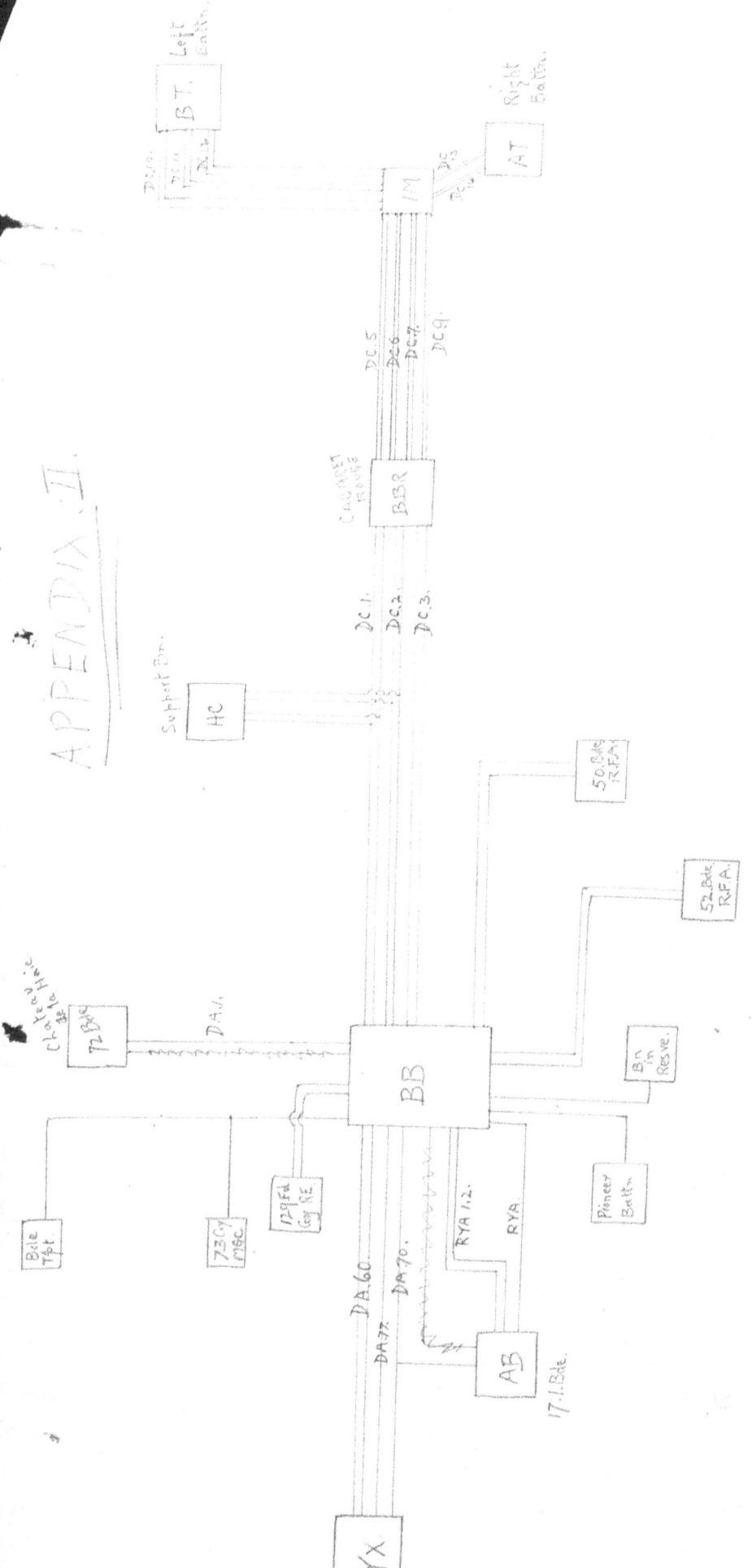

Army Form C. 2118.

Vol 15
1916 October 24

24th DIVISIONAL SIGNAL COMPANY. R.E.

WAR DIARY
or
INTELLIGENCE SUMMARY.
(Erase heading not required.)

Instructions regarding War Diaries and Intelligence Summaries are contained in F. S. Regs., Part II. and the Staff Manual respectively. Title pages will be prepared in manuscript.

Place	Date	Hour	Summary of Events and Information	Remarks and references to Appendices.
CAMBLAIN L'ABBE	October 1st to 13th		General maintenance, labelling and squaring up of lines. A good deal of work was done constructing a stable and testing slip for the purpose from Bruay. Wagons and equipment generally overhauled and deficiencies made up.	
	14th		Two parties of 4 men each employed salvaging disused cable in communication trenches. Part of Redoubt Road and part of Calais Road cleared.	Appendix VII
	15th		Two parties salvaging cable. Redoubt Road and part of Bayville line cleared.	

Army Form C. 2118.

WAR DIARY
or
INTELLIGENCE SUMMARY.
(Erase heading not required.)

(2)

Instructions regarding War Diaries and Intelligence Summaries are contained in F. S. Regs., Part II. and the Staff Manual respectively. Title pages will be prepared in manuscript.

Place	Date	Hour	Summary of Events and Information	Remarks and references to Appendices
	16th Oct		Two parties of men employed salvaging along 130 Road, Three Alley and Hospital Corner Road cleared.	See
	17th		Salvaging parties cleared 131 Hill Communication Trench.	Appendix
	18th		Salvaging parties cleared Albert Barge Road.	
	19th		Salvage parties cleared Worthy Avenue.	VII
	20th & 26th		General overhaul of lines and getting all lines correctly labelled preparatory to handing over to 1st Canadian Division.	WR
	27th		2nd Lieut W.E. Rhodes R.E. joined Company. Certain amount of stores sent over to New Keangro.	

Army Form C. 2118.

WAR DIARY
or
INTELLIGENCE SUMMARY.
(Erase heading not required.)

(3)

Place	Date	Hour	Summary of Events and Information	Remarks and references to Appendices
	28th October		Company moved out from CAMBLAIN L'ABBE and proceeded by march route to BRUAY taking up billets which had been vacated when previously in BRUAY. Route CAMBLAIN L'ABBE — ESTREE CAUCHIE — RANCHICOURT — HOUDAIN — BRUAY. Signal Office closed down at 10-0 am rejoining at the same hour in BRUAY. Completed handing over to 1st Canadian Division of the Signal area. One cable detachment left behind with 24th Divisional Artillery who remain in area.	Nil
BRUAY 29th			Party of one NCO & 7 men sent over to MAZINGARBE by lorry to take over exchange and lines at Report Centre established at Rio Place.	Appendix I

Army Form C. 2118.

WAR DIARY
or
INTELLIGENCE SUMMARY. (7)

(Erase heading not required.)

Place	Date	Hour	Summary of Events and Information	Remarks and references to Appendices
BRUAY	29th (cont'd)		Small party of fitters sent to New Divisional Headqrs. at NOEUX-LES-MINES to take over office and fit in new instruments.	
		5.00	Took over Signals from 40th Division in southern sector of LOOS Salient. Company proceeded by march route to NOEUX-LES-MINES via HALLICOURT and BARLIN and took over Lillers wires which had been worked by 40th Division.	
NOEUX-LES-MINES	31st		Rearranging Signal Office movements, clearing up yard & repairing parts of stables.	

WAR DIARY
or
INTELLIGENCE SUMMARY.

Army Form C. 2118.

APPENDIX I

OCTOBER 1916.

Exchange Connections

24th Division

CAMBLAIN L'ABBE

No			No		
1	Canadian Corps	RQ 5+6	11	175 Company R.E.	R.A.2 pair
2	17th Corps	R 29 pair	12	Canadian Corps	RQ 7+8
3	C.R.A.	Arty 1+2	13	{2nd Canadian Divn (Division on left)	C 577 S
4	{Central Exchange Mt. St Eloy	R 54 pair	14	Right Brigade	DA 74 pair
5	Left Brigade	DA 60 pair	15	C.R.A.	Arty 27+28
6	Rest Brigade	DA 87 pair	16	G.O.C.	—
7	C.R.E	R.A. 3 pair	17	'Q' Branch	—
8	Right Brigade	DA 75 pair	18	{Signal Company Office + O.C. Signals	—
9	'G' Branch	—	19	{D.A.D.S. (2 pairs) Divn Train (3 pairs)	DA 71 pair
10	182 Company R.E	182 pair	20	Resting Brigade	DA 80 pair

N.B:— Left Brigade at VILLERS-AU-BOIS
Right Brigade at CHATEAU D'ACQ
Resting Brigade at CHATEAU DE LA HAIE

Army Form C. 2118.

WAR DIARY
or
INTELLIGENCE SUMMARY

(Erase heading not required)

OCTOBER 1916

APPENDIX II

PAGE 1.

YX Lines in use by Division
(- and spares led in to YX)   CAMBLAIN
                                L'ABBÉ

DESCRIPTION OF WIRE	CIRCUIT	DESCRIPTION OF WIRE	CIRCUIT
DA 4 single	Right Brigade Sounder	DA 58 single	Divnl Artillery to 107 Bde RFA (vibrator)
DA 9 pair	Technical School Phone.	DA 60 pair	Left Brigade Phone.
DA 17 "	Spare YX to JC for Right Brigade (forward of earth point when vibrator between Right Brigade & Right Group Artillery)	DA 71 single	DADOS & Divisional Train (phone set) Right Brigade Sounder.
		DA 73 "	Right Brigade Phone
DA 18 pair	Divisional Artillery to 106th Brigade RFA. (vibrator)	DA 74 pair	"
		DA 75 pair	"
DA 46 pair	Spare (late Div Artillery to 16 Fld Ambulance doctor)	DA 75 A	Divnl Artillery to D.A.C. (earth phone)
		DA 76 B	" to Artly Wagon lines (vibrator)
DA 51 single	Divnl Artillery to 108th Brigade RFA (vibrator)	DA 77 single	Left Brigade Sounder
		DA 78 pair	Divnl Artillery to 108 Bde RFA (phone)
DA 57 pair	Spare (late Divnl Artly to 108 Bde RFA (New))	DA 85 pair (late RY 10)	Divnl Artillery to 116 Bde RFA (phone)

Army Form C. 2118.

WAR DIARY
or
INTELLIGENCE SUMMARY.
(Erase heading not required.)

October 1916   APPENDIX II   Page 2.

Summary of Events and Information

Description of Wire	Circuit	Description of Wire	Circuit	Remarks and references to Appendices
DA 86 Fair (late CH 7+8)	Phone to Resting Brigade	RA 1 Fair (French route)	Phone Divnl Artillery to No 8 Kite Balloon Section (artillery line)	Rush
DA 87 Fair (late RY 6)	"	RA 2 Fair (French route)	Phone YX to 175 Tunnelling Coy R.E.	
RQ 5 + 6	Phone to Canadian Corps	RA 3 Fair (French route)	Phone to C.R.E.	
RQ 7 + 8	"	182 Fair (French route)	Phone to 182 Company R.E.	
R 29 Fair	" 17th Corps	YFC 82	Sounder to CYB (Brown on Left)	
R 50 "	Phone Divnl Artly to No 8 Kite Balloon Section	Artillery 142	Phone to Divisional Artillery	
R 54 "	" to Central Exchange	" 27+28	" "	
CS 7 + 8 "	" YX to CYB (Brown on Left)	Artillery 13	Vibrator to "	
HA 7 + 8 "	" to Corps H.A. from Divnl Artillery			

N.B. :—

106th Brigade RFA to Right Group R.A.
107th " " " Left "
108th " " " Centre "

WAR DIARY
INTELLIGENCE SUMMARY
APPENDIX III

October 1916

Army Form C. 2118.

Instructions regarding War Diaries and Intelligence Summaries are contained in F.S. Regs., Part II. and the Staff Manual respectively. Title pages will be prepared in manuscript.

Place	Date	Hour	Summary of Events and Information	Remarks and references to Appendices

Wires on Artillery 20 Line Test Board Y X (OBAN ? 355)

Number of Wire		Circuit	Number of Wire		Circuit
Divnl Artly Side	Forward Side		Divnl Arty Side	Forward Side	
Arty 21 & 22	DA 78 (pair)	Phone Divisional Arty to 108 Brigade RFA	Arty 23 24	DA 18 (pair)	Divnl Arty to 108 Bde RFA subsid.
Arty 3 4	HA 7 8	Phone Divnl Arty to Corps R.A.	Arty 25 26	DA 40 (pair)	Phone (late Phone Divnl Arty to 13 Bde Balloon Section)
Arty 5 6	DA 76 & DA 76 ᵇ	Divnl. Arty. to DAC. (Phone) " to Artillery Officer i/c Routes	RA 1 (pair)	R 50 (pair)	Phone Divnl. Arty to Kite Balloon Section
Arty 7 8	DA 85 (pair (Arty 10) C. + D.)	Phone Divnl Arty to 106 Brigade RFA	Artillery 11	—	Spare
Arty 9	DA 58	Divnl Arty to 107 Bde RFA subsid.	Arty 13	—	Vibrator pro - Divnl Arty
Arty 10	DA 51 & DA 12	Divnl Arty to 108 Bde RFA alternative	—	DA 57 (pair)	Phone (late Phone Divnl Arty to 108 Bde RFA)

Artillery { Left, Centre, Right } Spare to 107 Bde RFA " " 108 " " 106 " "

OWN

Army Form C. 2118.

WAR DIARY
or
INTELLIGENCE SUMMARY.
(Erase heading not required.)

OCTOBER 1916

APPENDIX **IV**

Summary of Events and Information

40th DIVISION EXCHANGE
on handing over at FOSSÉ DE BRAQUEMONT

No.	OFFICE	WIRE	No.	OFFICE	WIRE
1	1st Corps Exchange	A 70/71	13	Signalmasters billet	DZ 20
2	"G"	DZ 29	14	R.A. Exchange	DZ 16
3	"Q"	DZ 30	15	Signal Officers Mess	DZ 15
4	C.R.E.	DZ 12	16	258 Company R.E.	DZ 18
5	"Minden" {120 Bde at Philosophe}	DZ 1a+3+ AM 22+24	17	Spare to T.P.	
6	"Marne" {119 Bde at Le Brebis}	DZ 2	18	173 Company R.E.	DZ 19
7	Mazingarbe Ex. (Div Report Centre)	DZ 4	19	Left Flank Divn (21st)	DZ 21
8	— do —	DZ 5	20	Emergency line to Corps	A 66+67
9	2nd Canadian Divn (Right Flanking Divn)	DZ 24	21	121st Bde Mazingarbe	RM 34+12
10	"Marne"	DZ 6	22	A.D.C.	DZ 17
11	Mine Noeux Les Mines Civil Exchange	DZ 13	23	D.A.D.O.S.	DZ 22
12	Company Office	DZ 14	24	Mazingarbe Exchange	AM 5+4+

N.B :- All Metallic circuits

Army Form C. 2118

WAR DIARY
or
INTELLIGENCE SUMMARY.
(Erase heading not required.)

Instructions regarding War Diaries and Intelligence Summaries are contained in F. S. Regs., Part II. and the Staff Manual respectively. Title pages will be prepared in manuscript.

OCTOBER 1916

APPENDIX V

Place	Date	Hour	Summary of Events and Information	Remarks and references to Appendices

Report Centre Exchanges at Magingarbe on Kithing Ass 30-10-16

No	OFFICE	WIRE	No	OFFICE	WIRE
1	40th Division	DZ 4 a+b	9	Centre Group R.A. Mazingarbe	BM 5 forward posn
2	"	DZ 5	10	Left Group R.A. Philosophe	DZR 22 a+b BM 1+2 forward posn
3	"	AM 5 +14	11	1st Corps H.A. Mazingarbe	
4	R.A. 40th Divn	DZ 3 a+b	12	Loos Garrison	No 1. Brown posn
5	Right Brigade "MARNS" 119 I.B. LES BREBIS	DZ 2 a+b	13	Brebis Exchange	BM 1+2 foot
6	Left Brigade MINDEN 120 I.B. Philosophe	DZR 21 a+b	14		
7	Centre Brigade MARATHON 121 I.B. MAZINGARBE	AM 7+8	15		
8	Right Group R.A. Le Brebis	BM 5 +3 Back portion			

Army Form C. 2118.

WAR DIARY
or
INTELLIGENCE SUMMARY

(Erase heading not required.)

OCTOBER 1916

APPENDIX VI

Place	Date	Hour	Summary of Events and Information	Remarks and references to Appendices

Diagram of Communications
CAMBLAIN L'ABBÉ

WAR DIARY
or
INTELLIGENCE SUMMARY.

(Erase heading not required.)

Army Form C. 2118.

October 1916

APPENDIX VII

Summary of Events and Information

REELED UP CABLE

COMMUNICATION TRENCH	PLACES FOR LABELLING	DATES ON WHICH TRENCHES WILL BE CLEARED	Remarks
Redoubt Road	1/ Junction Redoubt Rd and Hospital Corner Road. 2/ Junction Redoubt Rd and Bazille Line. 3/ Junction Redoubt Road & 7:30 Road	14th October	
Talbot Road	1/ Junction Talbot Road and Hospital Corner Road 2/ Junction Talbot Road and Bazille Line 3/ Talbot Ridge Road	14th October	

Army Form C. 2118.

WAR DIARY
or
INTELLIGENCE SUMMARY.
(Erase heading not required.)

Appendix VII Page 2

Place	Date	Hour	Summary of Events and Information	Remarks and references to Appendices
Communication Trench			Places for Labelling	Dates on which Trenches will be changed
130 Road			1/ Junction 130 Road and Redoubt Road. 2/ Junction 130 Road and Arras Alley. 3/ Junction 130 Road and Erantz Avenue	16th October
131 Hill C.T. and Bethune Road.			1/ Junction 131 C.T and Cabaret Road. 2/ Junction 131 C.T. and ~~Junction~~ Wortley Avenue 3/ Junction with Arthur Avenue	16th October	RCM

WAR DIARY
or
INTELLIGENCE SUMMARY.

Army Form C. 2118.

October 1916
Appendix VII page 3

(Erase heading not required.)

Place	Date	Hour	Summary of Events and Information	Remarks and references to Appendices
Communication Trench			Places for Labelling	Sites on which Transport to be shewn.
Worsley Avenue			1. Junction with Bethune Road. 2. Coliseum. 3. Sales des Zouaves.	19th October
Forsely Avenue			1. Cabaret Rouge 2. Alhambra 3. Kemp Trench 4. Salue des Zouaves	19th October

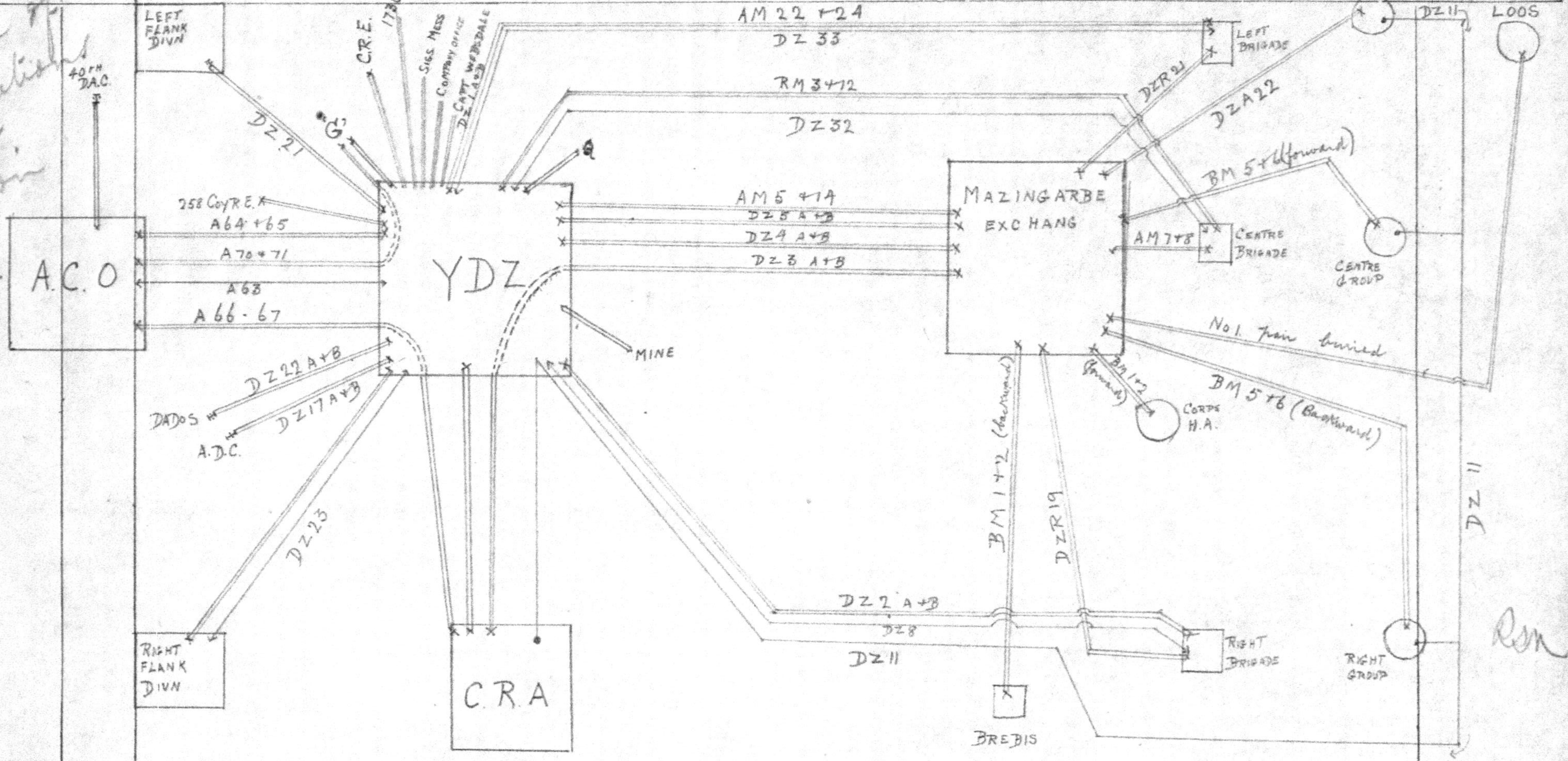

WAR DIARY
or
INTELLIGENCE SUMMARY.
(Erase heading not required.)

Army Form C. 2118

Place	Date	Hour	Summary of Events and Information	Remarks and references to Appendices.
	OCTOBER 1916			
CHEU D'ACQ	1		BERTHONVAL SECTION. Lines patrolled & maintained. Men from Sig ZQB to go over lines.	
W30b35 (France 3(B))	2		Relieved by Sig ZQB about 4 pm. Section to Reserve Bde Hqn	
Ch Ad de la HAIE W11c89 (do)	3—7		Section resting & refitting. Rifle & foot drill, musketry. Drying this time party of Os & 1B signallers went to aerodrome nr BRUAY for instruction by No 16 Sqdn RFC too bad for flying.	
"	8		2 men went to look over lines of Sig ZQC in CARENCY SECTION.	
VILLERS au BOIS X19a63 (do)	9		Relieved Sig ZQC 5pm. Bde Hqn as in margin. Advanced Hqn & report centre BBR, ar CABARET ROUGE 100x N7/A8R. All lines patrolled & maintained. Line to L group RA at X7C put through. Officers at BB (Betty) + BBR entirely re-wired, & all lines led in a trench. Visual from both hers to BBR, thence to stn on N.D.de LORETTE. Army stores to stn at X19a67 X5C14	

WAR DIARY
INTELLIGENCE SUMMARY

Place	Date	Hour	Summary of Events and Information	Remarks and references to Appendices
VILLERS au BOIS	10-24 Oct		On 14th labelling of all lines (according to GHQ OB 618) 10.11.15) began, starting with CABARET ROAD, working forward to lm, who also labelled all Coy lines at same time.	
	19th		Officer, 1 Some NCO of ZLA (40TH DIV) between MAZINGARBE and LOOS, inspected.	
	24		NCO + 3 Linesmen to ZLA to learn lines. 2 NCOs + 2 men of CZA to inspect own Buried Lateral containing 6 wires finished between ABR + BBR. During this tour, lemmen + billets were inspected every day - also cookhouse. Wagon repainted. Section relieved by Sig: CZA 5pm. all lines handed over.	
W12 c 89	25		Bde to CHÂt de la HAIE	
L23 c 27	26		Section marched to MAZINGARBE, L 23 c 27 to rm la le Ha⟨ie⟩	
L29 a 89	27		Relieved Sig ZLA at MAZINGARBE CHÂU	

WAR DIARY

INTELLIGENCE SUMMARY.

Army Form C. 2118.

Place	Date	Hour	Summary of Events and Information	Remarks and references to Appendices
MAZINGARBE CHATEAU	28TH – 31ST		On moving into MAZINGARBE Bde came under orders of 40 Div. All work to 24th Div through them till 24th took over on 30th. All lines patrolled & maintained. Several other reclaimed & put into use. System of working with a report centre to runners at MEETING HOUSE on BETHUNE–LENS road G27d18, where fresh men take DR.LS on to Bns. It Test point to cable at T.P. in northern most house of LOOS, G29 d 62. Came to say by buried line to Batterie S1 Telephone Post. Work in the reserve line with trench line extension into Coy hqrs. Cme with Bn. communicant, & Power Bn. Bn in cmr with Bns on their flanks. Cmr with Flank bdes + R A group through MAZINGARBE Exchange in chez harvever. Visual possible from hut [?] to VILLAGE LINE (Hut on side N.W. of LOOS & thence to FOSSES 9.19.5 thru there to Bde in Div HQ direct. CASUALTIES 1 NCO. Sick 2 OR.	SIGILIB [?] Strength [?] HE Honor [?]

Army Form C. 2118.

No. 3. Section
2nd April Coy R.E.
Appendix A

WAR DIARY
or
INTELLIGENCE SUMMARY.

(Erase heading not required.)

Place	Date	Hour	Summary of Events and Information	Remarks and references to Appendices
Chateau d'Aostoil	1-10-16		Reconnoitring lines in Right Bde area	S.7.A.
	2-10-16		Relieved Signals 17 I.B. in Right Bde area taking over at 4 p.m. Communication to Batties as follows. Dullerphone to Right Bhc - Left Batln & Battn in support all via A.B.R. Also speaking line to these same units. Buzzer & speaking line to Battn in support direct. (Circuit diagram enclosed)	S.7.A.
Vtla A.Aq	3-10-16		Extending lines and tracing buried routes.	S.7.A.
"	4-10-16		Patrolling and testing buried routes	S.7.A.
"	5-10-16		Tracing pair in buried route for use by T.M. Bty for registration purposes - found it in use by Arty.	S.7.A.
"	6-10-16		Arranged new system of D.R.L.S. to Battns via Relay stn at HOSPITAL CORNER.	S.7.A.
"	7-10-16		Laid pair from Rt. Batln H.Q. to Stokes gun Batty H.Q. arranging to lay line to O.P. in ALHAMBRA	S.7.A.
"	8-10-16		TRENCH. Laid Dr' Laid from H.Q. 72nd Trench Mortar Battery to 2/K O.P. in ALHAMBRA. Ret line through from 106 Bde R.F.A to T.M. Bty for registration purposes.	S.7.A. S.7.A.
"	9-10-16		Tracing TY10 a+b in trenches in which it is buried - chiefly old no communication trenches route found 3 trot boxes.	S.7.A.

WAR DIARY
INTELLIGENCE SUMMARY. 24th Signal Coy RE

W.S.3 Section

Army Form C. 2118.

Place	Date	Hour	Summary of Events and Information	Remarks and references to Appendices
Villa d'Acq	10-10-16		Joint taken out in new buried south traversed of ABR - Tracing 3 armoured pairs from ABR to Right Bn - Relabelling lines from AB to ABR.	S.P.R.
"	11-10-16		Continued labelling of lines (armoured) of AB to ABR. Tracing armoured pairs to R/ Bn. (continued) Joining in new buried route	S.P.A.
"	12-10-16		Tracing RY loach to find fault - located on junction pole. Testing and earthing new buried route from ABR Bn. Left Bn found faults on 2 prs.	S.P.R.
"	13-10-16		Continued labelling of lines from ABR to ABP. 3 prs. Armoured wire located and taken into R/ Bn office. Lateral bury between Right and Left Bns tested out and 3 spare pairs found. Lateral laid from ABR to BRR.	S.P.A.
"	14-10-16		Joint let in new buried route taken out and joint remade - finished labelling lines forward of ABR - Bn lines also labelled.	S.P.A.
"	15-10-16		All joints in 7 quad buried route waxed in and completed.	S.P.A.
"	16-10-16		Instructing linemen from 13rd Sig Section in lines in area	S.P.A.
"	17-10-16		Instruction of 73rd Bde linemen continued	S.P.A.
"	18-10-16		Relieved by Cyp. 73. 2B. Signals taken over at 4a.m. This section moving to Ref area and H.Q. Chateau de la Haie.	S.P.M.

Army Form C. 2118.

No 3 Section
24th Signal Coy R.E.

WAR DIARY
or
INTELLIGENCE SUMMARY.

(Erase heading not required.)

Place	Date	Hour	Summary of Events and Information	Remarks and references to Appendices.
Challan a la Haie	19-10-16		Patrolling lines in Reserve Area and reconstructing where necessary.	S.7.H.
"	20.X.16		Overhauling stores.	S.9.H.
"	21.X.16		Patrolling lines in Reserve Area.	S.9.H.
"	22.X.16		Patrolling continued and circuit diagram prepared showing same for area.	S.9.H.
"	23.X.16		Reconnoitring lines in NOEUX Sector from Pole H.Q. at CHIKOSOTHE G24 A 4 6 ref. sheet 36 C.	S.9.H.
"	24.X.16.		Interchip in lines in new area continued. R.E. section relieved at CHATEAU de la HAIE by 1st CAN. Bde. closing at 9.45 a.m. Moving to new area MAZINGARBE billeting for night. Came to Div. via 12/1st Inf Bde. and 4th Battn. by orderly.	S.9.H.
MAZINGARBE	25.X.16.		Moved to New Area relieving 12th Inf Bde. at H.Q.w - R.N.Hants and 9th Queens in line ref. sheet 36C. - Signals taken over at H.Q.w - R.N.Hants and 9th Queens in line. Kents in right - and Surreys in support with I.M. Staffs in reserve in billets in CHIKOSOTHE. Circuit diagram of same enclosed. Came to 24th Div via 40th Div at NOEUX LES MINES.	S.9.H.

Army Form C. 2118.

WAR DIARY
or
INTELLIGENCE SUMMARY.
(Erase heading not required.)

No. 3 Section
24th Signal Coy. R.E.

Instructions regarding War Diaries and Intelligence Summaries are contained in F. S. Regs., Part II. and the Staff Manual respectively. Title pages will be prepared in manuscript.

Place	Date	Hour	Summary of Events and Information	Remarks and references to Appendices
PHILOSOPHE	26.X.16		Patrolling airlines forward and back area lines. Blg wires and suggested improvements considered	S.9.2.
"	27.X.16		Corps buried cable - LE RUTOIRE patrolled with Corps Linemen - Spare leads in signal office tested - cable to T.P. and Hd. Batteries for new lines	S.9.2.
"	28.X.16		Overhauling A.V.1 6 units replacing poor cable	S.9.2.
"	29.X.16		" A.V.3 6 units - patrolling all airlines	S.9.2.
"	30.X.16		Batln wires and airlines patrolled	S.9.2.
"	31.X.16		All local lines patrolled. No linemen work on December line	S.9.2.

Sub-Appendix I

J.W.R.

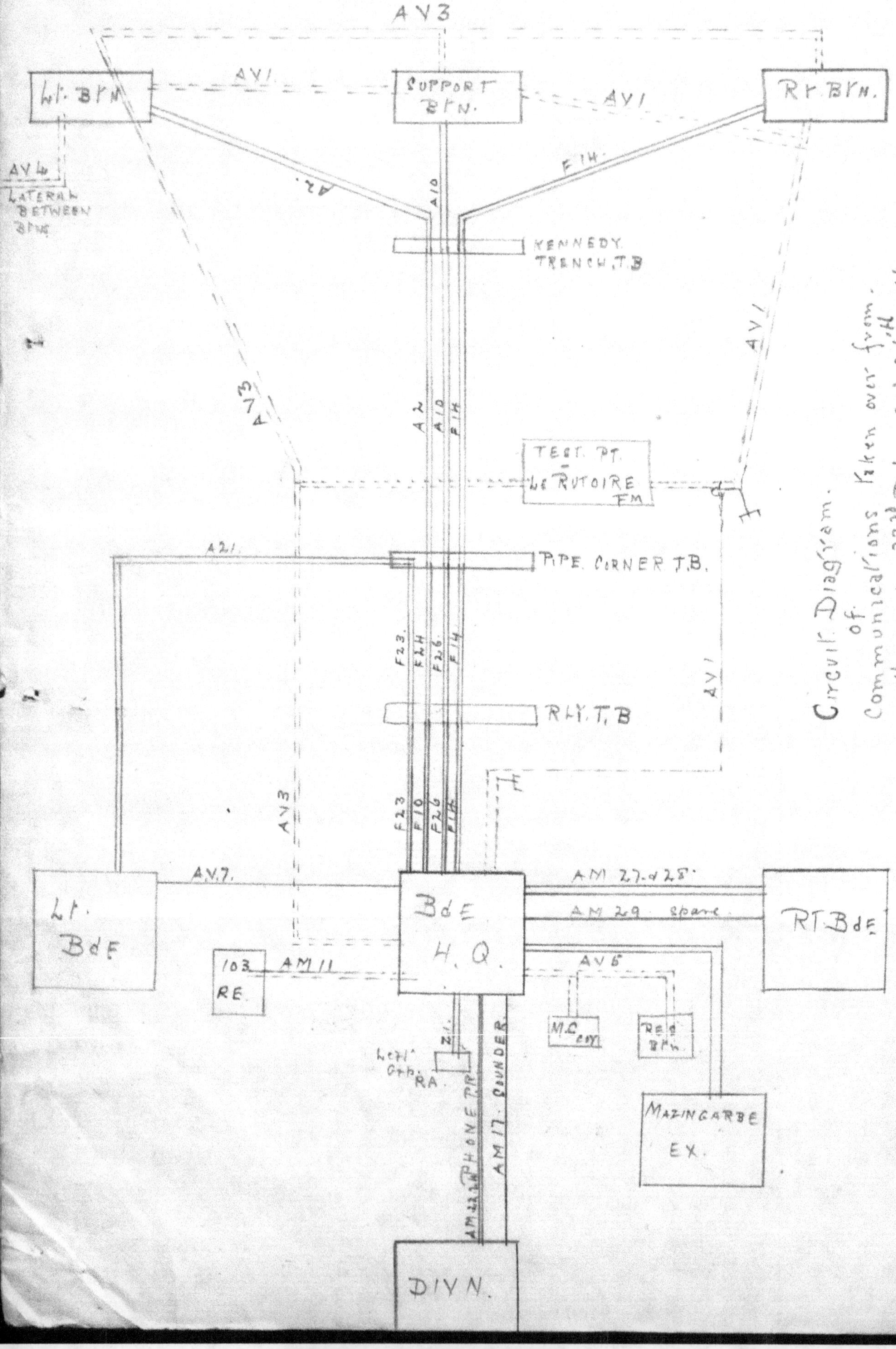

Circuit Diagram. of Communications taken over from 120th Bde. by 72nd Bde. Oct: 26th 1916.

Army Form C. 2118.

WAR DIARY
or
INTELLIGENCE SUMMARY.

(Erase heading not required.)

Instructions regarding War Diaries and Intelligence Summaries are contained in F. S. Regs., Part II. and the Staff Manual respectively. Title pages will be prepared in manuscript.

Place	Date	Hour	Summary of Events and Information	Remarks and references to Appendices

WAR DIARY

of

A Sec. 24 Sig. Coy. R.E.
for the month of
October 1916.

2353 Wt. W2544/1454 700,000 5/15 D. D. & L. A.D.S.S./Forms/C. 2118

Army Form C. 2118.

Sheet I

WAR DIARY
or
INTELLIGENCE SUMMARY.

(Erase heading not required.)

Place	Date	Hour	Summary of Events and Information	Remarks and references to Appendices
VILLERS-AU BOIS.	1.		Patrolled lines	agr
	2.		Patrolled lines. Telephone pair F.B.R (DC.3) disappeared reported 11.15am	agr
	3.		Patrolled lines.	agr
	4.		Reclaimed DA.16 from BBR to HOSPITAL CORNER	agr
	5.		Relaid DC.8 from BBR to IMTESS Station.	agr
	6.		Put DA16 through from BBR to B/108 R.F.A. Ear pairs from Bty right Battalion to Medium T.M.B. and to Light T.M.B. for rent.	agr
	7.		Received two pairs from right Coy right battalion to Bn. hqrs. Established wire from light Coy right battalion to BBR.	agr
	8.		Patrolled lines with Lieutenant of 17 Bde Sigs.	agr
	9.		Lost pairs from left Coy right battalion to L. T.M.B. and medium T.M.B. and two pairs to Bn. hqrs. Put through 108/306 R.F.A. & light battalion & DA16 ref DC.8	agr
	10.		Handed over to Sgt 17 Bde at 5pm moved to Rd. Bte area. CHAMPREIX AVE	agr

Army Form C. 2118.

WAR DIARY
or
INTELLIGENCE SUMMARY.

(Erase heading not required.)

Instructions regarding War Diaries and Intelligence Summaries are contained in F. S. Regs., Part II. and the Staff Manual respectively. Title pages will be prepared in manuscript.

Place	Date	Hour	Summary of Events and Information	Remarks and references to Appendices
CHAN. DE LA HAIE.	11		Put through line to 7 Northants Honours and 7.5 M.G.C and 131 I.B.A Mining	
	12.		Patrolled lines.	
	13			
	14			
	15.		Went to take over communications in 72 Bde area	
	16.		Sent four linesmen to 72 Bde. Advanced parties of 72nd Bde and infantry at No.16.Sqdn. R.F.C.	
	17.		Reconnoitred Communications in 72 Bde area.	
	18.		Took over from Sigs 72 Bde at CHAU. D'ACQ. Rear main groups ?	
CHAN. D'ACQ	19.		Laid pair to No.20.Kite Balloon Sec. patrolled lines.	
	20.		Put through line to transport at PETIT SERVINS.	
	21.		Patrolled lines.	
	22.		1.02. reported from Bde. Buried 6 yards from A.S.R. to B.S.R.	
	23.		Put through J.B.A 2. at col 6. left and right Bakalourg 18414 yards from ACRAS Rd test Box K test Box near right Battalion	

Army Form C. 2118.

Appx. 3

WAR DIARY
or
INTELLIGENCE SUMMARY.

(Erase heading not required.)

Instructions regarding War Diaries and Intelligence
Summaries are contained in F. S. Regs., Part II.
and the Staff Manual respectively. Title pages
will be prepared in manuscript.

Place	Date	Hour	Summary of Events and Information	Remarks and references to Appendices
CHAU. D'ACQ	24.		Reconnoitred communications in area of 119 Bde. Patrolled lines	a.R.
	25.		Sent men out and relabelled buried routes in office at ABR.	a.R.
	26.		Patrolled lines, tested out and labelled all spare lines from ARRAS Rd Toul Bge	a.R.
			to ABR	
	27.		Handed over to Sigs 3 Can Inf Bde at 4 pm. moved to CHAU. DE LA HAIE	a.R.
			sent 4 linesmen to 119 Bde Sigs.	
CHAU DE LA HAIE	28.		Marched off at 11 a.m. arrived NOEUX LES MINES 1.45 p.m.	a.R.
LES BREBIS	29.		Took over from Sigs 149 Bde in Les BREBIS at 4pm. Lines as in APPENDIX II	a.R.
	30.		Patrolled lines.	a.R.
	31.		Ran through lines to transfer end L.T.M. Battery	a.R.

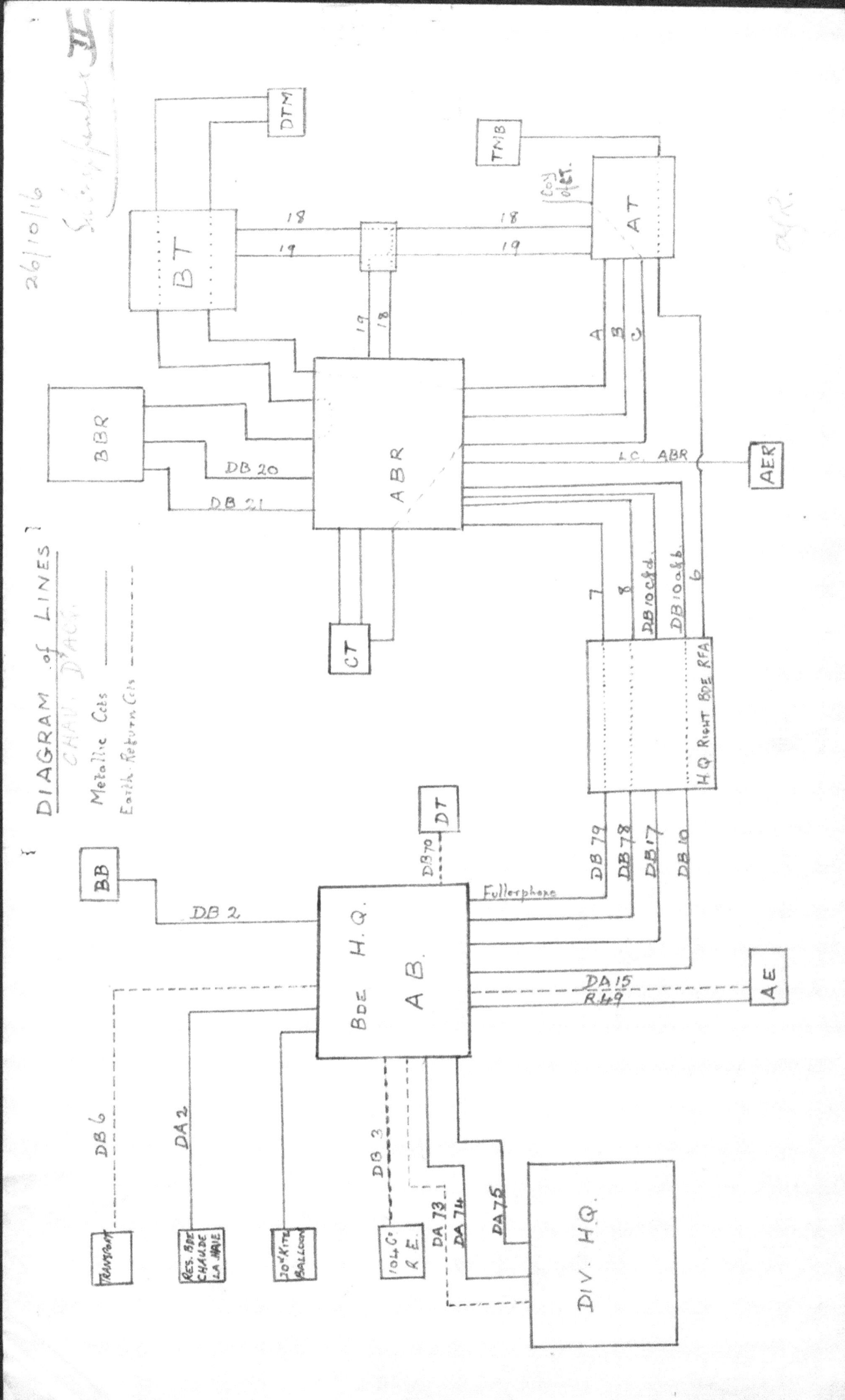

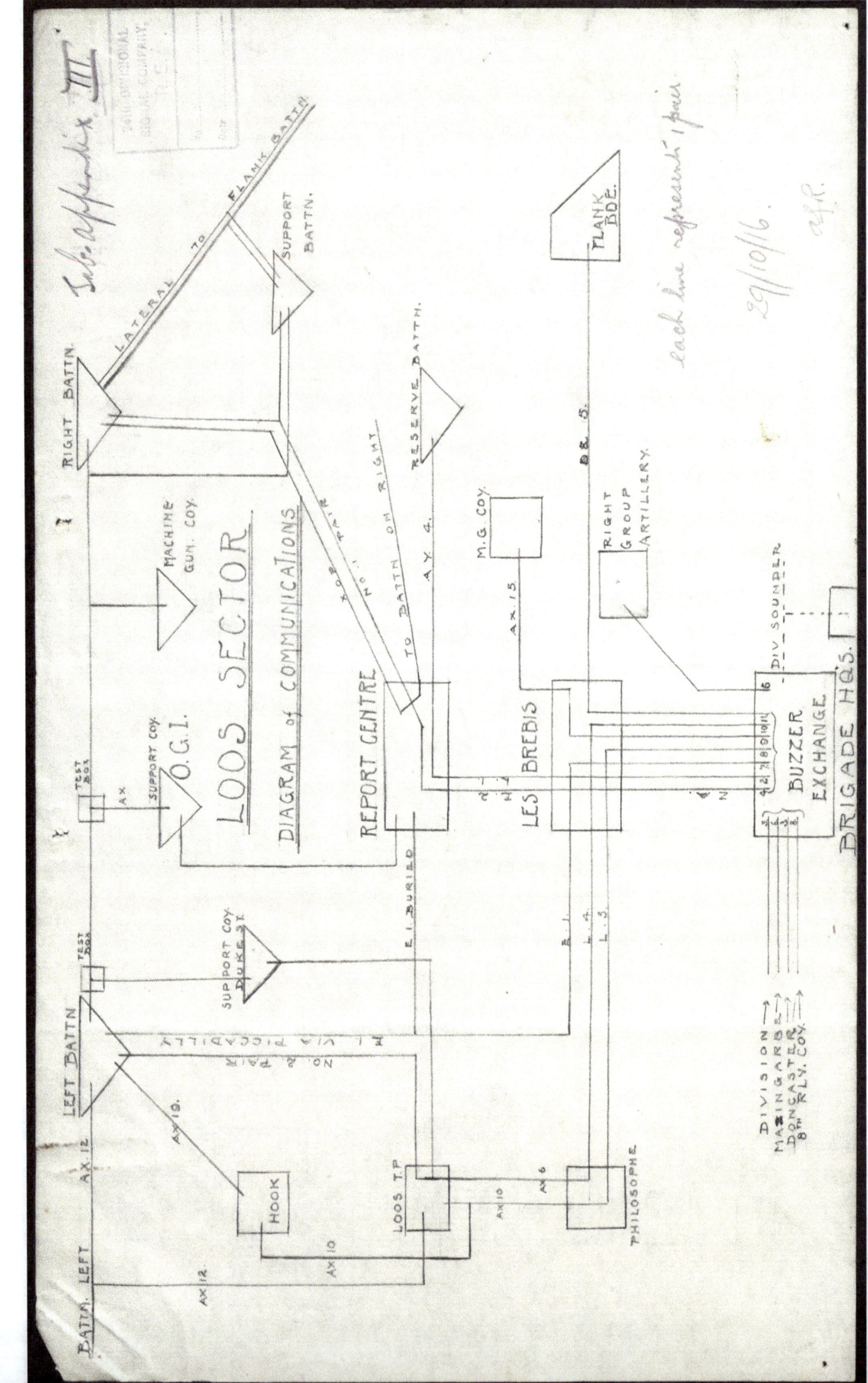

Vol 16

War Diary

29th Divisional Signal Company
R.E.

November 1916.

Army Form C. 2118.

WAR DIARY
or
INTELLIGENCE SUMMARY.
(Erase heading not required.)

24th DIVISIONAL SIGNAL COY.

NOVEMBER 1916

Place	Date	Hour	Summary of Events and Information	Remarks and references to Appendices
BRAQUEMONT (Noeux Les Mines)	1st – 3rd November		2/Lt Rhodes inspected all overhead routes in the area and made a programme of work to be done as well as making out a list of linemen patrols to ensure proper maintenance of all lines. A N.C.O. and four men were employed attending all overhead routes especially those to Brigades. Work on stables. The stables had a roof of canvas which were in a very bad condition. Half the stable was made good with canvas and remainder corrugated iron. New beams and bunks being put in the whole stable. Repairs to billet executed. Divisional Signal Office was squared up, all spare leads being cut away to give place to testboard.	WWH

Army Form C. 2118.

WAR DIARY
or
INTELLIGENCE SUMMARY.

(2)

(Erase heading not required.)

Instructions regarding War Diaries and Intelligence Summaries are contained in F. S. Regs., Part II. and the Staff Manual respectively. Title pages will be prepared in manuscript.

Place	Date	Hour	Summary of Events and Information	Remarks and references to Appendices
	November			
BRAQUEMONT	1st – 3rd (contd)		Staff employed to run communications in the Rear exclusive of Brigade Stations.	
			Divisional Signal Office	
			Telephone Operators 9	
			Telephone Operators 2	
			Linesmen 5	
			Signalmasters 15	
			Orderlies 6	
			Motor Cyclist 7	
			Mazingarbe Exchange O/C 1	
			Linesmen 2	
			Telephone Operators 3	
			La Rutoire Buried Route 1	
			Quality Street " 1	

2353 Wt. W2544/1454 700,000 5/15 D, D, & L. A.D.S.S./Forms/C. 2118.

Army Form C. 2118.

24th DIVISIONAL
SIGNAL COMPANY,
R.E.

WAR DIARY
or
INTELLIGENCE SUMMARY.
(Erase heading not required.)

(3)

Instructions regarding War Diaries and Intelligence Summaries are contained in F. S. Regs., Part II. and the Staff Manual respectively. Title pages will be prepared in manuscript.

Place	Date	Hour	Summary of Events and Information	Remarks and references to Appendices
	November			
BRAQUEMONT	1-3rd (cont'd)		Maroc trunk route	
	3rd		Corpl Lucas sent out to inspect and report on test points and boxes on the Quality Street trunk route. His report was that four test points were in a very bad state of repair, in some cases falling in, and many several circuits. Six men of the Sherwood Foresters were therefore applied for, to reconstruct these points.	
	4th		Pioneers commenced work on test boxes under Corpl Lucas. Four men employed making new frames and 3 repairing overhead cover and strengthening.	WNR
	5th		Spare trunk running along Route nationale from Noeux les Mines extended to Divisional Signal School and made use of as Phone to them.	

2353 Wt. W2544/1454 700,000 5/15 D.D.& L. A.D.S.S./Forms/C. 2118.

WAR DIARY or INTELLIGENCE SUMMARY

Army Form C. 2118.

(Erase heading not required.)

Place	Date	Hour	Summary of Events and Information	Remarks and references to Appendices
Noeux les Mines	6th		Sergt Bell with an Qrmt Lineman and an Qrmt Lineman assistant per Lynes commenced work on Questionnaire Buried Cable overhead tracing lines and making diagrams of test boxes.	Ration
		7pm	2/Lt E. J. New joined company. Work on buried route continued.	
		8^3	Riding Class commenced for all NCOs and Officers who have joined the Company since Last Embarkation and who are unable to ride. Small party of 1 NCO and 4 men digging in dead lines in communication trenches.	
		9pm	Work on buried route and hiking up line continued. Chalk pit alley cleared.	

Army Form C. 2118.

24th DIVISIONAL
SIGNAL COMPANY,
R.E.

WAR DIARY
or
INTELLIGENCE SUMMARY
(Erase heading not required.)

Place	Date	Hour	Summary of Events and Information	Remarks and references to Appendices
NOEUX LES MINES.	10th November – 13th		Work on buried routes continued also working parties picking up cables. Gun trench.	
	14th + 15th		R.A. Heights Signal Office and Dugout repaired. New leading in pearly fitted at each relay and all wires which were in any poor condition cut out up to this date there had been no interruptions on Divisional lines in this area. Work on buried routes continued. Some test pounds repaired and new frames and test pounds fitted. Pattersons	
	16th to 20th		Work on buried routes continued lines on Quality Street route tested out and five more frames and test boxes put in between Lens road and Village line trench.	(A)

2353 Wt. W2544/1454 700,000 5/15 D. D. & L.   A.D.S.S. Forms/C. 2118.

Army Form C. 2118.

WAR DIARY
or
INTELLIGENCE SUMMARY.
(Erase heading not required.)

Instructions regarding War Diaries and Intelligence Summaries are contained in F. S. Regs., Part II. and the Staff Manual respectively. Title pages will be prepared in manuscript.

Place	Date	Hour	Summary of Events and Information	Remarks and references to Appendices
NOUEX LES MINES	20th (cont)		Party of 48 men continued for buried cable from Henry Trench across the change behind South Reserve.	
	21st and 22nd		Small party probing up on the front on buried cable continued. Digging party of 48 men at night.	
	23rd		Work on buried route continued. Party probing on buried route buried cable N of L3 and buttress rail in North L3 and buttress. Digging party at night. Range trench dug 6ft deep about 90 yards and 6ft deep.	
	24th		Party removed dense between rails. Doubled duty dugouts. Night digging continued.	

2353 Wt. W2544/1454 700,000 5/15 D. D. & L. A.D.S.S./Forms/C. 2118.

WAR DIARY
or
INTELLIGENCE SUMMARY.

(Erase heading not required.)

Army Form C. 2118.

24th Div Army
SIGNAL COMPANY.
R.E.

Place	Date	Hour	Summary of Events and Information	Remarks and references to Appendices
NOEUX LES MINES	25th	—	Line between Druel Hqrs and Artillery Hqrs completed. Work on quality of lines route continued. New test boxes fitted between in Railway alley. Trench Party picked up cable in Gun Trench and Railway alley.	MM
	26th to 29th		Work on buried radio continued. Test boxes put in on Kennedy Trench and Gun Trench. Party picked up cable in Kingsbridge and Northern app. Digging at night continued.	MM
	30th		Vibrator line between Divnl arty and Artillery Group made metallic. Spare line used between Hqrs and Le Brebis and then D3 cable run on same poles as existing line. Night digging party completed trench for buried cables. No interruptions on Divnl Lines during month.	MM

Army Form C. 2118.

WAR DIARY
or
INTELLIGENCE SUMMARY

(Erase heading not required.)

24th DIVISIONAL SIGNAL COMPANY, R.E.

NOVEMBER 1916

APPENDIX I

Instructions regarding War Diaries and Intelligence Summaries are contained in F. S. Regs., Part II. and the Staff Manual respectively. Title Pages will be prepared in manuscript.

Place	Date	Hour	Summary of Events and Information				Remarks and references to Appendices
			Emergency August for Signal Office at NOEUX LES MINES				
			Description	Name	Description	Name	
			Quad brass bound cable	DZ 6 a+t forward, DZ 7 forward, DZ 7 back, DZ 1 a., DZ 1 k	Quad brass bound cable	None, DZ 4 a+t forward, DZ 5 a+t	Rush
			D 5		D 5	DZ 8 forward, DZ 9 "	
			Quad brass bound cable	4 wires marked Inland 2	D 5	A 64, A 65	

WAR DIARY

Army Form C. 2118.

APPENDIX II

NOVEMBER 1916

Wires on Testboard at 24th Division Headquarters at Noeux les Mines.

LABEL No.	TESTBOARD No.	EXCHANGE No.	To	LABEL No.	TESTBOARD No.	EXCHANGE No.	To
A {66/67}	20	20	Emergency telephone to Corps	DZ 4 (pair)	7	8	Mazingarbe Exchange telephone
A 68	35	—	1st Corps Sounder	DZ 5 (main)	8	—	Spare pair to Mazingarbe Exchange
A {70/71}	1	1	1st Corps telephone	DZ 6 (pair)	10	13	Les Brebis Exchange
RM {3/12}	21	10	Centre Brigade (17th Inf. Bde.) telephone	DZ 7 (single)	29	—	Spare
LM {5/14}	24	17	Mazingarbe Exchange telephone	DZ 8 (single)	30	—	
AM {22/24}	5	5	Left Brigade (72nd Bde) telephone	DZ 11 (single)	28	—	RA groups (strapped to DZ 31)
DZ {2} (pair)	6	6	Right Brigade (73rd Bde) telephone	DZ 12 (main)	4	4	C.R.E. telephone
				DZ 13 (pair)	11	11	Mine Office Civil Exchange

Army Form C. 2118.

WAR DIARY
or
INTELLIGENCE SUMMARY

(Erase heading not required.)

Appendix II Page 2

Place	Date	Hour	Summary of Events and Information								Remarks and references to Appendices
			LABEL No.	TESTBOARD No.	EXCHANGE No.	To.	LABEL No.	TESTBOARD No.	EXCHANGE No.	To.	
			DZ 14 main	12	12	Signal Company Office	DZ 22 main	23	15	DADOS telephone	
			DZ 15 main	15	—	Spare to Officers Mess	DZ 23 single	34	1	Spare wounded line to 2nd Canadian Division	
			DZ 16 main	14	14	C R A Exchange	DZ 24 main	9	9	2nd Canadian Division telephone	
			DZ 17 main	22	18	G.O.C. telephone	DZ 25 main	17	7	Colonel Doyle telephone (Q branch)	
			DZ 18 main	16	16	258 A.T. Company R.E. telephone	DZ 28 main	25	1	G Branch telephone (emergency)	
			DZ 19 main	18	16	173 A.T. Company R.E. telephone	DZ 29 main	2	2	'G' Branch telephone	
			DZ 20 main	13	—	Spare to Capt Wabadabo Miller	DZ 30 main	3	3	"Q" Branch telephone	
			DZ 21 main	19	19	21st Division telephone (left Division)	DZ 31 single	27	1		
							DZ 32 single	32	1		
							DZ 33 single	31	1.	C.R.A (stripped to DZ 11)	

Army Form C. 2118.

WAR DIARY
or
INTELLIGENCE SUMMARY

APPENDIX III

(Erase heading not required.)

Place	Date	Hour	Summary of Events and Information	Remarks and references to Appendices
			Connections on 24th Division Telephone Exchange at Bruay, October 28-30th	
			1. Canadian Corps 6. 1st Corps	
			2. 7.	
			3. G. Staff 8. Office Phone	
			4. C.R.E. 9.	
			5. 10. Q Branch	

CORPS W/T STATIONS

CORPS DIRECTING STN - ZAA.
SUB-DIRECTING STN - ZM.

6-11-16

November 1916
APPENDIX IV

- ZR̄ — A26 b 6-8
- ZC̄H̄ — G3 c 4-1
- ZAA — L18 a 0-3
- ZM — L35 a 7-7
- ZW — G36 a 2-3
- ZH — M3 a 9-5

λ 350, λ 350, λ 550, λ 550, λ 550

BRITISH FRONT LINE

ZAA } Keep continuous watch.
ZM }

ZR̄ }
ZC̄H̄ } Close down from Midnight till first call next morning, unless specially warned. They are always available for transmitting messages to the Directing Stations.
ZW }
ZH }

ZAA calls:
- ZM — 0730 — every 2 hrs till Midnt
- ZR̄ — 0800 " " " " "
- ZC̄H̄ — 0830 " " " " "
- ZW — 0900 " " " " "

ZM calls ZH — 0800 " " " " "

Army Form C. 2118.

Appendix VI

WAR DIARY
INTELLIGENCE SUMMARY
(Erase heading not required.)

No R Section 24th Div Sig. Coy R.E.

Place	Date	Hour	Summary of Events and Information	Remarks and references to Appendices
MAZINGARBE CHATEAU L23c75 [Sheet 36b FRANCE] "14 BIS SECTOR"	NOVEMBER 1916 1–7		Lines to 17 M.G. Coy, Bde Transport, at LES BREBIS, but though all trench + air-lines patrolled + maintained. Great difficulty with trunk lines in the wet weather owing to constant falling in of sides. Following buried routes reconnoitred. I. MAZINGARBE to TEST POINT (LOOS) via QUALITY ST. Route good to latter, but was had found. This was taken in hand by Div Sigs. II. TEST POINT to G36a67, thence to R Bn HQ G36a 33½ + L BN HQ G36a 89. Routes switch good. III. T.P. to LOOS POST OFFICE G35d 6¾ 5½. Hqr L Bn of Bde on our Right – 73rd. Good route, with armoured trench line test off on pair at BOND ST to HOOK (Hqrs Cinds LOOS).	
	8–14		Later buried routes from R Bn to TPs 8 & 9 reconnoitred. Some trouble with the former at TOWER BRIDGE power house, owing to part of the power cable (which formed part of the circuit) being cut out to make way for water tanks. This was made O.K. There lines were mostly reconnoitred with a I Corps linesman in place, they were practically invisible. The lines found?	

Milton Kramer Lt
R. Sig. 17/1/18

WAR DIARY

INTELLIGENCE SUMMARY

Army Form C. 2118.

Place	Date	Hour	Summary of Events and Information	Remarks and references to Appendices
MAZINGARBE CHATEAU. 14 BIS SECTOR	NOVEMBER 1916 8-14 ctd.		Left Bn Hqrs were also thoroughly reconnoitred. These included a main lateral route, following the line of LOOS - HULLUCH road, Athens branching off to junction of CHALK PIT ALLEY & RESERVE TRENCH, thence following the latter past HUGO LANE & the old L Bn Hy at G.30.6.33, to MINERS TRENCH, across POSEN ALLEY, on N boundary & So NW to Hqrs in CURZON ST. of R Bn of Bde on our L. - 72 I.B. This route was used as lateral & also to the L Support Coy in old L Bn Hqs. From there a "pipe route" with 3 pm in an armoured guard & turn up HUGO LANE to MEATH TRENCH, to T.P.11,at H.25.b.6.9. Also from L Bn Hq 3 pm ran to a T.B. at G.30.d.11, on the main route, thence in a 3 pm "pipe route" up RAILWAY ALLEY to T.P.10, at H.25.c.3.1, with 1 pm going from a T.B. at junction of R.A. & RESERVE TRENCH to R support Coy Hqrs at G.26.6.7.1.7. In all 4 front companies then hqs were some way from their T.P. The only one where it was practicable to work with Coy Sigr linemen in T.P. was at No.8, the R Coy Y Bn All the others were 300 or more from the TP. The extensiveness	
	15 - 21			

WAR DIARY / INTELLIGENCE SUMMARY

Army Form C. 2118.

24th DIVISIONAL SIGNAL COMPANY, R.E.

III

Place	Date	Hour	Summary of Events and Information	Remarks and references to Appendices
MAZINGARBE CHATEAU 14 BIS SECTOR	NOVEMBER 1916 15-21 ctd		to strive corps were all of D☰ & I when taken over, but during the 2nd & 3rd weeks there were gradually replaced by armoured cable that had been salved. Directly the corps D & F Bn were put on to the trunk route, all trunk lines were reeled in & returned to Sig. Farm they were done from T.P. to Rm, & in the R lm where trunk line still existed. One common armoured trunk pair to be was left down. Rather all trunk tracks to brigade except I D☰ f - Aw 11, in the track part of RAILWAY ALLEY, & in NORTHERN UP, were reeled in by Sw Engrs. Aw 13 was left as far as QUALITY ST. The Support Bn Hqrs, but they & MEETING HOUSE were put on to No I Fm track at QUALITY ST T.B. That route gave considerable trouble while work on new	11 17 12 3/1
	22-30		T.B.s & lm was in progress, in going on & off. On 17/15 the delivery of all Mor tattoos was taken over from Z.G.C, also the 17 L.T.M.R.G at G 36c 27 was put through by trench lim to R Im Hy, also FURNEYS LANE & NORTH ST. During 3rd & 4th weeks T.P. was re-wired entirely, & new	

WAR DIARY
INTELLIGENCE SUMMARY.
(Erase heading not required.)

Army Form C. 2118.

Instructions regarding War Diaries and Intelligence Summaries are contained in F.S. Regs., Part II. and the Staff Manual respectively. Title pages will be prepared in manuscript.

Hour, Date, Place	Summary of Events and Information	Remarks and References to Appendices
MAZINGARBE CHATEAU. 14 BIS SECTOR 22-30	**NOVEMBER 1916.** Terminal boards fitted. During this period work was begun on cleaning the the Exchange approaches & all spare lines. The office was fitted with a new heading in board. 2 linesmen were detailed from each Bath. to be attached to Bde. Signal Section to form the permanent maintenance personnel of the telephone Posts in Bde. Area. Telephone posts were labelled at each entrance. All trunks in Bde. area were surveyed & a report of all cables was forwarded to Division. Sappers ASHTON, COMPTON & WILDGOOSE proceeded to Divisional School were replaced by Sappers HATSEY, LITTLE and Pte HARDY. Rifle, gas helmet & respirator returned. Relief Cookhouse cleaner & survey done.	
Sunday 19	Gen Sir W. HORNE only I Army presented Military Medal when in Conmettia. Spr HARDSTAFF relieved by Cpl MARSHALL. to Sgt SHEPPARD, CplCLARKE YCpl SUMMERS & Spr LEITCH, at Div HQ. Spr SUMMERS site returned 18th. Sapper TOPP to be attested for + conjoining QUALIFESE & T.P. ADOS Sapper	

Appendix VII

Army Form C. 2118.

No. 3 Section
4th Signal Coy R.E.

WAR DIARY
or
INTELLIGENCE SUMMARY.
(Erase heading not required.)

Instructions regarding War Diaries and Intelligence Summaries are contained in F. S. Regs., Part II. and the Staff Manual respectively. Title pages will be prepared in manuscript.

Place	Date	Hour	Summary of Events and Information	Remarks and references to Appendices
Hilhoek Ph	1-11-15		Patrolling airline forward. AV.7. & Lifts Pole repaired and overhauled	S.7.H.
"	2-11-		Patrolling AV.3. where trench line and repinning came.	S.7.H.
"	3-11-		Reconstructing AV.1. making it metallic circuit of earth return	S.7.H.
"	4-11-		Laying line to R.T.O at Kingsbridge Jn.	S.7.H.
"	5-11-		Reconstruction of AV.1. proceeded with	S.7.H.
"	6-11-		All line patrolled and repegged & trench walls where necessary	S.7.H.
"	7-11-		All airlines (patrolled) and (laying) where required	P.7.H.
"	8-11-		Line to transportation at Lt. Brebis laid and manned by Both sparklers	S.7.H.
"	9-11-		Picking up abandoned south chiefly gunner lines	C.7.H.
"	10-11-		Running local line over broad gang railway patrolling airlines.	S.7.H.
"	12-11-		Finished reconstruction of line portion of AV.1. salving old circuit	S.7.H.
"	13-11-		Picking up local lines abandoned & Patrolling local lines	S.7.H.
"	14-11-		Leaving AV.1. and finished reconstruction as trench line	S.7.H.
"	15-11-		Salving local lines not in use.	P.7.H.
"	16-11-		Salving French lines in TENTH AVENUE	C.7.H.
"	17-11-		Salving trench line in POSEN ALLEY	S.7.H.

Army Form C. 2118.

WAR DIARY
or
INTELLIGENCE SUMMARY.
(Erase heading not required.)

Instructions regarding War Diaries and Intelligence Summaries are contained in F. S. Regs., Part II. and the Staff Manual respectively. Title pages will be prepared in manuscript.

Place	Date	Hour	Summary of Events and Information	Remarks and references to Appendices
PHILOSOPHE	18-11		Raising local lines over new bridge of aerial railway	C.7.A.
"	19-11		Salving local lines in back area	C.7.A.
"	20-11		Raising and reconstructing lines over various gauge railways	C.7.A.
"	21-11		Altering burnt road to more two telephone lines on its own side	C.7.A.
			and also "bus" speaking circuit	C.7.A.
"	22-11		All lines patrolled and made good where necessary	C.7.A.
"	23-11		Salving lines on top of TENTH AVENUE	C.7.A.
"	24-11		Reconstructing French entrance to Signal office	C.7.A.
"	25-11		Dulloghone service established to Coys & Light batts	C.7.A.
"	26-11		Commenced renewing Bat Signal office local lines (patrols)	C.7.A.
"	27-11		Started to relay line 6-Tol., replacing D1 by D5.	C.7.A.
"	28-11		Repairing AV3 in C.E. TUTOIRE ALLEY and TENTH AVENUE, AV3 cut off from O.P.	C.7.A.
"	29-11		Carried on with reconstruction of AV6-TpT line.	C.7.A.
"	30-11		Broke fault on Dullophone line joined up spare pair between B but box and	C.7.A.
			KENNEDY TRENCH test box.	

C.7. Stephens Lieut.
1(o o No. 3. Section 24H. Div.) Sig Coy.

Appendix VIII

Army Form C. 2118.

No 4 Section   2nd Sheet

WAR DIARY
or
INTELLIGENCE SUMMARY.

(Erase heading not required.)

Place	Date	Hour	Summary of Events and Information	Remarks and references to Appendices
LES BREBIS (sheet 36b)	1.		Patrolled lines	a/R
	2.		Patrolled lines. Traced buried routes.	a/R
	3.		Started out buried route from Loos Test Point to Left Batt.	a/R
	4.		Traced out E₁ and E₂ in the buried routes	a/R
	5.		Put through pair from right battalion to Brigade to L/F battalion line.	a/R
	6.		Pair to R.E. Dump. (AX20) on der BREBIS.	a/R
			Replaced the pair and X O P line from Test Box 16 in Artillery Row to right battalion	a/R
			by Nos 2 & 4 in the new buried route.	a/R
	7.		Patrolled lines.	a/R
	8.		AX6. and AX10. broken by trench falling in. AX10. repaired.	a/R
	9.		AX6. repaired but signals on that line weak.	a/R
	10.		relaid part of AX6. which was broken by trench falling in	a/R
	11.		Mr started to use A/F as the South Africa buried route to T.P.	a/R

Army Form C. 2118.

WAR DIARY
or
INTELLIGENCE SUMMARY.
(Erase heading not required.)

Instructions regarding War Diaries and Intelligence Summaries are contained in F. S. Regs., Part II. and the Staff Manual respectively. Title pages will be prepared in manuscript.

Place	Date	Hour	Summary of Events and Information	Remarks and references to Appendices
LES BREBIS.	12.		Patrolled lines	
	13.		Ens. Pat. through to Left Bath. in Loos via the (and) 1st Kensit road	
	14.		Patrolled lines.	
	15.		Patrolled lines.	
	16.		Took over of No.5 2. and 4 Coys. and routes from T.No. 16 & 17 Regt Inf. Bathn. on Sunset. Battalion. Used No 2 → H₂ → E₂ as Intelligence line & my own rood necessarily this and H₃ → L₁ as speaking line. Cut out A.X.9. from No 16 & 17 Regts on O.91 L.C.	
	17.		Picked up A.X.9.	aSR
	18.		Replaced A.X.8. from right Inf. battalion to O.G.1. by No 2 on E.Y.A 90 as centre Brigade —	SR
	19.		Put through A.X.19. from Pioneer Bn in LOOS to left Bn.	aSR
	20.		Patrolled lines.	aSR
	21.		Patrolled lines.	a. Mitchie 2/RE

Army Form C. 2118.

7th DIVISIONAL
SIGNAL COMPANY
R.E.

Sheet III

WAR DIARY
or
INTELLIGENCE SUMMARY.
(Erase heading not required.)

Place	Date	Hour	Summary of Events and Information	Remarks and references to Appendices
Les Brebis	22		Picked up front of AX8 from right battalion to O.E.1. WSR.	
	23		A.H. dis at intervals during the day. Patrolled lines WSR.	
	24		A.H. put through and E2 cleared. Fullerphone put on A.H. to left battalion, and on E.2 to right and support battalions. Picked up remainder of AX8 from right battalion to O.G.1. Picked up AX6 from the railway to Bilerophe. The Reserve battalion moved to Les Brebis and took on to DZR.8 WSR.	
	25		Repaired DZR.7. Reserve battalion taken off DZR.8 and put on DZR.7. WSR.	
	26		Picked up the front of DZR.7 beyond Reserve battalion headquarters which has not in use. Fullerphone at Support battalion right done. WSR.	
	27		Picked up spare lines in Les Brebis labelled DZR.5 and DZR.6. Fullerphone at Support battalion went dis.	
	28		Repaired Fullerphone at Support battalion. Picked up more spare lines in Les Brebis labelled DH3 and DH14.	
	29		Les Brebis labelled DH1 and DH4. Picked up more spare lines in Les Brebis labelled DH1 and DH4.	
	30		Picked up spare and unlabelled lines in Les Brebis. WSR.	

W.J. Phobro? Lt.
2/Lt. W. R.E.

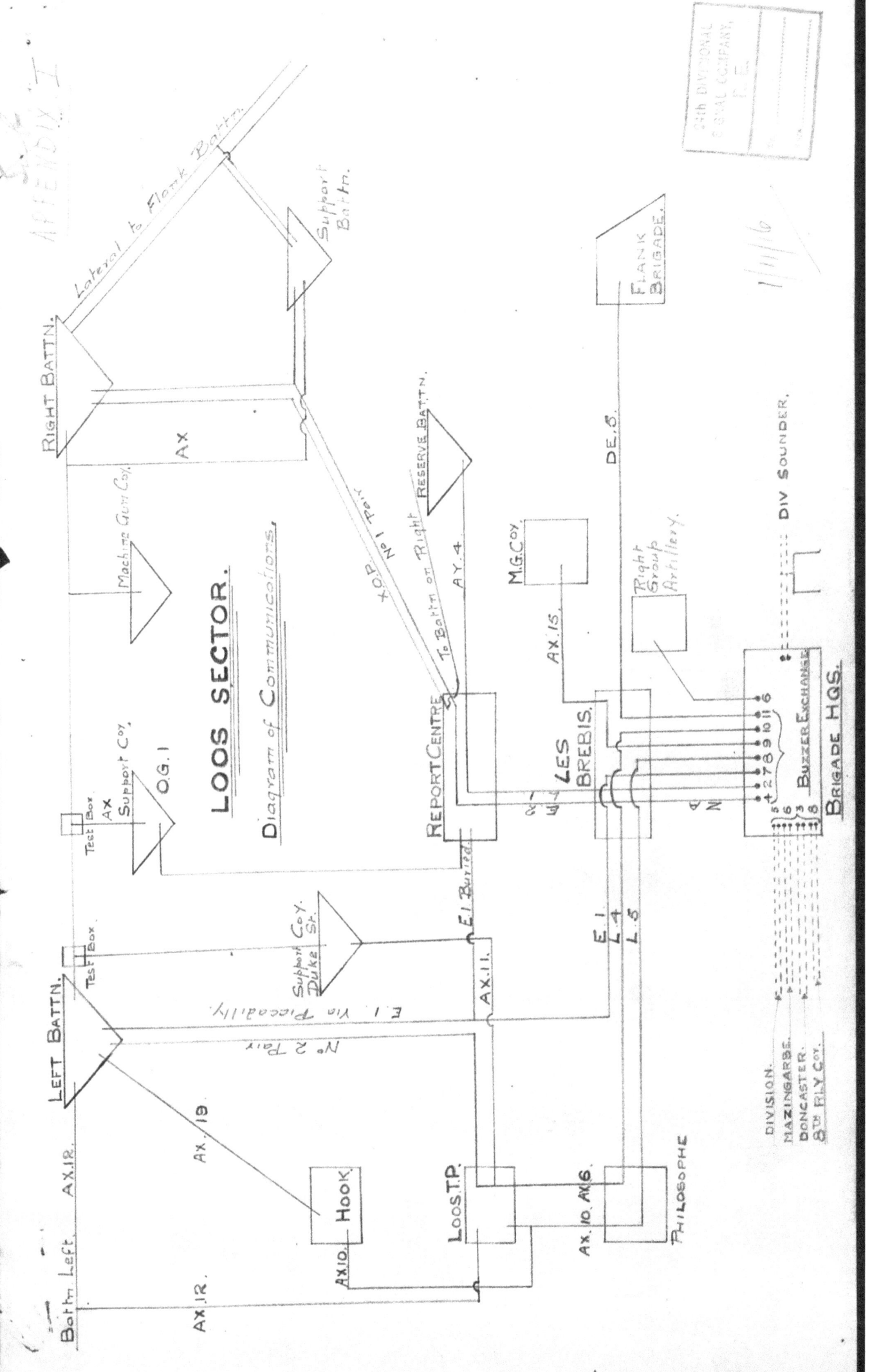

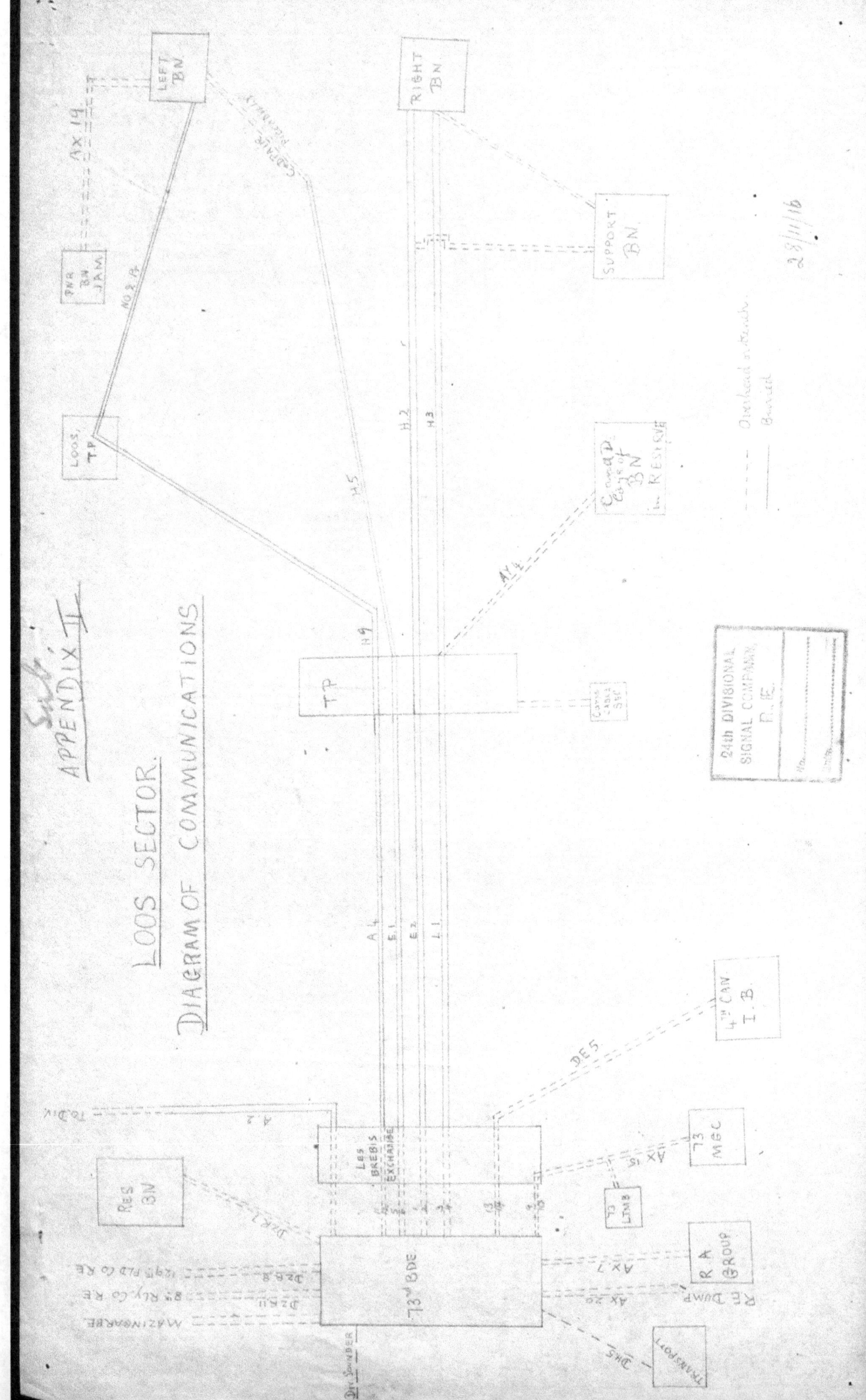

Army Form W. 3091.

Vol 17

Cover for Documents.

Nature of Enclosures.

War Diary
24th Divisional Signal Company
R.E.

Notes, or Letters written.

December 1916.

Army Form C. 2118.

24th DIVISIONAL SIGNAL COMPANY R.E.

WAR DIARY
or
INTELLIGENCE SUMMARY.
(Erase heading not required.)

24th Divisional Signal Coy R.E.

December 1916.

Place	Date	Hour	Summary of Events and Information	Remarks and references to Appendices
Bracquemont Noeux-les-Mines	1st-2nd		Party completing trench for cables between Kennedy Trench to La Haie Exchange. Telegraph cork of armoured twin cable laid in trench. Tested and labelled. Work on Quality Street buried route continued. New Test Boxes fitted at points in Railway alley, Tool alley, & in Reserve Trench. Number of men under instruction at Divnl Signal School 7 - 80.	Appx
	4th 5th		Party testing and labelling line to D.A.C. Cable section left behind on last move with Divnl	

WAR DIARY or INTELLIGENCE SUMMARY

Army Form C. 2118.

Place	Date	Hour	Summary of Events and Information	Remarks and references to Appendices
BRAQUEMONT NOEUX LES MINES	April (contd)		Divl. Artillery reported taking place of distion of 10th Signal Coy who moved out. Cable and Riding Drill also commenced consisted of men drawn from Brigade Sections.	
	5th	6pm	Party employed laying line from La Bose Exchange to Bhad Inf O.P. New Test Boxes fitted at test points in Scottish Alley and Reserve Trench.	Pssh
	7th	10am	Party making up derived cables in Northern Work on Quality of buried route continued. Scott boxes put in at points in Railway alley Vendin Alley and Poyak Alley.	

Army Form C. 2118.

24th DIVISIONAL SIGNAL COMPANY, R.E.

No. ....
Date. ....

WAR DIARY
or
INTELLIGENCE SUMMARY.
(3)
(Erase heading not required.)

Instructions regarding War Diaries and Intelligence Summaries are contained in F. S. Regs., Part II. and the Staff Manual respectively. Title pages will be prepared in manuscript.

Place	Date	Hour	Summary of Events and Information	Remarks and references to Appendices
BRAQUEMONT NOEUX-LES-MINES	11th — 12th		Party employed thirty fifty up Visual Signal report on trench stretched & Party picking up cables.	Nich
	13th		Work on Visual Station and Buried Lines continued.	
	14th		New ground cable between Kennedy Trench and Enfare Garden Brought into use. Also 4 Pairs between Kennedy Trench and Sulford Battalion H.Q. (Keft Br.) brought into use.	
	15th & 16th	19.0	Party extending buried routes from Test Box (27) into La Stove Exchange. Work on Visual Station continued.	

2353 Wt. W2544/1454 700,000 5/15 L D, D. & L. A.D.S.S./Forms/C. 2118.

Army Form C. 2118.

WAR DIARY
or
INTELLIGENCE SUMMARY.
(Erase heading not required.)

Instructions regarding War Diaries and Intelligence Summaries are contained in F. S. Regs., Part II and the Staff Manual respectively. Title pages will be prepared in manuscript.

Place	Date	Hour	Summary of Events and Information	Remarks and references to Appendices
Bueenoult Noeux les Mines	20th	10pm	Telephone from Brindle saying to Exchange tonight in is in use.	
	21st		Went over trenches with Co...	
	22nd		Party employed laying new electric wire-head-wire and putting in cable buffers by the exchange in Reserve trench. New tunnels for wire in our support trenches between 24 & 25 & between 29 & 30 and 17 Twins between. Exchange brought into use. In this exchange received.	P.M.L.
	23rd-29th		March commenced 7 PM. Formally this Battalion on the front S & S 27 a (Sh 36c) In relief of bodies of 1 Devon, 2nd D. and party took over from the Party fully of cable in trenches up 21 by 4 pm & takes over 16 Marine etc	

WAR DIARY or INTELLIGENCE SUMMARY. (5)

Army Form C. 2118.

(Erase heading not required.)

Place	Date	Hour	Summary of Events and Information	Remarks and references to Appendices
Bray-sur-Somme Trenches	25/12		Xmas Day. Working parties suspended for today.	
	26/12		Working parties continuing work of support & Hazgto in Reserve Trench and also tunnelling party testing up cable.	Rain
	27/12		Carry party went out lately line at daylight to Reserve Trench. Party picking up spare artillery lines	
	28/12		Large carry party picked up about 1200 yards of armoured cable. Work on service cable continued. Party filled sand bags with hurdles to Kennedy Trench + 40 stakes carried up	

WAR DIARY
or
INTELLIGENCE SUMMARY

Army Form C. 2118.

(Erase heading not required.)

Instructions regarding War Diaries and Intelligence Summaries are contained in F. S. Regs., Part II. and the Staff Manual respectively. Title pages will be prepared in manuscript.

Place	Date	Hour	Summary of Events and Information	Remarks and references to Appendices
Brigumont Thiennes to Thour	29th – 31st		Work on turning and extension of Infy Bde Sig Office continued. Buried cable being laid throughout length of Bde front. Depot strength for month – 50 miles. Average daily number of messages passing thro' Sig Office during month – 836. A.D.S.O. admitted to hospital sick Nov 11. Have reported unit officers could act as strong month to maintain efficiency and mobility usefully employ. More efficiently and trained further for 31st December 1916 — 70.	Run

Army Form C. 2118.

WAR DIARY
of
INTELLIGENCE SUMMARY
(Erase heading not required.)

J. G. R. Sulivan
Appendix No 1.

24th DIVISIONAL SIGNAL COMPANY, R.E.

Hour, Date, Place	Summary of Events and Information	Remarks and References to Appendices
DECEMBER 1916.		
MAZINGARBE & H.TY (Ben 14) L.23.c.80. (Ham 36b) XIV BIS SECTOR.	1-7. Telephone hut. 8-11 Wall of arch entrance with number plates. 3 men to Div Riding School, who were replaced by 3 Div men. Headquarters at Div. Sig. office much improved by substituting 2. 5ft cables from road to windows, also a 10ft route from main gate (alternative) to the existing wire of lines running in front of the STAY. T.M. line on R of R.bn sector relaid in, also one at H.Q. system of "position cases" started, + calls for most officials allotted. Plates were fixed above instrument with calls painted on them. Great difficulty with fieldphone to lines over QUALITY ST EAST routes; these were improved by running airlines between boxes 17 & 23. 9th Entrance to test box in RAILWAY ALLEY just E of T.P. dug down to level of trench floor + roofed with corrugated iron. 6 of the 8 new pairs which had been buried from T.P. to that box were but straight through, giving a line to each box if necessary.	Attachments hereto V/ SIGS 17 18

(9.29.6) W.2794 103,000 S/14 H W V Forms/C. 2118/11.

WAR DIARY
INTELLIGENCE SUMMARY

Army Form C. 2118.

(Erase heading not required.)

[Stamp: 24th DIVISIONAL SIGNAL COMPANY R.E.]

Place	Date	Hour	Summary of Events and Information	Remarks and references to Appendices
"XIV BIS" SECTOR	DEC. 1916			
	11th		A good deal of trouble was experienced with the substation line, due mainly to intermittent faults at T.B. of QUALITY St E route	
	13		TP 10 (H25 c 3.4.) occupied by 70th A.R. coy. Sp. Inf. Awll (French line for Chateau (to TP from Bde.) re-layed from Vos 3 on Q. or W route to Anti-aircraft clar (L23 G 92. [36 g])	
	14		2 Special linesmen (for duty at T.Pots.) & 1 R.F. attendant for exchange at Sn then complete. Establishment of 2 men per Sn.	
	15		Work begun on leading all main lines into cellar behind "MAZINGARBE EXCHANGE" (in chau basement). 6 good buried farm wires found running from box 2 (just outside gate) under the house & were led through a went into the cellar behind the exchange. This would give enough lines, in case of shelling, to carry on main circuits.	
	16		6p terminal board fitted up at BA7. & linesman in gcall wire improved. Work begun on 10p board at BA33.	
	17		Arrangements made to change over 3pr (telephone 6tm to 2 R.A. hq) at Box 15 (QUALITY St) from Q St E to MinRoc route, & thence by at Box 15 (QUALITY St) to TP. 13 B.12. Sh. J.C.&8. Work at BA33 continued.	

Army Form C. 2118.

WAR DIARY
or
INTELLIGENCE SUMMARY.
(Erase heading not required.)

Instructions regarding War Diaries and Intelligence Summaries are contained in F. S. Regs, Part II. and the Staff Manual respectively. Title pages will be prepared in manuscript.

24TH DIVISIONAL SIGNAL COMPANY. R.E.

Place	Date	Hour	Summary of Events and Information	Remarks and references to Appendices
XIV Bis SECTOR	DEC 1916 19th		Lines changed from Q. & E. to MAROC route as arranged, all working well	
	20th		Points selected, as near Coy Hqrs as possible, from which to work visual to "CRAIGOWEN" O.P. in CATALK PIT ALLEY (G29.b 25.45.)	
	22nd		Six men working on BA10 (G30.b 33) leading 25pr head covered in pipes, into signal office to cut out test box at entrance.	
	23rd		1 NCO & 1 man to Rfc. Sig. Hq. RESIGNEUL for instruction in contact patrol work. 2 men returned from riding school. AW11 dis	
	24th		General round of TPs. Visual Stn near TP8 fixed to come to CRAIGOWEN O.P (G29.b 35.)	
	25th		All men on duty. Lt Chitcom Brown at Bde Hq.	
	26th		Men at BR12. & MEETING HOUSE returned. Site of trench for S.O.S line from TP11 to R Town Coy Hq. 1 hour Coy Hq (H25c98½) surveyed. Bell line from sentry post at head of NORTH Pt to R Town Coy Hq fixed, & one from head of SCOTT ALLEY to do. begun.	
	27th		Bell line in R.m. annex completed.	
	28th		Office at BA33 labelled at tar board, & lines tested to box at junction of CATALK PIT ALLEY & RESERVE TRENCH	
	29th 30th		Workshop on S.O.S. trench from TP11. Work abandoned owing to rain with 40' at 4'4" & 50' at 2'6" & etc. 40' completed & filled. 30" at 4'6". 2 men to Div riding school. Casualties NIL.	

WAR DIARY or INTELLIGENCE SUMMARY

Army Form C. 2118.

(Erase heading not required.)

Place	Date	Hour	Summary of Events and Information	Remarks and references to Appendices
PHILOSOPHE	1.12.15		AV3 re-hauled in LE PREOL TRENCH	
"	2.12		All local lines patrolled – no faults reported	
"	3.12		Recovering local buried lines and air wire	
"	4.12		Testing buried route from Guyson Street to Brew Alley	
"	5.12		Testing buried route from VICKERY ALLEY to MYERS AVENUE	
"	6.12		AV.1 and AV.3 W jammed in handles where fallen away	
"	7.12		Cabling and re-hauling all local lines	
"	8.12		Completed Renaming Office	
"	9.12		Recovering removed lines between types 3 and type 2	
"	10.12		Recovering removed lines at tops of types 3	
"	11.12		Completed line to Hqts at Les Brebis. old line recovered	
"	12.12		Cut new buried lines through from KENNEDY TRENCH T.B.4. Sgt. BATTN B.04.7	
"	13.12		F31. faulty – fault located and renewed	
"	14.12		Clearing faults on Dulleph's line to Coys. RI. Bthn. AV.3. patrolled	
"	15.12		AV.3. patrolled and re-stapled in some larger streets –	
"	16.12		(Recovered) buried lines between KENNEDY TRENCH T.B. and Hay Exchange.	

Army Form C. 2118.

WAR DIARY
or
INTELLIGENCE SUMMARY. No. 3 Section. 4th S Coy RE

(Erase heading not required.)

24th DIVISIONAL SIGNAL COMPANY

Place	Date	Hour	Summary of Events and Information	Remarks and references to Appendices R.E.
GHILSSOPHE	17/12/16		Found lines from T.B.37 to Advd. Bde. HQ. recovered. Local lines patrolled.	8.7.H.
"	18-12		Clearing faults on telephone line to Rt. Btn.	8.7.H.
"	19-12		Pipe lead to Left Coy - Rt. Btn found faulty and changed over.	8.7.H.
"	20-12		Buying cable from Bde. Sig. Office to No. 1 T.B. to replace French lines.	8.7.H.
"	21-12		A.V.1 and A.V.3 patrolled - Continued burying cable by office.	8.7.H.
"	22/12		Telephone line faulty - cleared - test box by Lt. Btn. Adv Q overhauled and new prepared for putting in test board - Spt. line repaired.	8.7.H.
"	23-12		Continued bury by Bde office - all local lines patrolled.	(8.7.H.
"	24/12/16		Commenced Cables put in bury by Bde. Sig office.	8.7.H.
"	25/12/16			
"	26/12/16		Test board put in in test box by Lt. Bath.S/O and all lines numbered.	8.7.H.
"	27/12/16		Lines tested and numbered in bury from Lt. Btn. H.Q. to Stay H.L.E.Y. Test box.	8.7.H.
"	28/12/16		A.V.1 and A.V.3 patrolled and stayed where necessary	C.7.H.
"	29.12		Filling in cable trench	8.7.H.
"	30-12		Sounds line faulty - part P.K.	8.7.H.
"	31.12		Local lines patrolled.	8.7.H.

Appendix No. 3

WAR DIARY
of
No 4. Section 24th Signal Coy. R.E.

for the month of

DECEMBER 1916

WAR DIARY No 4 Section Sheet I.

INTELLIGENCE SUMMARY

24th Divl Army Signal Company, R.E.

Place	Date	Hour	Summary of Events and Information	Remarks and references to Appendices
Les Brebis	1.		Patrolled lines. WSR	
	2.		Picked up spare lines in St James' Street. Laid a new pair from Test Box in South Sheet to Coy. Hdqrs in Corbeil Avenue, via St James Street. WSR. Two pack horses returned and one Maltese cart received to replace them. AJR	
	3.		Patrolled lines. AJR	
	4.		Patrolled lines. AJR. Relaid pair to 73 MG Coy in Les Brebis. AJR	
	5.		Patrolled lines.	
	6.		Patrolled lines. 1 O.R. returned to HQ and 24 Sig Coy R.E. AJR	
	7.		Cleared spare lines round right Battalion hqrs. AJR	
	8.		Witnessed testing of new Maroc-Loos route by corps cable section. AJR	
	9.		Put through HQ. to Loos 9. and H.S. to Loos 5. HQ used as telephone line and No 5. as speaking line from Bde to left Battn. Right Bn No 5 put through to Loos as a lateral line. AJR.	
	10.		Patrolled lines. AJR	
	11.		Put through Right Bn. 1. to Loos 3. and Loos 3. to No. 3. to Talbot 6. Right Battalion extended No. 5 from telephone box 6 to their left Coy. AJR	

Army Form C. 2118.

WAR DIARY
or
INTELLIGENCE SUMMARY.
(Erase heading not required.)

Sheet 1

Place	Date	Hour	Summary of Events and Information	Remarks and references to Appendices
LES BREBIS.	13.		Joined through night Battalion from SOUTH ST. Tpk Box to Telephone Post N.1. Put up Light around St James St. AJR	
	14.		Put through A.X.P. from left Batth to horse Box in LOOS, tried AX.19, as BoS Queen line. picked up cable in SOUTH ST. AJR	
	15.		Picked up cable in SOUTH ST. and ST JAMES ST. AJR	
	16.		No.2. LOOS MAIN route joined through from LOOS to Support Box north Ice way to Cry in	
	17.		O.G.1. No2 MAIN LOOS Route joined [crossed out] in LOOS X.C.1.D from around Piccadilly to Cozan Duke St. Leaving Spare AX.8. round Piccadilly from O.G.1. to DUKE ST. AJR picked up AX.8. AJR	
	18.		Extended No 16 from Telephone Post 5 to 2" T.M. in Queen St. Extended 18 from Telephone post 4 to 2" T.M. in Cardwell Avenue. AJR	
	19.		Laid Tees off 16 & 18 from South By Post box to 2" T.M. O.P. in SOUTH ST. AJR	
	20.		L.O.G.1 joined through 16 from T.M in Queen St to LOOS 13 and 18 from T.M in Cardwell Av to No. 14. R. LOOS. AJR	

WAR DIARY or INTELLIGENCE SUMMARY

Army Form C. 2118.
24th DIVISIONAL SIGNAL COMPANY, R.E.
Sheet III.

Place	Date	Hour	Summary of Events and Information	Remarks and references to Appendices
LES BREBIS	21		Laid pair from Left Bn Hqrs to Medium T.M. Officer in ENCLOSURE.	AGR
	22.		7AB.1. and 1.AC.3. substituted by Nos 9 & 10 in the Master Loop Route.	AGR
	23.		Tested and renumbered routes from left Bn to Telephone point 64.7.	AGR
			Bell substituted for telephone from officers dugout DOUBLE CRASSIER to right supporting right Battn.	AGR
	24.		Pair to R.E. Dump dis and repaired	AGR
	25.		Line to Bde Transport restayed	AGR
	26.		Picked up 7AB.1. Brazier lamp emplacement at Right Coy dugin, right Bn. too mistry to align the pipe.	WR.
	27.		Replaced the telephones from the Double CRASSIER to the right support Cy.	AGR
	28.		Patrolled lines.	AGR
	29		Patrolled lines.	AGR
	30		Line to R.E Dump relaid	AGR
	31.		Line to 129 Field Coy R.E. broken and repaired	A Ritchie Lt.

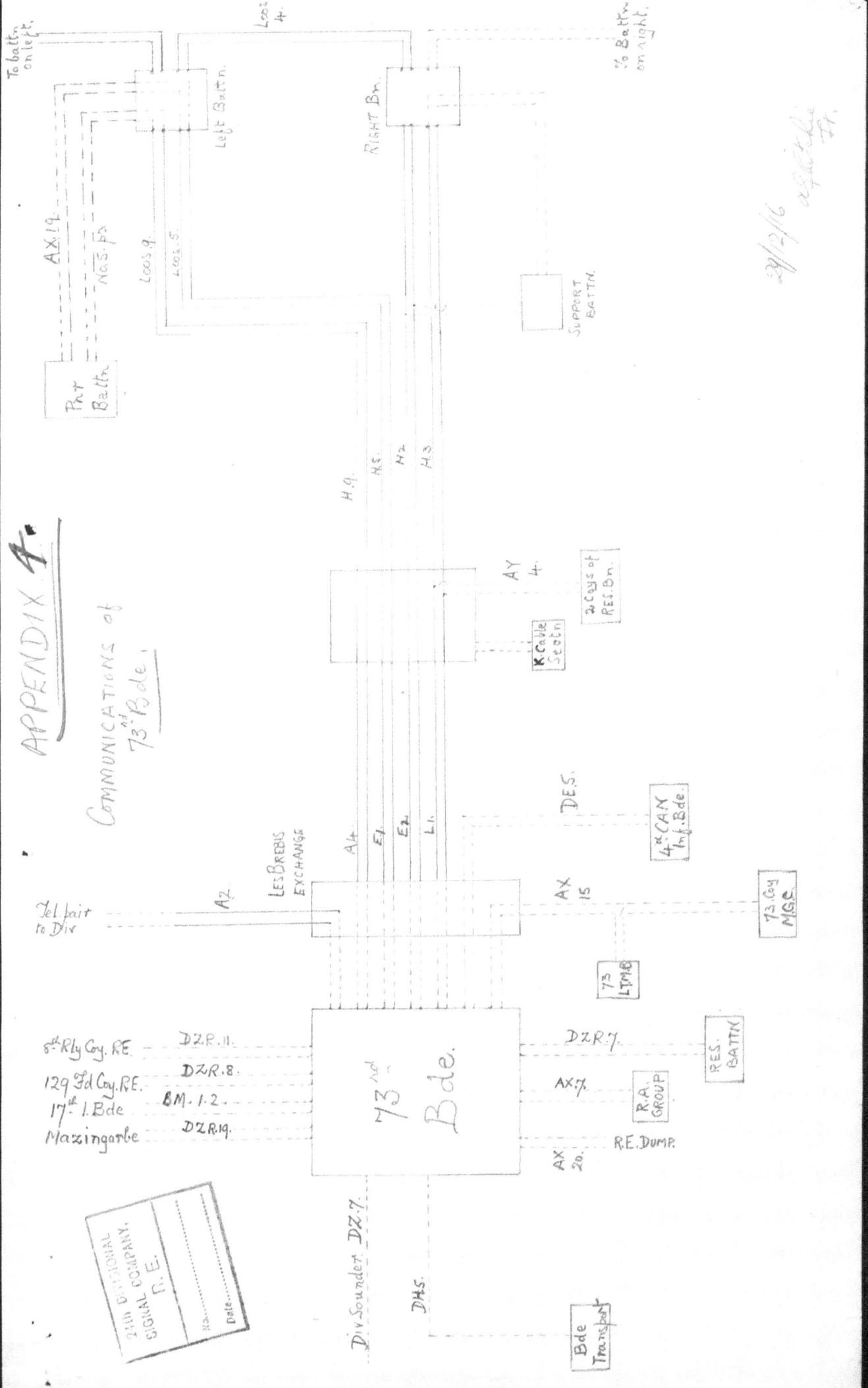

www.ingramcontent.com/pod-product-compliance
Lightning Source LLC
Chambersburg PA
CBHW080808010526
44113CB00013B/2343